FOOD FROM WASTE

An industry–university co-operation Symposium organised
under the auspices of the National College of Food Technology,
University of Reading

THE SYMPOSIUM COMMITTEE

GORDON G. BIRCH, B.Sc., Ph.D., F.R.I.C., M.R.S.H., F.C.S.
Reader at National College of Food Technology, Reading University, Weybridge, Surrey.

R. DAVIES, B.Sc., Ph.D.
Senior Lecturer at National College of Food Technology, Reading University, Weybridge, Surrey.

J. A. FORD, B.A. (Oxon.)
Secretary at National College of Food Technology, Reading University, Weybridge, Surrey.

R. D. KING, B.Sc., Ph.D.
Lecturer at National College of Food Technology, Reading University, Weybridge, Surrey.

K. J. PARKER, M.A., D.Phil. (Oxon.)
General Manager, Tate & Lyle Ltd, Group Research and Development, Philip Lyle Memorial Research Laboratory, Reading University, PO Box 68, Reading, Berks.

H. VIZARD ROBINSON, A.C.I.S.
Former Secretary at National College of Food Technology, Reading University, Weybridge, Surrey.

E. J. ROLFE, B.Sc., M.Chem.A., F.R.I.C., F.I.F.S.T.
Principal, National College of Food Technology, Reading University, Weybridge, Surrey.

Mrs B. A. SHORE
National College of Food Technology, Reading University, Weybridge, Surrey.

R. H. TILBURY, B.Sc., Ph.D.
Tate & Lyle Ltd, Philip Lyle Memorial Research Laboratory, Reading University, PO Box 68, Reading, Berks.

J. T. WORGAN, B.Sc., Ph.D.
Lecturer, National College of Food Technology, Reading University, Weybridge, Surrey.

FOOD FROM WASTE

Edited by

G. G. BIRCH, K. J. PARKER
and J. T. WORGAN

APPLIED SCIENCE PUBLISHERS LTD
LONDON

APPLIED SCIENCE PUBLISHERS LTD
RIPPLE ROAD, BARKING, ESSEX, ENGLAND

ISBN: 0 85334 659 3

WITH 80 TABLES AND 61 ILLUSTRATIONS

Printed in Great Britain by Galliard (Printers) Ltd Great Yarmouth

List of Contributors

D. E. Brown
> *University of Manchester Institute of Science and Technology, PO Box 88, Sackville Street, Manchester, M60 1QD, England.*

S. G. Coton
> *Milk Marketing Board, Thames Ditton, Surrey KT7 0EL, England.*

H. O. W. Eggins
> *University of Aston in Birmingham, Biodeterioration Information Centre, 80 Coleshill Street, Birmingham B4 7PF, England.*

S. W. Fitzpatrick
> *University of Manchester Institute of Science and Technology, PO Box 88, Sackville Street, Manchester M60 1QD, England.*

C. F. Forster
> *Wessex Water Authority, Techno House, Redcliffe Way, Bristol BS1 6NY, England.*

R. A. Grant
> *Ecotech Systems (UK) Ltd, Balena Close, Creekmoor, Poole, Dorset, England.*

B. von Hofsten
> *Institute of Biochemistry, Box 531, 75121 Uppsala 1, Sweden.*

F. K. E. IMRIE

Tate & Lyle Ltd, Group Research and Development, Philip Lyle Memorial Research Laboratory, University of Reading, PO Box 68, Reading RG6 2BX, England.

J. C. JONES

Wessex Water Authority, Techno House, Redcliffe Way, Bristol BS1 6NY, England.

D. T. JONES

Viscose Group Ltd, Development Division, South Dock, Swansea SA1 1UT, Wales.

G. D. KAPSIOTIS

Development Strategy Service, FAO, Via delle Terme di Cara-calla, 00100 Rome, Italy.

B. J. OOSTEN

Koninklijke Scholten-Honig Research NV, Foxhol (GR), Postbus 1, KL Nieboerweg 12, The Netherlands.

G. W. PACE

Tate & Lyle Ltd, Group Research and Development, Philip Lyle Memorial Research Laboratory, PO Box 68, Reading RG6 2BX, England.

N. W. PIRIE

Rothamsted Experimental Station, Harpenden, Herts., England.

L. G. PLASKETT

Biotechnical Processes Ltd, Skilmoor House, Cadmore End, High Wycombe, Bucks. HP14 3PJ, England.

G. PRIESTLEY

Western Biological Equipment Ltd, Sherborne, Dorset DT9 4RW, England.

C. RATLEDGE

Biochemistry Department, University of Hull, Hull HU6 7RX, England.

R. C. RIGHELATO
Tate & Lyle Ltd, Group Research and Development, Philip Lyle Memorial Research Laboratory, University of Reading, PO Box 68, Reading RG6 2BX, England.

E. J. ROLFE
National College of Food Technology, University of Reading, St George's Avenue, Weybridge, Surrey KT13 0DE, England.

K. J. SEAL
University of Aston in Birmingham, Biodeterioration Information Centre, 80 Coleshill Street, Birmingham B4 7PF, England.

H. SKOGMAN
AB Sorigona, Box 139, 24500 Staffanstorp, Sweden.

G. SOBKOWICZ
Institute of Storage and Food Technology, Agricultural Academy, ul. C. Norwida 25, 50-375 Wrocław, Poland.

S. R. TANNENBAUM
Department of Nutrition and Food Science, Massachusetts Institute of Technology, Cambridge, Massachusetts 02139, USA.

P. VAN DER WAL
Institute for Animal Nutrition Research (ILOB), Wageningen, Haarweg 8, The Netherlands.

J. T. WORGAN
National College of Food Technology, University of Reading, St George's Avenue, Weybridge, Surrey KT13 0DE, England.

Contents

Session III (Chairman: Dr. Magnus Pyke)

Session IV (Chairman: Professor F. Aylward)

Contents

1

Food From Waste in the Present World Situation

E. J. Rolfe

*National College of Food Technology, University of
Reading, Weybridge, Surrey, England*

The occurrence of famine has always been the lot of man, and has not been restricted to the distant and remote parts of the world. The Irish famine of 1846 was caused by the complete failure of the potato crop—the staple diet of the people—through attack by the parasitic fungus *Phytophthora infestans*. The population of Ireland in 1700 was only 1¼ million. It reached 4½ million in 1800 and this rapid rate of increase continued for nearly the first half of the nineteenth century, reaching 8 million in 1841. In 1846 within the space of a few weeks the abundant potato harvest was replaced by a waste of putrefying vegetation. Death and hardship followed in spite of relief aid. It is said that the total Irish mortality for the five years ending in 1851 was close on a million and in the decade that followed 1847 more than 1½ million persons emigrated. The failure of crops aggravated by population increase still causes widespread death and misery and unfortunately represents an unresolved problem in the world today. At present there is extensive famine in the Indian subcontinent, Ethiopia and Sahel, and because of a succession of years of bad harvests in the world due to unfavourable weather, the world's granaries are nearly empty. The expanding population, accompanied by demands for a higher standard of living and for more material goods, is giving rise to a deeply disturbing and lengthy list of economic and environmental crises of apparently unmanageable proportions. We are all too familiar with the oil crisis, balance of payments crisis, unemployment, inflation, the energy crisis, and the shortage of fertilisers and of food and water. All are interrelated and impinge on and aggravate each other. The degree of success of any attempt to help solve the food crisis will be influenced by the extent to which account is taken of these other factors.

1

Man has proved himself to be the most successful animal to inhabit our planet, and through the application of science and technology, particularly medicine, agriculture, and an ability to exercise some control over his environment, his numbers are showing what is to a great many people an alarming rate of increase. The population of the world at the beginning of the Christian era has been estimated at about 250 million. Growth rate was slow until the mid-seventeenth century by which time it had doubled to 500 million. It doubled again to 1000 million by 1850—only 200 years later. Within 80 years, by 1930, the population doubled again to 2000 million and now by the mid-1970s the population has doubled once more.[1] In order to help meet the need for a vast increase in food supplies, the plant breeders introduced new high-yielding varieties of wheat and rice, and the consequent Green Revolution enabled food production to keep pace with the increase in population. But the high yields from these crops are dependent on what have now become expensive and scarce inputs, fertiliser and water, through the energy crisis and the dramatic increase in the cost of oil. Large energy inputs and advanced technology are needed to produce chemical fertilisers. Of necessity the price of the latter has increased and consequently their use is inhibited, particularly in the poorer countries. This, coupled with the higher cost of diesel fuel required for irrigation pumping, is causing the Green Revolution to wither. Most emphasis to increase food supplies is placed on the traditional ways of persuading the soil and the sea to yield more food. A welcome addition is the effort being devoted to exploiting the substantial potential of factory production of protein and to create food from waste. Presently the effort is relatively small but the signs are that expansion in this important area is occurring.

Lack of food, absence of employment, the shortage of arable land and capital for investment in the country areas has produced the urbanisation crisis, the irresistible growth of the world's cities due to the drift of people from the land to the towns, there to be herded into shanty towns on the perimeter. The cities must be fed and their expansion creates a demand for an ever greater supply of food from the rural areas. Sufficient is not available and so hunger and lack of work persist in the cities. Calcutta has become a familiar example of such circumstances where perhaps one million people without support live and die in the streets.

The growing population supported by a developing technology is demanding and getting an improved standard of living in many parts of the world, if this is interpreted in terms of an adequate diet, provision of labour-saving equipment in the home and factory, and availability of material things for comfort and pleasure. The food factory prepares convenience foods and has taken much of the drudgery out of the kitchen. The manufacturers vie with each other in presenting their goods in alluring wraps of plastic, paper or foil in order to attract and persuade the housewife to select their goods from the supermarket shelf. The expensive wraps, after completing their other function of protecting the food during retailing and distribution, will finish in the dustbin, possibly with some of the food. The avoidance of such waste of energy and material resources is a matter for urgent investigation, and recycling, together with greater care to reduce waste, can ameliorate the situation. This policy is given ready endorsement by the environmentalists who are particularly alert to the threats to our environment of effluents from factories and the waste that accumulates and accompanies living in a civilised community. Our daily national newspapers consume vast quantities of timber as newsprint—use it more quickly than it can be replaced by Nature—but after the newspaper has been read it quickly becomes waste which absorbs further effort and energy for its collection and disposal together with other rubbish from the home. Greater efforts are being made to utilise waste newsprint. A new de-inking process permits it to replace a proportion of the wood pulp in newsprint manufacture. The use of cellulose from waste paper as an energy source for micro-organisms to synthesise fat or convert inorganic nitrogen into protein is an interesting possibility that could make a noteworthy contribution to our food supply.

Other wastes which give rise to concern because of pollution (but also have potential for conversion into food) include those from agriculture, particularly where intensive farming methods are used, *e.g.* battery hens and broilers, effluents from food factories, and residues from meat, poultry and fish processing plants. All such materials merit consideration as a means of providing food for human consumption. Some residues can be readily upgraded into a food suitable for human consumption, *e.g.* a considerable amount of fish muscle tissue remains on the bones and head of fish after filleting. This residual tissue can be removed mechanically but has a pink colour. Nutritionally it is the equal of the fish fillet and it shows no flavour abnormalities. Hence, provided the consumer will accept pink fish fingers, a substantial quantity of extra fish can be provided for human consumption at the expense of a small drop in fish meal production. Other residues can be converted into animal feeding stuffs and help to maintain our supply of poultry, eggs and milk and reduce the requirement of imported feeding stuffs.

Wastes and residues unsuited for either of the above uses may be converted into food for animals or man through their conversion by means of micro-organisms. An early attempt of this kind was the preparation of food yeast from molasses in Jamaica during World War II. During the last few decades a new biotechnological industry has emerged and developed based on the large-scale commercial culture of micro-organisms. They are used to produce a wide range of biochemicals and pharmacologically active substances, *e.g.* steroids, vitamins and antibiotics. Also a substantial part of the new fermentation industry has been oriented towards meeting the need of the food industry for essential raw materials. It uses large quantities of acetic, lactic and citric acids of microbial origin, and amino acids from such a source may become important for supplementation or upgrading of proteins from new sources. Enzymes for the food industry are also prepared by fermentation. This new knowledge and expertise in biotechnology is available and is being applied to microbial biosynthesis as a means of adding to our food supply. To convert waste or surplus organic material and a cheap nitrogen source into microbial protein is an attractive proposition, and a considerable part of this symposium is devoted to a critical study and evaluation of the process and its possibilities using various waste materials as substrate. The traditional fermentation is a discontinuous batch process, but the potential advantages of a continuous fermentation process for large-scale production are clearly obvious and important. But whereas the selection of chemically and physically induced mutants has provided the means to achieve dramatic increases in yields in a wide range of fermentations, the occurrence of a spontaneous mutation in the microbial population in a continuous fermenter which escaped detection could be a serious hazard, particularly if the end-product is intended for human consumption. The acceptance of foods from microbial biosynthesis must be preceded by extensive clinical and toxicity feeding tests, and only following favourable reports will approval for their use as human food be given. Such approval cannot apply to the product obtained from a new mutation of the original micro-organism, and stringent checks to detect mutation, should it occur, become essential.

The nucleic acid content of a cell is dependent on its rate of growth, a consequence of the fact that nucleic acids are involved in the synthesis of proteins. Microbial cells in the favourable environment provided in a fermenter grow and multiply rapidly and their content of nucleic acids may be up to 15% (on a dry weight basis), which is much greater than occurs in protein foods of animal origin such as meat or fish. Nucleic acids after ingestion give rise to uric acid in the blood, and because of low solubility and possibility of precipitation may give rise to disorders similar to gout. Accordingly the Protein Advisory Group of FAO have recommended that the ingestion of nucleic acid from such sources should not exceed 2 g/day.[2-4] If microbial protein is to be used as a major source of protein in the diet its nucleic acid content must be reduced by some suitable treatment. This will affect yield and add cost to the product, as will also any treatment which may be required to remove flavour or to build in special textural characteristics. Such considerations cannot be overlooked as the economics of the process and cost of product must always be under surveillance. It is obviously simpler to use microbial protein for animal feed and often this is the initial target of present commercial operations.

The value of imported animal feeding stuffs into the UK is substantial and partial replacement by organic wastes is being explored and represents a valuable means of producing food from waste. Proper treatment to render such wastes free from pathogens and safe for animal feeding is essential. The incidence of salmonellosis has increased markedly over the past two to three years in most countries and contaminated animal feed is a major source of infection.[5] The chain of events leading to disease in man is from contaminated feeding stuff to infection of the animal, through to our food and to man. Inadequate treatment of animal waste products converted to feedstuffs perpetuates the cycle of salmonellae back to the living animal. Most feedstuffs come from overseas, *e.g.* fish meal, meat unfit for human consumption and animal, poultry and vegetable wastes of various kinds which are ground, sterilised and dried. They are rendered quite safe provided the treatment is properly controlled, but such is not always the case. A procedure for converting poultry manure into an animal feed ingredient has been developed in Denmark. It is stated to contain up to 30% protein, and it is relevant in this context to point out that Denmark has a pathogen-free poultry scheme.[6] Since the big increase in protein prices which began about two years ago it has been estimated that processed poultry manure has been used in compound animal feeds manufactured in the UK at the rate of about 50,000 tons per annum. Potential UK production from laying units only (broiler units are excluded because of drug residue problems) is estimated to be about 800,000 tons per annum which would significantly reduce the cost of beef and dairy rations. Once dried and sterilised it can be utilised by cattle and sheep, it is stated. Chickens are a reservoir for salmonellae but this does not imply that the use of the manure for feeding should be prohibited on bacteriological grounds; rather the hazard should be recognised and due precautions taken. The latter remark applies to any waste which may be fed to animals; it must be properly processed to ensure freedom from pathogens.

When considering the production of food from waste, due regard must be paid to its applicability and objectives relevant to the proposed location of the operation. Waste material is available universally, *e.g.* sewage, waste paper, food factory effluents in the technologically advanced countries, and primarily agricultural residues in developing countries, *e.g.* sugar cane bagasse, olive press cake and citrus waste. A successful process will have taken into account all the local factors. The conversion of waste into a food material is not the most difficult of the problems. It is susceptible to solution by scientific study and it is encouraging that scientific interest is being generated in this area, with some of the more important developments being reported at this symposium. But the world food crisis cannot be solved without also solving the problem of world poverty. People without work cannot earn money to buy the cheapest of available foods, and consequently the market for the produce will not be available. It is the solving of the human, social and economic issues which presents the greatest difficulty and it is to be hoped that they will also receive extensive study in the appropriate quarter. In the developing areas where the need for additional food supplies is greatest it is perhaps going to be most difficult to implement such schemes. A large-scale operation can be successful only if assured of a reliable and adequate supply of waste material, if appropriate services such as electricity, water, etc., are available together with suitable labour to operate plant, and if an efficient infrastructure exists to permit distribution of the finished product. The product will be consumed only if it is attractive and can be absorbed into the local social culture. This is an aspect that cannot be ignored. Though the food produced from the waste may have excellent nutritive value, it will not benefit man unless it is eaten. The objective must therefore be to produce palatable cheap food which will be accepted by the indigenous population. For developing countries the new food should be stable and easy to distribute without the need for elaborate food distribution chains such as exist in the technologically advanced countries. However, traditional societies will eventually need to change if the projections of world population materialise. Change must come, *e.g.* in food habits, if only to cope with the much greater numbers of children which now survive with the aid of modern medicine. Traditional methods and inputs will be unable to provide even a meagre living. New methods of food production must be ready to support the world's population as the need arises.

REFERENCES

1. Bridger, E. and de Soissons, M. (1970). *Famine in Retreat?* Dent, London.
2. Edozien, J. C., Udo, U. U., Young, V. R. and Scrimshaw, N. S. (1970). *Nature, London,* **228**, p. 180.
3. Rolfe, E. J. and Spicer, A. (1973). In: *The Biological Efficiency of Protein Production,* ed. J. G. W. Jones, Cambridge University Press, pp. 363–70.
4. PAG Guideline No. 7, FAO/WHO/UNICEF Protein Advisory Group, *Guideline for Human Testing of Supplementary Food Mixtures,* 10 June 1970.
5. Hobbs, Betty C. (1974). *Food Manufacture,* **49**(10), p. 29.
6. Wollen, A. (1974). *Food Manufacture,* **49**(10), p. 3.

2

Food from Waste: An Overview

S. R. Tannenbaum and G. W. Pace*

*Department of Nutrition and Food Science,
Massachusetts Institute of Technology, Cambridge, Massachusetts,
USA*

ABSTRACT

The concept of producing food from waste has become of great interest within the last few years as a result of increasingly frequent food shortages and price rises. Direct human food production by fermentation of most waste materials is unlikely at present due to the problem of meeting safety requirements. Feed production is more likely, and the presentation will focus on schemes for fermentation of waste to animal feed ingredients. Economics is the overriding factor in the decision to implement any process. Although many waste streams appear to have zero or negative costs, there are often hidden costs in additional processing necessary to prepare the material for fermentation. Another significant consideration is the availability of raw material with respect to quantity and distribution in time. These and other economic factors will be reviewed for a number of waste processing proposals with a view towards generating a unified approach to the problem.

INTRODUCTION

Millennia ago man was a hunter and gatherer, and there was no conception, let alone problem, of waste. He used what he required, and whatever remained was readily absorbed into the ecosystem and recycled.

It was only when man began to settle the land and congregate in groups, and ultimately to live in cities, that waste became a problem. The Industrial Revolution not only exacerbated the existing problem, but also created new types of industrial waste, including materials which were foreign to the ecosystem.

Today we have come to the point where a new type of Industrial

---

* Present address: Tate & Lyle Ltd, Philip Lyle Memorial Research Laboratory, University of Reading, Reading, England.

8

Revolution is required—one in which the waste of the old system becomes the raw material of the new system. In the keynote to this symposium on Food from Waste, we will try to indicate briefly where the opportunities and pitfalls lie. The more important indications of progress in specific areas will be given in the papers of the symposium.

ORIGIN AND TYPES OF WASTE

Many types of waste result as a consequence of the production and consumption of food. To understand the problem of waste in the general sense one needs to consider for each type of food the total production, distribution and consumption system as depicted in Fig. 1. One can imagine from this picture the varied nature of the opportunities that may arise.

For example, in a country with scarce land resources and a primitive food distribution system, there would be great incentives to collect and recycle at the farm level all materials which could be converted to animal feed. At the same time, expense or unavailability

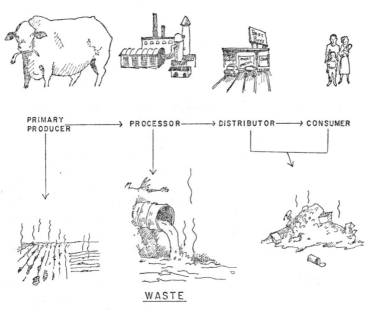

FIG. 1.   Formation of waste in the food distribution system.

of a local energy supply might dictate that part or all of the waste be converted to methane or hydrogen. Materials which in years past served as mulch or fertiliser are no longer utilisable with modern agricultural practice. In addition, concentration of production facilities, such as in modern poultry houses or cattle feedlots, has created concentrated waste streams which had not previously existed.

Waste streams from food processing operations can be divided into two general categories on the basis of their biological oxygen demand (BOD) or soluble and suspended solids content, as shown in Fig. 2. Low BOD streams (less than about 5000 ppm) are usually

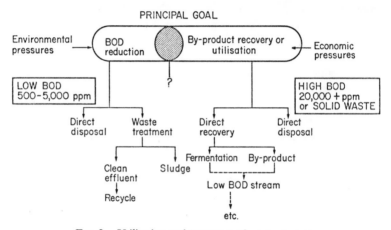

FIG. 2.   Utilisation and treatment of waste streams.

treated because of environmental pressures. Where severe economic penalties are incurred for direct disposal, by-product recovery or fermentation may prove to be the more desirable disposal route. However, because these streams are so dilute, at present disposal by microbial processes necessitates either preconcentration of the waste stream, or a large capital investment per pound of BOD disposed. As will be seen later, many food plants which operate at a marginal profit would not be able to assume the cost of disposal, by microbial processes or any other procedure, without raising the sales price of their product to an uncompetitive level. Low BOD streams must have a negative cost associated with their disposal.

High BOD streams (20,000+ ppm) or solid wastes (which also arise at the distribution–consumer end of the system) may be treated because of environmental pressures, but economic opportunities may also exist in the form of a marketable by-product which may either be recovered directly from the waste stream (*e.g.* whey protein) or indirectly by fermentation. It is possible that the treatment process may result in a 'spent substrate' stream which will require additional processing to lower BOD to meet regulatory standards. Two possible approaches to this final stream include recycling all or part of the water within the plant, or total evaporation of the exit stream to produce solids which may or may not be added to the product. In any case, the economics of treating high BOD streams by fermentation follow those of other single-cell protein (SCP) processes, and an economically successful process will generally depend upon the relative (local) value of the substrate.

WHEN IS A WASTE?

The economic considerations of high BOD waste disposal schemes leave us with the semantic conundrum of whether something is a waste or a by-product. Obviously, once a waste stream achieves some measure of value it is no longer waste, even though the original impetus for processing was the cost of disposal. In fact, the assigned value for a waste is often a question of locale, as, for example, the fuel value of bagasse or sulphite waste liquor. Depending upon tax laws and investment incentives, it might be more profitable for a company to assign a negative (or positive) value to a waste stream at the expense of the main process.

ECONOMIC CONSIDERATIONS

Important economic considerations applicable to the processing of different waste streams are summarised in Table 1. For liquid wastes from fruit and vegetable processing plants, Olson *et al.*[1] have conducted an economic survey and listed four approaches to liquid waste control:

1. Treatment by lagoons or aeration, *i.e.* involving fermentation processes and possibly leading to recoverable SCP.
2. Disposal by irrigation.
3. Disposal to municipal sewage plants.
4. In-plant changes to reduce waste water flows or the generation of BOD or suspended solids.

TABLE 1
Economic considerations in the processing of waste streams according to principal aim

BOD reduction[a]	Waste utilisation[b]
1. Extent and type of treatment required: fixed by environmental limits, nature of stream, available plant 2. In-house versus municipal treatment 3. By-product recovery to partially off-set treatment costs (*e.g.* CH_4, SCP, fertiliser, B_{12})	1. Availability: volume, strength, seasonality, location 2. Manufacturing costs versus sales price: product demand and saleability intrinsic value of waste hidden costs—further disposal of resultant low BOD stream

[a] Typically low BOD waste streams.
[b] Typically high BOD of solid waste streams.

Economic aspects of the fermentation approach are shown for plant size and extent of BOD removal in Fig. 3.

The pollution control cost in $ per ton of raw material processed is influenced strongly by the above two factors. The pollution control cost that would cause a plant to go out of business, assuming no price increase, was named the 'critical pollution control cost'.

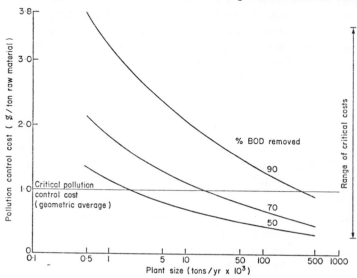

FIG. 3. Pollution control costs versus plant size (calculated from data of Olson *et al.*[1]).

This varied among the plants surveyed with a geometric average of $1 and a range of $0·25 to $3·6. Taking the geometric average, a plant processing about 5000 tons per year could afford about 60% BOD removal, and in general small plants would be hard put to operate their own treatment systems at a high rate of BOD removal.

SCP PRODUCTION

A general scheme for SCP production is shown in Fig. 4. The inputs into any SCP fermentation include the inoculum, essential nutrients and energy, and the outputs include heat, carbon dioxide and cells. The major operating costs in the fermentation are related to cost of nutrients, oxygen transfer and heat removal. In addition to the fermentation cost, we must also consider unit operations concerned with collecting and utilising the cells in the fermenter effluent, and the unit operations connected with conversion of the waste into a suitable substrate for the organism. The blocks in Fig. 4 represent all possible operations, but one would not expect all to be present in any one process.

What are the special problems for conversion of waste to SCP? First, it is well recognised that the greatest biomass productivity for a fermentation plant is achieved when the process is run on a continuous basis. Many food processes are highly seasonal, producing 75% of their annual BOD in less than four months. Even during the season these plants might operate only five days a week. And even if the plant processes more than one type of raw material, the nature and concentration of the waste streams will vary on a temporal basis. A continuous process could not be used under these conditions. An interesting approach to these problems is the recent tendency to explore inexpensive fermenters of plastic or concrete construction which operate at low pH to avoid the need for sterile operation, and which are based upon fungal fermentations with organisms that are not 'finicky' and are adaptable to unsteady-state operation.[2,3] This approach could be adapted to food processing or farm waste, but economically is still in the exploratory stage.

A different type of problem is presented by solid wastes containing large amounts of cellulose. In these cases, although the waste is apparently free, the fermentation substrate is not free because a significant cost arises in the form of conversion of the waste to a fermentable form, *i.e.* glucose. Therefore, one must ask the question: will the cost of producing fermentable sugar from waste cellulose compete with other available substrates which could be used in the fermentation? Thus far, the cost of converting cellulose to sugar has been economically marginal, although future expectations for process improvements are high.

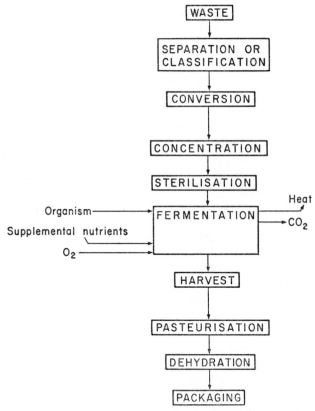

Fig. 4.   General scheme for SCP production from waste.

Another problem in the case of many wastes is their content of non-fermentable substances which may accumulate in the cells or fermenter effluent and which may be non-nutritive or even toxic. Examples include lignin degradation products, heavy metals, agricultural chemical residues, etc. It is hardly likely that one could afford the extra processing necessary to guarantee safety.

COMBINED PROCESSES

In many instances there has been considerable interest generated by wastes that offer combined opportunities. An outstanding example of this type of waste is the whey that is a by-product of cheese manufacture, containing both a high-quality protein (0·6%) and a readily fermentable sugar, lactose (5%). The quantity of whey annually produced in the United States is of the order of 12 million tons, but the industry is highly dispersed and there is also some variability in the characteristics of the whey depending upon the type of cheese being manufactured.

There are a number of proposals for combined processes which recover protein and ferment the lactose to SCP. One such process utilises membrane ultrafiltration to remove protein and feeds the lactose-containing permeate to a fermenter for SCP production from *S. fragilis*. The final products are this dried food-grade yeast and dried whey protein. The economic feasibility of such a process has been explored,[4] and the authors have indicated that the profitability of any part or all of the combined operation of ultrafiltration/ fermentation depends upon how one wishes to distribute the total cost of sales. That is, one could (a) ferment whole whey; (b) recover whey protein and discharge lactose; or (c) use a combined process. Although (c) provides the most useful manner in which the whey could be processed, it also requires the largest capital investment and would need fairly large quantities of whey for optimum scale of operation. A further complication is that mentioned earlier, a waste becoming a by-product. With the recent price increases in dried milk, dried whey has become a valuable material in its own right, and in some localities is no longer available.

WASTE INTO FOOD OR FEED?

Increasingly frequent food shortages and increases in the price of food, as well as environmental pressures, are the basis of our interest in reusing waste. However, can waste be directly converted to food? There is obviously a serious problem of public concern about what is going into our food, and sources of waste which are not in themselves food grade will have difficulty becoming recognised as direct food precursors. Substances like cheese whey, for example, if handled under appropriate conditions of microbiological quality, can be considered foods as such or serve as precursors for other food products. Other types of food waste (not food grade in themselves), or SCP produced under non-aseptic conditions, would have to be considered for use as animal feed.

There are now guidelines available from the Protein and Calorie Advisory Group of the United Nations for SCP intended as food or animal feed, notably PAG Guideline No. 6 on the requirement for pre-clinical testing, Guideline No. 7 on food specifications and human testing, and Guideline No. 15 on animal feeds. Typical testing protocols are given in Dr I. P. van der Wal's paper in this volume. In 1975 prices it is likely that a complete testing protocol will cost on the order of US $500 000, which is a significant part of the necessary research investment. Moreover, it is also likely that a given organism grown on distinctly different types of waste will be considered as different products, and therefore require separate testing. Although these costs will act as a deterrent to the application of certain types of waste utilisation schemes, it would be irresponsible to the health and safety of future generations to forgo or lower these standards.

Although the problem is purely semantic in nature, publicising the idea of food from waste could in itself be anti-productive as a result of public misunderstanding. It would perhaps be better to talk in specific rather than generic terms when describing such processes, to avoid entirely the necessity of explaining how that which is clearly not food, *i.e.* waste, can be reconverted or reclaimed.

ULTIMATE DISPOSAL

The utopian goal is to maximise our food production, minimise our energy input and simultaneously protect our environment. Some have suggested the creation of the 'city-farm', shown in Fig. 5, as one approach to the solution of the waste problems generated at all stages of the food distribution system.[5]

As we all know, no system operates in perpetual motion. No matter where we draw our boundaries we require an external source of energy and somewhere along the way our system will also ultimately produce unusable waste in the form of heat. It is not at all clear that optimisation of waste disposal systems from an energy point of view would produce the same solutions as optimisation from other economic points of view, particularly if the cost of energy is externally subsidised by local authorities.

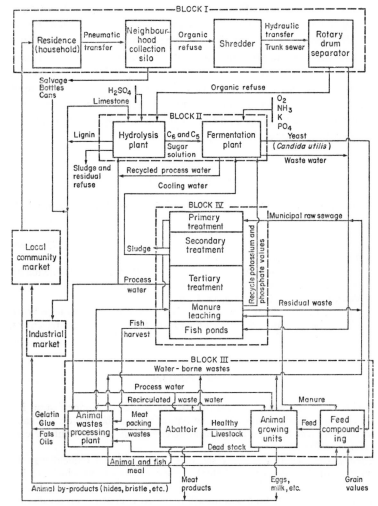

FIG. 5. The 'city-farm' concept.[5]

CONCLUSIONS

The concept of producing food from waste is attractive and creates many opportunities for inventive proposals, such as will be heard at this symposium. At the same time it is likely that a significant number of waste problems will not be immediately amenable to by-product recovery or recycling. Nevertheless, these problems too will require solution. It is apparent that under the impact of continued strong pressures to protect our environment, small inefficient plants will disappear. To avoid a significant additional energy expenditure to treat these waste problems, a great deal more attention will have to be paid to more efficient plant and process design. In some cases the way to generate food from waste is to minimise the formation of waste in the first place; in others it may entail SCP production or by-product recovery. There is no ideal solution, only the most appropriate solution for a given situation.

REFERENCES

1. Olson, N. A., Katsugama, A. M. and Rose, W. W. (1974). In: *Fifth National Symposium on Food Processing Wastes Proceedings*, Environmental Protection Agency, Washington, DC, p. 280.
2. Church, B. D., Erickson, E. E. and Widmer, C. M. (1973). *Food Technol.*, **27**, p. 36.
3. Imrie, F. and Vlitos, A. J. (1975). In: *SCP II*, ed. S. R. Tannenbaum and D. I. C. Wang, MIT Press, Cambridge, Mass.
4. Pace, G. W. and Goldstein, D. J. *Ibid.*
5. Meller, F. W. (1969). *Conversion of Organic Solid Wastes into Yeast*, US Public Health Service, Bureau of Solid Waste Management, Rockville, Maryland.

DISCUSSION

Parker: One question I would like to ask Professor Tannenbaum, if I may, is do you identify any particular type of waste as being most amenable to development from an economical or commercial standpoint for conversion to food?

Tannenbaum: There are many schemes, but I felt that effluent was the purpose of this symposium. I think there are many ideas which are just marginally economical at this point, but I think there are many factors which could change that situation. Very often it depends on locale—for example, I could cite the case of General Electric which has a process for recycling waste, which is basically manure, back into animal feed for the calf. Right now it appears to be uneconomical in the United States but it appears it may be economical in Europe simply because of the differential in the price of animal feed in the two different locations. So that is an example, and I think there are other examples, such as in the processing of whey, where, given the right conditions, that is given enough whey in the locale, and given that the whey comes from the right kind of cheese process, it might be feasible to recover whey protein. But with a small cheese plant that is not operating with a whey of good microbiological properties, the chances are that the odds are against it, so it is very locale-dependent both from the point of view of the source of the raw material and from the point of view of where you are going to sell the product.

Parker: Thank you, Professor Tannenbaum. In other words it depends where the waste is and how valuable it is.

Tannenbaum: Yes.

Lalla: Can Professor Tannenbaum comment on the possibility of concentrating small quantities of waste available from small factories.

Tannenbaum: It has been suggested, for example, that all plants have evaporation capacity, and so might use their evaporators to preconcentrate the whey and then to ship it, to reduce the shipping cost. Is this what you are talking about? And it has been suggested that even reverse osmosis could be used to concentrate directly. These are interesting suggestions, but I think that one simply has to sit down and look at it in a hard way. (I didn't intend that as a pun.) For example, I think it is generally accepted that if you are going to build a fermentation plant to make single-cell protein you are going to make a high-quality product and you are going to make it for food material. So it has to be of sanitary construction and it has to be a continuous plant, for there are certain minimum criteria that these plants would have to meet, and really there are certain minimum sizes which the plant would have to meet before it could hope to begin to operate economically. I think that a number that is often given is around 10 000 tons a year and that requires a lot of whey. It is not that there aren't any places where it can be used, but if you have a situation, for example where you have some plants producing acid whey and other plants producing sweet whey, and the microbiological quality varies, then it is difficult. People have looked at it and it often turns out to be marginal. Furthermore there is the problem of capital investment. Companies are usually short of capital and what they want to do is put their capital where it will bring the greatest return, and the idea of fermenting lactose to yeast has most often not been the best way to place their capital. It is as simple as that. Given an infinite amount of capital there would be no problem in the economic incentives, and then I think you would see many more people going into the idea of producing single-cell protein. I would point out that there are other fermentation alternatives. It is fairly well known now in the United States that the Kraft Co., which controls more whey than any other company in the United States, some years ago started to make alcohol and vinegar which they could use within their own company. They still make a fair amount of vinegar which they use in their mayonnaise and salad dressings, from their whey, but those economics are now dependent upon the fact that those plants were built a long time ago, and I'm not certain that one could afford to build a new plant at this point.

Questioner: Should we not lower our sights and produce animal feed protein rather than produce protein of a higher quality?

Tannenbaum: I was trying to give a flavour of this in my talk. I think that the returns in terms of the potential sales price of the product is obviously going to be much harder in a human food product, so therefore most animal feed projects tend to operate at a very much smaller margin, but at the same time would allow you, I think, a smaller capital investment. That is, you could get away with building simpler plants which don't have to operate so strictly and aseptically and you might be able to get away with some organisms. I think there are many organisms, for example, which would be tolerated by animals, and particularly certain types of farm animals, that wouldn't be tolerated necessarily by humans and which would create flavour problems which would preclude say utilisation in food, whereas it could be used for example in animal feeds. So often where this has been successful it has been in a local situation where one can't get rid of the material, because usually one wants to avoid, if one can, in that kind of a situation, the drying cost. The drying cost is often very expensive and if you can get away with just basically pasteurising the product, giving it to some local pig farmer to let him add to his slops or something like that, then you can operate more easily.

Butcher: Professor Tannenbaum, coming back to SCP from whey, I believe you have done a fair bit of work on DNA reduction of yeasts produced from this kind of material. A lot of people have been rather worried about human subjects—I believe people at MIT—being able to take high levels of DNA, and I wonder if you have any comments?

Tannenbaum: RNA is really the problem, because DNA is at a low concentration. The problem of nucleic acid levels in general is a problem which is related primarily to usage of the materials in fairly high concentrations of foods. If you want to use materials as a food additive with, let us say, 3–5 % concentrations of nucleic acids, then the amount being added to the diet would be so small as not to be of any significance, but if one wanted to consider using single-cell protein directly as a human food in large amounts, then I think one has a problem in getting rid of the RNA. We have done some work at MIT and most of this has been published, but I also think there has been a lot of work done in other places and I think it has definitely been a problem. It has not been a problem to develop processes which will reduce RNA. It has been a problem to develop processes which are as economical as one would like to reduce RNA, and this is a general problem with single-cell protein production and not one that is specifically related to the question of food from waste. I think a detailed discussion of this problem would be outside the context of this talk.

Edelman: You said that by 1985 it is possible that no waste water will be mandatory in the United States. On that basis the companies concerned will be required to spend money on reducing their waste. Do you see a very large increase in food from waste, or feed from waste, or waste elimination, around the middle 1980s?

Tannenbaum: I think we can still separate these two points because, for example, what will be important is to have no waste water. But you could still distribute solids from the plant. Once again getting back to whey, which is just an easy one to come back to, what really held up the whole problem of whey treatment is what do you do with the lactose, and up until now it has just been cheaper to burn the lactose than to build a plant to ferment it. Now this is beginning to change. For example, if you concentrated your lactose stream to a very high solids content there is no reason why you couldn't just use it as fuel, or there's no reason why you couldn't convert it to methane and put the methane back into the plant. So there are many schemes which one could envisage which would not create waste water but would still discharge solids in some way, and what one does with those solids is very much locale-dependent. I'll give you one example. In the United States the Campbell soup company, which is a company that has plants all over the United States, has plants in some parts of the United States, for example in Texas, where they are growing the most beautiful grass you ever saw by just taking the waste water from the plant and using it to irrigate a field, and then they are harvesting the grass and selling the grass off for local cattle feed, but try doing that in the middle of New Jersey. Exactly the same plant in a different locale creates very different kinds of problems. I think one still is going to have to sit down, even in 1985, and say what is the cheapest way out of this thing, and if one sees an opportunity in a new product then I think this will be pursued, and it is also a way to get rid of the waste. I think in general, when it comes to the crux, that people tend to separate these problems.

Wimpenny: You were talking about the problems of this high-technology single-cell protein production and the necessity for very large plants. We found the same thing in our study of this sort of thing that has been going on in Great Britain. We find there are only very few wastes capable of being economically converted to protein, but I was very interested in what you said about the possible low-technology approaches, so what do you think of the future of the low-technology approach using cheap fermenters, and where do you think the cut-off might be for low-technology single-cell protein?

Tannenbaum: Well, I think this is an idea that has really only just got started, and just looking at the programme I think there are a number of people who are going to be talking about this. This is something that Tate & Lyle's have been interested in, and there is a group in the United States which is interested. The idea here is that it is still a very complicated problem. The first goal is to get rid of the waste, not to produce protein. If one could produce protein at the same time, so much the better. I think the beauty of things like fungal fermentations is that they are slower-growing and they do tend to have a certain amount of stability, that they are less finicky and you can just rake the stuff out under awkward conditions, and furthermore they seem to have some pretty good nutritional properties, at least in some species. So I think that there will be more done along these lines. I think, for example, although I didn't mention it, that ensilage once again is a way of getting rid of waste. When you look at silage you see that really almost nothing has been done, I think, for four years on the microbiology of silage. I use that as an example of another way of putting stuff into a pit and letting it become converted to something potentially useful. I think that the reason that approach is going to be attractive is because it is going to require a minimal capital investment, and the reason why the high-technology approach is going to be unattractive is simply because it is going to require a high capital investment.

Wimpenny: There's plenty of room for both, really.

Tannenbaum: Well, I know that in the petrochemical industry, for example, there are many schemes that are being held up, not just single-cell protein, but plant construction, simply because the money isn't there. And I know specifically of some single-cell protein schemes which simply hadn't got the go-ahead because the company has been unwilling to commit the capital. So I would say—I hate to make predictions that go too far into the future—I don't know what the situation is going to be like in 1985. Maybe we will all have to go to Saudi Arabia to build our plants, I don't know.

Questioner: Could I ask one final supplementary question on the high-technology approach: what about the possibility, since cellulose is so important, of farming cellulose as well?

Tannenbaum: I think that ultimately cellulose is going to be a very important substance, whether it comes from waste or whether it comes directly from producing cellulose to produce waste, because you can produce it in very high yield on a very wide variety of different types of land resources, and I think that once we really put our minds to it we are going to solve some of those problems, but right now there are some very serious technological problems, such as the other things that come along with the cellulose, for example the cost of hydrolysing the cellulose. Also there is the fact that the optimum fermentation conditions for degrading cellulose to glucose are not the same as the optimum conditions for producing cell mass. But I think we are getting round those problems. I think that when one thinks of cellulose, at the same time one ought to think of starch, because there is another case of something which we have had in excess from time to time in certain situations, and certainly it is much more readily convertible and presents far fewer problems than cellulose. Yet there have been great problems in finding ways to use it economically, and the thing that saved starch, certainly in the United States and I think to an extent in Europe, was the fructose technology; basically that someone discovered how to convert glucose into fructose by fermentation at a reasonable cost, and that took companies which were almost on the verge of bankruptcy in the United States and made them into the hottest stocks on the New York Stock Exchange. So I think that it is difficult to predict what technology will produce, but I think that ultimately cellulose will be very important.

3

Wastes from Crop Plants as Raw Materials for Conversion by Fungi to Food or Livestock Feed

J. T. WORGAN

National College of Food Technology, University of Reading, Weybridge, Surrey, England

ABSTRACT

Neither synthesis nor conversion of the fossil fuels can produce sufficient food for the increasing world population. Supplies must therefore be provided from agriculture and since less than one-quarter of current production is consumed as food, greater use must be made of agricultural output.

The short-term solution is to convert wastes from established processes to food. A more fundamental approach is to treat the whole of crop plants as sources of food raw materials. Examples are the separation of oil and protein from oilseeds and leaf protein extraction accompanied by microbiological conversion of the remainder of the crop.

Fibrous residues form the bulk of agricultural and food processing wastes and are resistant to microbiological conversion. Chemical methods of treatment can reduce this resistance and examples are given of the preparation of culture media for fungal protein production.

Nutritional value and the safety of the product as food or feed are the important criteria for the selection of microbial species. If a species shows any indication of growth on a non-fibrous waste, then both growth rate and protein yield can be increased by adaptation to the substrate. By applying this principle Fusarium semitectum *has been adapted to utilise lactose and starch. Studies on mycelial protein production by the fungal species* Aspergillus oryzae, F. semitectum *and* Trichoderma viride *from the following wastes are reported: citrus pulp, cheese and soya bean wheys, olive and palm waste liquors, leaf protein residual juice and starch processing effluents.*

In several of these examples the reduction of the biological oxygen demand of the waste is an essential part of the process. Although most of the products are initially intended for livestock feed, toxicity trials and food textural studies indicate that F. semitectum *mycelium could be a safe and acceptable food product.*

INTRODUCTION

Every year the world's population increases by 75 million and to keep pace with the additional demand for food, annual production must be increased by three times the total output of UK agriculture.[1] Although the synthesis of food is scientifically feasible, the amount of energy required makes this method of food production impracticable. The USA, for example, would have to divert more than half the present amount of energy consumed to food production and most other countries would have to use amounts far in excess of their present total consumption.[2,3]

As an alternative to synthesis the fossil fuels can be converted to food by chemical or microbiological methods. The energy consumed, including that of the fossil fuel raw materials, is less than that required for synthesis[2,3] and the method has the advantage over agriculture that arable land is not essential. There are, however, competing demands for the fossil fuels and we are now well aware that supplies are not unlimited. Agriculture will therefore continue to provide the bulk of our food supplies and the output of food can be increased by making more effective use of agricultural production, since less than one-quarter of the material produced by crop plants is currently used as food.[4]

SEPARATION OF NUTRIENTS FROM CROP PLANTS

Most of the under-utilised materials occur as crop residues from agricultural production or as wastes from subsequent processing. The short-term solution is to convert wastes from established processes to food or to upgrade their value as livestock feed. For some crops a more fundamental approach is to regard the whole of the crop plant as a source of food raw material. An example of this approach is the leaf protein process described in a later paper by N. W. Pirie. The separation of oil and a high-quality protein from oilseeds is a further example. In the processes currently in use the oil is regarded as the primary product and although the residues after oil extraction have a high protein content, they are frequently unsuitable for human consumption. In 1970 it was estimated that 22 million tons per year of largely under-utilised oilseed proteins were produced.[5]

Recovery of Sesame Protein

Sesame protein is of particular interest because it is one of the few plant sources of protein which has an excess of the sulphur amino acids, cystine and methionine. Most microbial sources of protein are also limiting in these sulphur amino acids. From the conventional method of oil extraction from sesame seeds the approximate composition of the residue is 50% protein, 8% fibre and 5% oxalate. Both the fibre and the oxalate are located in the outer seed coat, the removal of which is difficult by purely mechanical methods. A preliminary steep for approximately 1 min in hot dilute alkali (0·6% NaOH) facilitates decortication and the residue after oil extraction has been found to contain 4·4% fibre and 0·9% oxalate. Although some foods do contain this amount of oxalate[6] it is advisable, particularly for child feeding, that the level should be reduced.

TABLE 1

Limiting amino acids in sesame, soya and F. semitectum *proteins*

Protein	Amino acid (g/16 g of N)			
	Lysine	Methionine	Cystine	Total S
Sesame[8]	3·2	3·3	2·1	5·4
Soya[8]	6·9	1·4	1·4	2·8
Sesame and soya 1:1	5·5	2·3	1·8	4·1
Sesame and *F. semitectum*[a] 1:1	4·1	2·3	1·5	3·8
FAO reference[9]	4·2	2·2	2·0	4·2

[a] See Table 2.

Studies to improve the method for the removal of oxalate and to investigate the properties of sesame protein are in progress.[7] The complementary nutritional effect of the limiting amino acids in soya and sesame proteins is illustrated in Table 1.

MICROBIOLOGICAL CONVERSION OF WASTES TO FOOD OR LIVESTOCK FEED

The bulk of the wastes which occur from agriculture or food processing are not suitable for food or livestock feed because they are too fibrous to be digested by monogastric animals or because the cost of the separation of the organic matter from large volumes of liquid is not justified by the value of the product.[10] Micro-organisms are capable of utilising the organic matter in wastes as their source of energy for growth and as carbon compounds for the synthesis of cell biomass.

Nitrogen can be supplied in the form of inorganic compounds and is converted by the micro-organism to protein. Food yeast (*Candida utilis*) has been the traditional micro-organism to study for this possibility. It has the disadvantage that it is only capable of using a limited range of relatively simple organic compounds. Molasses and waste sulphite liquor are two of the few examples of wastes which are suitable.[11,12]

Most of the fungi have a wide range of enzyme systems and are capable of utilising the more complex mixtures of organic compounds which occur in most wastes. They also have the advantage that they can be harvested by simple filtration methods which are not applicable to bacteria or yeasts.[13-15] Although fungi are frequently reported to be slower-growing, and to yield biomass with lower protein contents, several fungal species grow as rapidly and give yields of protein equivalent to those of food yeast.[15] In general from 100 g of carbohydrate substrates the maximum practical yield of true protein by bacteria is 35 g and by yeasts and fungi 25 g.[16]

Provided micro-organisms show any indication of growth on a waste product, then the two most important criteria for further selection are the nutritional value of the protein and the safety of the product as a food. Almost the same standards of safety must be applied if the product is to be considered as monogastric livestock feed. Any trace of adverse symptoms throughout the extensive series of feeding trials will mean that the whole programme of work with a particular species of micro-organism may have to be abandoned. Both toxicological and nutritional studies have been made on the mycelium of *Fusarium semitectum* 1M1 135410.

TOXICITY TRIALS WITH THE MYCELIUM OF *FUSARIUM SEMITECTUM*

In an acute toxicity trial 40 g *Fusarium semitectum* mycelium per kg body weight was administered over a 24 h period to a group of five rats (Wistar strain). The animals showed no adverse symptoms and were normal in all respects on post-mortem examination when they were slaughtered seven days after the mycelium was administered.[17]

Chronic toxicity trials with rats as the test animals have been conducted over a period of two years through three successive generations, feeding *F. semitectum* mycelium as the sole source of protein in the diet. The procedure for the tests made throughout the trial was as outlined in the UN Protein Advisory Group Guideline No. 6 (1972),[18] although the number of animals used was less than that recommended in the Guideline. No significant difference was observed between the test group of animals and a control group in which casein was fed as the sole source of protein.[19].

Feeding trials with both pigs and poultry have also shown no adverse effects. These results suggest that *F. semitectum* mycelium is a safe feed for livestock and that it is improbable that it would have any harmful effect if it were to be used as a component of the human diet.

NUTRITIONAL STUDIES ON THE MYCELIUM OF VARIOUS SPECIES OF FUNGI

Nutritional data[20] on the mycelium of four fungal species is summarised in Table 2. The nucleic acid content of the mycelium of all four species is significantly lower than that reported for food yeast

TABLE 2
Nutritional data on the mycelium of various species of fungi[20]

	Aspergillus oryzae[a]	*Fusarium semitectum*	*Gliocladium deliquescens*[a]	*Trichoderma viride*[a]
Nucleic acid (g/100 g mycelium)	3·4	3·2	3·9	4·7
Essential amino acids (g/16 g of N):				
Lysine	5·2	5·0	5·3	5·4
Total S	2·2	2·4	2·3	2·8
Digestibility (%)	71·0	83·0	78·0	83·0
Amino acid (N as % of total N)	82·1	71·7	77·1	83·6
NPU value:				
Crude protein basis (N × 6·25)	0·34	0·42	0·38	0·40
+ Methionine	0·55	0·66	0·62	0·52
True protein basis	0·41	0·59	0·50	0·48
+ Methionine	0·67	0·92	0·80	0·62

[a] Strains adapted to grow rapidly on starch substrates by Scholten-Honig Research BV, The Netherlands.

(10 g per 100 g cells). Although the content of nucleic acid is a function of growth rate, it has been found that *F. semitectum* mycelium does not contain more than 5 % nucleic acid when it is grown at the same growth rate as yeast, namely at a mean protein doubling time of less than 5 h.[15,16]

The Net Protein Utilisation value (NPU) of 0·92 calculated on a true protein basis for *F. semitectum* confirms that only the sulphur amino acids are limiting and that in spite of the presence of chitin the protein of the mycelium is almost completely digested and utilised. The particular sample of *F. semitectum* mycelium which was used for these trials was produced under conditions which were initially standardised in a series of pilot plant studies.

In other experiments the chitin content has been reduced and nearly 90 % of the mycelial nitrogen has been recovered as amino acid nitrogen after protein hydrolysis.[15] That variations can occur in the proportion of non-protein nitrogen is evident from the results presented in Table 3, Experiment A.

TABLE 3
Effect of the period of incubation on the composition and shear value of F. semitectum *mycelium*[20]

Mycelial component	Mycelial composition (%)	
	24 h culture	96 h culture
Experiment A:		
Total N	9·1	5·8
Chitin N	0·8	1·2
Chitin N as % of total N	8·8	20·3
Experiment B:		
Cell wall	24·0	37·0
Protein (N × 6·25)	52·0	29·0
Chitin	11·7	18·0
Glucan	7·3	9·4
Shear value (kg)	11·4	3·5

Variations in the chitin content can also be produced by changes in the composition of culture media and by altering the conditions of mycelial growth.[21] Any reduction in the chitin content of the mycelium of any of the species listed in Table 2 would increase the NPU values calculated on a crude protein basis. This finding accounts for variations in the NPU values previously reported for *F. semitectum*.[4,11,12,15,16]

With the exception of the limitation in sulphur amino acid content the mycelium of all four species would be good sources of protein as human food or livestock feed. The complementary nutritional effect of combining sesame protein with *F. semitectum* mycelium is illustrated in Table 1.

FOOD TEXTURAL STUDIES ON *F. SEMITECTUM* MYCELIUM

In addition to nutritional value, acceptability is also a factor if a product is to be considered as human food. Texture is one of the important properties which contributes to the pleasant sensation given when eating fibrous foods such as meat. Unlike bacteria, yeasts or algal cells, fungal mycelium has a cohesive structure which in the case of *F. semitectum* does confer a meat-like texture.

One of the important components which contributes to texture is the resistance of the material to shear forces when it is chewed in the mouth. Measurement of the force required to shear a food sample under standard conditions can therefore be used as a method of texture assessment.

Table 3, Experiment B, shows the difference in the shear value of mycelium when it is produced over different periods of incubation. The values are below the limits at which a food product would be classified as tough and the sample with the higher shear value can be considered to be more acceptable. Although under standardised conditions the results obtained are reproducible, other parameters than the period of incubation, such as media composition and pH value, also have an influence on the shear value.

From a comparison of the quantitative composition, only the decrease in protein content appears to correlate with a reduction in shear value. Although this suggests that protein is the main component responsible, extraction of 90% of the protein does not cause any significant change in textural properties. It is concluded from this and from other experimental evidence that it is the cell walls of the hyphae which confer the textural properties.[21]

The main components of the cell walls are chitin and glucan together with about 10% of protein. No significant correlation between the quantitative composition of the cell walls and the resistance of the hyphae to shear has been found and it is probable

J. T. Worgan

that the strength of the cell walls is determined by the interlinked structure of chitin and glucan.[21]

That protein does not play a significant part in contributing to the textural properties of mycelium is confirmed by the effects of heat summarised in Table 4, since denaturisation at higher temperatures would be expected to alter the characteristics of protein fibres.[21]

TABLE 4
Effect of heat on the shear value of F. semitectum *mycelium*[21]

Heat treatment		Shear value (kg)
Time (min)	Temperature (°C)	
2	80	4·5
20	100	4·8
30	121	5·0

F. semitectum mycelium is therefore a material which can be produced with considerable variation in texture. Once, however, the most desirable texture has been determined by sensory assessment this texture can be consistently reproduced and is not influenced by processing conditions.

ADAPTATION OF *F. SEMITECTUM* TO GROWTH ON WASTE PRODUCTS

If a micro-organism shows any indication of growth on a particular waste then it is probable that rapid growth can be achieved by adaptation of the culture and by an investigation of optimum growth conditions. Only relatively slow limited growth on lactose or starch takes place with the original strain of *F. semitectum* 1M1 135410.

A strain of this species has been developed which grows as rapidly with lactose as the carbon source as it does with glucose. This culture has been grown on deproteinised whey for periods greater than 1000 h in a 25 litre continuous culture system.[22] A strain adapted to the rapid utilisation of starch has also been developed and has been grown in a 2500 litre pilot plant fed directly with a processing effluent containing starch.[23]

CONVERSION OF FIBROUS WASTES TO FOOD
OR FEED BY FUNGI

Other factors than the adaptation of micro-organisms are involved when attempting to use the fibrous materials which form the bulk of the waste products from agriculture and food processing. The annual production of some of these wastes is listed in Table 5. Although they are often termed cellulosic materials, only about one-third may be cellulose and they consist of ligno-cellulosic plant tissue, which is resistant to rapid degradation by micro-organisms due to the protective effect of lignin and the partially crystalline structure of cellulose. The general aspects of the degradation of ligno-cellulosic materials by micro-organisms have been summarised.[1,4,11,16] Various fungal species are capable of growth on these wastes, although the rate of growth is too slow to form the basis of a production process.

TABLE 5

Annual world production of carbohydrates in wastes from crop plants[1,4]

	Carbohydrate ($\times 10^3$ ton)	
	Agricultural waste	Processing waste
Wheat straw	286 600	
Wheat bran		57 300
Maize stover	120 000	
Maize cobs		30 100
Sugar cane bagasse		83 000
Molasses		9 300

In general woody tissue is the most resistant to chemical, enzymic or microbiological degradation and temperatures of 160–180°C may be necessary to dissolve the lignin of some types of wood, whereas the lignin of some annual plants is soluble in 1·5% NaOH at 20°C. By heating with dilute acid at 160–180°C cellulose is hydrolysed to glucose and after the removal of furfural or its derivatives from the hydrolysate this can be used for the growth of food yeast. The main effects of less drastic chemical treatments are summarised in Table 6.

These methods of degradation have been applied to the preparation of culture media for fungal growth.[15,24] The main products of acid hydrolysis are pentose sugars, uronic acids and partially hydrolysed polysaccharides. Oxidation reactions yield a complex mixture containing aromatic compounds from lignin and saccharinic acids and oxidised carbohydrate polymers from cellulose and hemicellulose. Provided conditions are controlled when heating with dilute acids to avoid the formation of furfural, no other products appear to inhibit fungal growth.

TABLE 6

Summary of the action of chemical reagents on ligno-cellulosic wastes

Type of treatment	Main effects
Heat with dilute acid at temperatures below 100°C	Sterilises
	Separates and partially hydrolyses hemicelluloses
	Hydrolyses some cellulose to glucose
	Converts cellulose to hydrocellulose
Steep in alkali solution	Dissolves hemicellulose, hydrocellulose and lignin
	Strong solutions disrupt crystalline cellulose structure
Steep in urea solution	Breaks H-bonds disrupting cellulose structure
Oxidation in air:	
In acid conditions	Degradation of cellulose; hydrocellulose more readily degraded
	Products soluble in alkali
In alkali conditions	Cellulose, hemicellulose and lignin oxidised; hydrocellulose more readily degraded than cellulose
	Products soluble in alkali

In order to reduce the cost of treatment, acid and alkali compounds of the nutrient elements required by fungi are used as the reagents.[15,24] Urea can be used as a source of nitrogen by several fungal species and as a chemical reagent has the effect of breaking H-bonds in the crystalline regions of cellulose. Sterile culture media can be prepared without the use of the pressure-resistant equipment required for heating at temperatures above 100°C. The heat-resistant spores of *Bacillus cereus*, *B. licheniformis* and *B. subtilis* on oat husk, for example, were destroyed in 3 min at 43°C in the presence of a mixture of phosphoric and sulphuric acids which lowered the pH value to 0·45.[25]

Yields of mycelial protein obtained by the growth of *F. semitectum* on culture media prepared from various plant by-products are given in Table 7.

TABLE 7
Yields of mycelial protein (F. semitectum) *from various ligno-cellulosic wastes*[15]

Waste	Yield of mycelial protein	
	g/100 g waste	g/100 g C source
Oat husk	11·0	16·0
Sugar cane bagasse	5·6	9·9
Cocoa shell	5·9	9·1
Spent hops	5·4	9·5
Glucose as C source		10·0

CONVERSION OF LIQUID WASTES TO FOOD OR FEED BY FUNGI

From the processing of many natural commodities large volumes of liquid wastes are produced which have a high biological oxygen demand (BOD). Because of more stringent regulations against pollution these wastes can no longer be freely discharged into local river systems. Most of these wastes contain a complex mixture of organic compounds consisting mainly of carbohydrates the value of which does not justify the use of separation methods for their recovery.[10]

By the growth of fungi on these wastes the BOD can be reduced and the mycelium harvested for use as livestock feed or human food. The protein content of the mycelium can be increased by the addition to the waste of an inorganic source of nitrogen. A summary of the results of the fungal treatment of a number of wastes of this type is given in Table 8. At the level of BOD which exists in the effluents listed, no economical method of waste treatment is currently available, and if the cost of treatment is offset against the cost of producing mycelium, the product should be competitive with other sources of animal feed.

Although BOD is the ultimate measure of the polluting intensity of a waste, measurement of the chemical oxygen demand (COD) is a more rapid and convenient method and for most wastes from food processing gives a good indication of BOD level. COD reduction has therefore been used in assessing the changes brought about by fungal growth.

TABLE 8
Fungal treatment of liquor wastes

Waste and fungal species	COD reduction	Yields (g/litre)	
		Mycelium	Protein
F. semitectum:			
Palm waste[26,27]	72	28·7	—
Citrus molasses[28]	—	22·8	9·0
Lucerne leaf liquor[29]	65	22·9	8·3
Maize leaf liquor[30]	—	14·6	7·1
A. oryzae:			
Olive waste[31]	—	19·5	10·5
Lucerne leaf liquor[29]	68	17·6	12·0

For maximum growth, protein yield and COD reduction it is essential to have an optimum balance of inorganic nutrients in culture media. An inorganic source of nitrogen and in some cases relatively small quantities of phosphate and other inorganic compounds have therefore been added to the wastes listed.

Palm waste consists of an aqueous sludge and a condensate which are produced in volumes equivalent to those of the oil extracted from the palm fruit. In Malaya the discharge of these wastes is causing serious problems where the river water is subsequently used for irrigation of rice fields. Olive waste occurs when the oil is separated from the juice which has been expressed from the olive fruits. The quantity produced is about 40% of the weight of the olive and the annual production in Greece is estimated to be 320 000 tons. Citrus molasses is the liquid expressed from waste citrus pulp after the pulp has been treated with a calcium compound such as lime. For each 100 tons of oranges used for juice extraction, 30 tons of molasses are produced.

From the liquid wastes listed and from other similar wastes which occur, substantial quantities of protein for livestock could be produced. In many cases it is now essential to find methods of reducing the polluting intensity of these wastes.

From the leaf protein process waste liquors remain after the protein has been precipitated from the leaf juice. These liquors have a high BOD and could present a disposal problem. Waste liquors from the leaves of several crops have been investigated and found to give good yields of mycelial protein with a correspondingly significant decrease in COD.[29,30]

That the output of food per unit area of land can be increased by making more effective use of crop plants is illustrated by the results presented in Table 9. For each crop the yield of protein from the combined system is about six times that of the conventional crop which is still available as food.[1,4,12]

TABLE 9
Comparison of protein yields from conventional crops and food production systems[1,4,12]

			Yield of protein (kg/ha)			
	Seed	Leaf protein	Fungal protein from			Total
			Leaf juice	Leaf fibre	Maize cobs	
Maize:						
Conventional crop	352	—	—	—	—	352
Combined system	352	300	110	1 290	80	2 132
Peas:						
Conventional crop	400	—	—	—	—	400
Combined system	400	625	125	1 366	—	2 546

A MULTI-STAGE SYSTEM FOR THE PRODUCTION OF FUNGAL MYCELIUM FROM LIQUID WASTES

For maximum productivity in a conventional vessel for growing micro-organisms the concentration of the carbon source in the culture medium should be between 5% and 8%. Most processing effluents, although they are considered to be strong pollutants, are usually more dilute than this. To deal with a continuous flow of a dilute effluent the system illustrated in Fig. 1 has been investigated.

The inoculum is initially introduced into vessel 1 and the effluent stream, supplemented if necessary with inorganic nutrients, is allowed to flow into the vessel. Growth and COD reduction take place as the vessel fills. When vessel 1 is full the contents are transferred to vessel 2 to serve as inoculum, maintaining the same rate of flow as the effluent stream which is redirected into vessel 2. When vessel 2 is full the same procedure is followed into vessel 3.

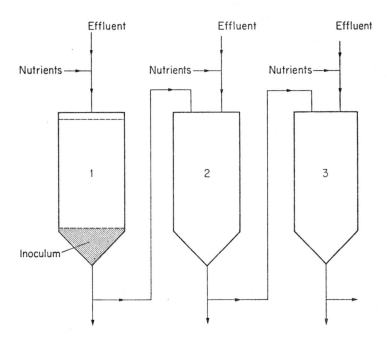

Fig. 1.   Multi-stage fungal treatment of a liquid waste.

In the meantime vessel 1 will be half full and the contents are discharged from the system. On a laboratory scale it is feasible to begin a fresh cycle by transferring the contents of vessel 3 to vessel 1. In practice on a large scale it would be advisable to have a fourth vessel in order that each vessel could be taken out of the cycle in sequence to be cleaned and sterilised. The introduction of freshly prepared inoculum would also be an advantage at the beginning of each cycle.

TABLE 10
Multi-stage fungal treatment of liquid wastes by Aspergillus oryzae[32]

Waste	COD reduction (% of original value)		Mycelial yield (g/100 g source)
	Vessel 1	Vessel 2	
1% glucose solution	98	96	45·0
Effluent containing 1% potato starch	91	84	46·2

This system was tested with *Aspergillus oryzae* on a 1% glucose culture medium and conditions optimised to give the results reported in Table 10. On the time scale operated, vessel 1 was filled in 18 h, vessel 2 in 9 h. Similar periods of time would apply on a large scale. When glucose was replaced by a waste potato starch effluent both mycelial yield and COD reduction were considerably less. This problem was overcome with the results shown in Table 10 by developing an inoculum which had good extracellular amylase activity.[32]

CONCLUSION

Wastes which arise from agriculture and from the processing of biological materials, including food, can be converted by fungi to nutritionally valuable sources of protein. Because of the extensive tests required to ensure their safety for human consumption it is probable that the products will initially be used for livestock feed. Where wastes have to be treated because they are a pollution hazard the mycelial product from fungal treatment can probably be produced at a cost competitive with that of other sources of protein.

ACKNOWLEDGEMENTS

Grateful acknowledgement is made to the following for their help and financial support: Brooke Bond Liebig Ltd, Ecotech Systems (UK) Ltd, the National Research Development Corporation and Scholten-Honig Research BV, The Netherlands.

REFERENCES

1. Worgan, J. T. (1973). In: *By-products of the Food Industry*, Symposium Proceedings No. 16, British Food Manufacturing Industries Research Association, p. 11.
2. Worgan, J. T. (1975). In: *The Man–Food Equation*, ed. A. Bourne, Academic Press, London.
3. Worgan, J. T. (1975). In: *Human Food Chains and Nutrient Cycles*, ed. J. G. W. Jones and A. N. Duckham, North-Holland Publishing Co., Amsterdam.
4. Worgan, J. T. (1973). In: *Proteins in Human Nutrition*, ed. J. W. G. Porter and B. A. Rolls, Academic Press, London, p. 44.
5. Altschul, A. M. (1970). In: *Evaluation of Novel Protein Products*, ed. A. E. Bender, B. Lofqvist, R. Kihlberg and L. Munck, Pergamon Press, Oxford, p. 41.
6. Davidson, S., Passmore, R. and Brock, J. F. (1973). *Human Nutrition and Dietetics*, 5th ed., Churchill Livingstone, London, p. 380.
7. Suleiman, T. E. S. M. and Worgan, J. T. Unpublished results.
8. UNIDO (1974). *Review and Comparative Analysis of Oilseed Raw Materials and Processes Suitable for the Production of Protein Products for Human Consumption*, United Nations, New York, p. 10.
9. FAO (1957). *Protein Requirements*, FAO Nutrition Study No. 16.
10. Worgan, J. T. (1974). 'Interactions: the environment and the food processor', Institute of Food Science and Technology Symposium, Cambridge, UK, Abstracts p. 12.
11. Worgan, J. T. (1974). *Plant Foods for Man*, 1, p. 99.
12. Worgan, J. T. (1974). 'Conventional and unconventional sources of proteins', IX International Symposium of Zootechny, Italian Society for the Advancement of Zootechny, Milan, Italy.
13. Worgan, J. T. (1968). In: *Progress in Industrial Microbiology*, ed. D. J. D. Hockenhull, Churchill, London, 8, p. 74.
14. Worgan, J. T. (1971). *1st International Congress of Mycology*, Exeter, UK, Abstracts p. 106.
15. Delaney, R. A. M. and Worgan, J. T. (1970). *3rd International Congress of Food Science and Technology*, Washington, DC, Abstracts p. 113.
16. Worgan, J. T. (1972). In: *The Biological Efficiency of Protein Production*, ed. J. G. W. Jones, Cambridge University Press, p. 339.
17. Feuell, A. J., Tropical Products Institute, London. Unpublished results.
18. UN Protein Advisory Group (1972). Guideline No. 6, *Preclinical Testing of Novel Sources of Protein*, United Nations, New York.
19. Smith, R. H. and Palmer, R. M. (1974). *2nd International Symposium on Food and Work*, Vittel, France.
20. Smith, R. H., Palmer, R. M. and Reade, A. E. (1975). *J. Sci. Fd. and Ag.* (in press).
21. Hunston, M. J. and Worgan, J. T. Unpublished results.
22. Whey Developments Ltd, High Wycombe, Bucks, UK. (1974). Published booklet.

23. Scholten-Honig Research BV, Foxhol (GR), The Netherlands. (1974). Internal report.
24. Worgan, J. T. (1967). British Patent Specification 1 220 807.
25. Beswick, N. A., Reynolds, A. J. and Worgan, J. T. Unpublished results.
26. Barker, T. W., Kauer, P. and Worgan, J. T. Unpublished results.
27. Grant, A. A. and Worgan, J. T. (1974). British Patent application.
28. Barlow, C. and Worgan, J. T. Unpublished results.
29. Pain, S. E., Tye, R. and Worgan, J. T. Unpublished results.
30. Mehta, M. and Worgan, J. T. Unpublished results.
31. Drouliscos, N. J. and Worgan, J. T. Unpublished results.
32. Croxford, J. A. and Worgan, J. T. Unpublished results.

DISCUSSION

Wimpenny: I am sorry you couldn't tell us something about the cellulose treatment, because I think that cellulose is perhaps one of the most important of these wastes. I wonder if you could tell us something about the way you treat cellulose?

Worgan: I think that Fig. 1 summarises the main chemical methods of degrading cellulose which don't go to the extreme of actually converting it to sugar. The other point I would make is that when we are talking about cellulose there is a whole spectrum of materials which differ in their resistance to both enzymes and micro-organisms. We go right from woody tissue to soft plant tissue which is very much more easily broken down. I don't think you can generalise about the susceptibility of cellulose to either chemical or microbiological degradation. Some materials will be much more readily degraded than others. There are also oxidation reactions which are used in the manufacture of rayon, for example. The point about many of these reactions is that they are complementary to one another—cellulose initially heated with acid, for example, becomes more easily oxidised.

Burrows: A lot of work has been done on the toxicity of dried materials which have been sterilised, but I am worried about the process workers in low-technology systems where things like *Trichoderma* species might be grown. May I have any information on what happens when a process worker gets a big dose of the living organism?

Worgan: You mean they may breathe the spores?

Burrows: Yes.

Worgan: We don't use spore inocula; the mycelium before it sporulates is macerated. This is the way in which most processes using fungi now operate. Unless material was spilt and left lying about you would not get spores produced. Everything would have to be very dry; it would only happen if some material was spilt and left to dry. It is only then that spores would become dispersed. I think there would be very little likelihood of it happening in developed countries. I don't myself think these processes are answers to the immediate problems in developing countries in any case— I think there are other things which can be done first.

Emery: You refer to shear value of fibres and mycelia and talked about control in which you removed 90% of the protein and retained very similar shear value. Can you comment on the technique which you used in order to achieve that removal without affecting shear value?

Worgan: It is fairly easy to remove the protein from mycelium by treatment with alkali. I think this would explain why the presence of chitin doesn't have much effect on the digestibility of the protein. It does not appear to be the same situation that you get in plants where the ligno-cellulose can prevent you from digesting protein. The protein of mycelium seems to be much more freely available and can be more readily removed. About 10% of the protein does remain in the cell wall and this is more difficult to remove.

Garrett: I should like to raise a note of caution in relation to the use of BOD and COD as indices of the polluting potential of a waste. It is worth remembering that algal productivity in most of our inland waters is nutrient-limited, and that the secondary BOD of a waste may greatly exceed its primary BOD due to the promotion of algal growth. Therefore in considering the topic of food from waste we should be concerned with optimising nutrient removal as well as protein production and BOD removal.

Worgan: I think this will have to come later on. To date we have been concerned with reducing a BOD of 40 000 or 50 000 down to say 5000 or 6000 ppm. There may have to be some process to follow or we may be able to get further fungal growth to reduce it to a level where it could be regarded as a treated waste. Fungal growth also removes a good deal of the inorganic elements in wastes.

Thomson: Have you done any calculations on how much fermentation capacity you need to deal with the effluent from an average dairy processing plant?

Worgan: Not directly, but obviously, the more rapidly you can treat the waste the smaller the capacity you would need, so the more rapidly your COD reduction takes place the smaller the capacity of the system you would need. Incidentally, in relation to continuous growth of micro-organisms, this is incompatible with complete COD reduction because in a continuous system you are bound to be removing some of the incompletely treated waste when you harvest mycelium. I don't know whether that specifically answers your question about capacity.

Clift: Can you tell us something about the specific toxins found in fungi, and secondly tell us whether you feel that if you grow a similar organism on a slightly different substrate the toxicological testing you carried out on the first organism on the first substrate can be related to the second?

Worgan: There are over 100 000 different species of fungi and very few of these are toxic. This is not to say we shouldn't test them. Although I think there are a large number of species of fungi which are quite safe, we have to prove this. Now so far as the growth on one substrate or another is concerned, I think it is improbable that the organism would produce toxins on one substrate or another if the substrate itself was a reasonable one—dairy waste, for example, or starch waste. It would be unlikely, I would think, but I agree that this doesn't prove the case. If you adopt a new substrate then you may well have to do at least some toxicity trials which would establish that the new substrate was not producing any changes. You may even have to go through another complete toxicity trial, which is a problem in the development of all these type of processes.

Edelman: May I ask you a question: the material you are producing you see as an animal feed and not as human feed—or both?

Worgan: We work on both. Where we are dealing mainly with the elimination of a waste where the COD reduction is the important factor, then I think the initial outlet will be as an animal feed. Eventually I think that mycelium might well be used as human food, which is why we have been studying its texture.

Pace: In the case of a starch effluent treatment plant, what was the fermenter design used?

Worgan: For this we have used a conventional type of fermenter design. We are looking at the possibilities of ways of eliminating the mechanical agitator and of using an airlift or air-agitated system, because I think this may be necessary from a capital cost point of view.

4

Yeast from Molasses

G. Sobkowicz

Institute of Storage and Food Technology,
Agricultural Academy, Wrocław, Poland

ABSTRACT

Molasses, for a long time a waste product of the sugar industry, has found application as a raw material for the production of baker's and feed yeast. Besides this, yeast may be recovered as a by-product of alcohol fermentation on molasses.

The chemical composition and physical properties of molasses vary, depending on agronomic factors, weather conditions during the growth of the sugar beets, storage of their roots before the slicing, and most of all on manufacturing processes applied in the sugar industry. Different samples of molasses produced in the same sugar factory and in the same campaigns can have different chemical compositions. Molasses have both harmful and advantageous properties and components for the growth of yeast. Numerous investigations have proved that molasses from the first part of the campaigns were better raw material than those from the second. Some authors have confirmed that in the last twenty years molasses have become worse as a raw material for yeast. Nevertheless molasses are still a major raw material for the production of baker's and feed yeast.

Yeast manufacturing processes have also undergone continuous change. Present-day development of the methods of yeast production depends on improvement of the preparation of molasses, its clarification, the feeding of yeast, application of continuous processes instead of batch ones, modernisation of the aeration system of mash, and the separation and filtration of yeast. All these procedures allow yields of baker's and feed yeast to be increased from 10% to 40% in comparison with the classic processes. Particularly important is the selection of a proper strain of yeast that is capable of taking advantage of the constituents other than sugars from molasses mash during the manufacturing processes.

These and other problems are very important for production of baker's and feed yeast from molasses.

INTRODUCTION

Production of baker's yeast from molasses was begun about sixty years ago. In the beginning, natural nutrients such as malt and malt sprouts were added to the molasses wort, and later mineral nutrients such as ammonium, phosphorus and magnesium salts, which have been used to the present day. Production of food and feed yeast was begun during World War I, but actually its development followed World War II. Yeast is a rich source of protein and vitamins of the B group which because of the current deficiency of these substances are of great importance. The production of food and feed yeast is based mainly on *Torulopsis utilis*, whereas baker's yeast is *Saccharomyces cerevisiae*. The latter from the substrate metabolises hexoses, lactic, tartaric, succinic, acetic and glycolic acids, and ethanol aerobically.[1] The aim of the production of baker's yeast is to obtain a live cell mass capable of dough fermentation in bread-making. The most important property of baker's yeast is its 'raising power', measured in time of raising of dough.

The great demand for baker's yeast and high requirements concerning its quality oblige scientific workers and engineers to carry out the investigation of all factors which affect yield and quality of the yeast. One of these factors is molasses as a raw material for the production of baker's yeast.

CHARACTERISTICS OF CHEMICAL COMPOSITION AND PROPERTIES OF BEET SUGAR MOLASSES

Molasses is a by-product of sugar production from the sugar beet as well as from sugar cane. In white sugar factories the average yield of molasses with 50% sugar content ranges from 3·2% to 4·0% on beets. Sugar (saccharose) content in molasses amounts to about two-thirds of all losses of the sugar factory. The quantity of molasses and its sugar content depend upon the amount and kind of non-sugars of the beet not eliminated by the juice purification process, the soluble impurities added in processing, and the degradation products formed during processing.[2,3] The amount and quality of non-sugars in beet depend upon various factors, such as strain of beet, agronomic factors of soil and fertilisation, weather conditions during growth and the treatment between harvesting and slicing. These factors all affect, also, the composition of molasses.

The quality of a technological process applied has a great influence on quantity and quality of substances formed and added during sugar production.[2,3] Some of these substances may be harmful to the yeast. Not all factors that may have influence on chemical composition and properties of molasses were mentioned above.

There are three types of beet sugar molasses: raw sugar, white sugar and refinery molasses. Their composition is practically similar, apart from the content of colloidal materials, suspended matter and colour.[4] The chemical compositions of some kinds of Polish molasses are given in Table 1. The analytical values presented in the table show how large variations from average values in respect of properties and components of molasses reported by different authors[4-8] may be demonstrated as depending on their origin.

MOLASSES AS A RAW MATERIAL IN BAKER'S YEAST MANUFACTURE

Molasses used in yeast culture is not only a source of organic carbon but also of other essential nutrients such as nitrogenous and mineral compounds and growth substances. Apart from the advantageous components for the growth of yeast, molasses may contain harmful ones which are deleterious to yeast production. The lability of the chemical components of molasses governs its quality as a raw material for the manufacture of yeast. Poorer quality molasses causes various kinds of technological difficulties and therefore its processing requires costly manipulations without which the yield and quality of yeast become lower.[4,9-13]

Some Compounds and Properties of Molasses Advantageous to Yeast

A low dry substance content of molasses (below 75%) indicates such disadvantageous properties as a large infection with microorganisms, high content of volatile acids, reducing and colour substances, and pH lower than 7·0.[4,6,9,10,14-16] These molasses can undergo further deterioration during storage at higher temperature.[6,11,17]

Saccharose is the main constituent of molasses and determines its price. Commercial molasses contains 47–52% sugar. Other sugars contained in molasses, such as glucose and fructose, are fermentable. Raffinose, in varying amounts, occurs in beet molasses, and only one-third of its quantity is assimilated by baker's yeast.

The purity coefficient is a quality indicator of the molasses because it shows sugar content in its total dry substance, usually in percentages. Molasses of good quality have purity coefficients ranging from 60% to 63%. Between these limits, purity coefficients ensure a good buffering capacity of molasses and stability of pH during fermentation

TABLE 1

Composition of Polish molasses originating from various seasons[10,16,19]

Constituent	Season and conditions affecting molasses quality			
	1956–7 Partly frozen and thawed beets	Vegetation season		1966–7 Studied Oct. 1966–Jan. 1967
		1959–60 Dry and warm	1962–3 Wet and cool	
Dry substance (refr.), wt %	70·30–80·60	74·20–79·80	74·90–77·70	78·90–86·20
Sugar (polarimetric), wt %	32·30–52·20	19·50–49·30	47·10–54·90	43·80–54·50
Purity coefficient, %	46·08–67·29	25·86–63·76	61·64–67·66	51·80–65·10
Raffinose (chromat.), wt %	0·00–1·17	0·27–1·05	0·10–2·24	0·00–2·75
Invert sugar, wt %	0·32–12·06	0·15–18·34	0·04–0·85	1·19–4·50
pH	6·40–9·50	5·40–8·50	6·00–9·32	6·40–8·10
Total nitrogen, wt %	0·43–1·74	1·38–2·20	1·31–1·80	0·82–1·90
Volatile acids as acetic acid, wt %	0·96–1·96	0·79–1·51	0·89–1·42	1·12–1·95
Colloids, wt %	3·52–10·50	2·10–4·95	2·22–3·52	1·40–12·90
Colour of 2 % solution in 1 ml of 0·1n J$_2$	1·27–2·86	1·42–3·75	1·23–2·15	1·90–5·80
Carbonate ash, wt %	4·07–8·82	7·84–10·0	7·67–10·65	5·30–9·60
K$_2$O, wt %	—	3·43–4·65	2·91–4·36	1·35–5·00
Number of samples	14	18	15	20

of yeast.[4,7,8,11,18] Stros and Syhorova[8] noted the inversely proportional dependence between the yield of yeast and purity cofficient, whereas Sobkowicz[15,16] stated the same dependence for yield of alcohol from molasses.

Total nitrogen contained in molasses ranges from 0·82%[19] to 2·2%. Nitrogen is a component of various substances such as protein, amino acids, amides, betain, ammonium salts, nitrates, sometimes nitrites and others.[4,5,7]

Molasses produced in the first half of a campaign contains a higher amount of total nitrogen than that from the second half.[8,10,19] The assimilation of molasses nitrogen is varied. Classen[20] believed that only 0·7–0·9% of the nitrogen was assimilable by the yeast, while Malanowska et al.[14] reported 0·02–0·9%, Stuhlik et al.[21] 0·351–0·643% and Underkofler and Hickey[22] 0·3–0·6%. White[23] held that approximate molasses nitrogen contents ranging from 10% to 20% of the total allowed one to obtain a high yield of baker's yeast. Malanowska et al.[14] stated the real dependence between the amount of assimilable nitrogen and yield of the yeast. This dependence is presented in Fig. 1. The same dependence was also stated by Stros and Syhorova.[8] These results show that organic nitrogen content in the molasses is of great importance to processing of the yeast.

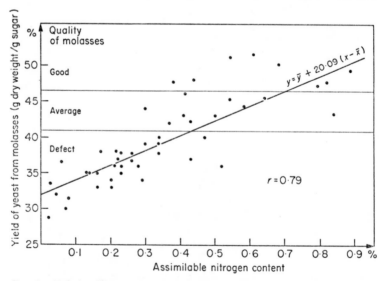

FIG. 1.   Relationship between the amount of assimilable nitrogen and yield of the yeast.

Ash in beet molasses ranges from 8.0% to 10.0%. Malanowska *et al.*[19] and Sobkowicz[24] reported that the content of ash and K_2O in molasses became lower in the course of a sugar campaign. K_2O is of great importance to yeast metabolism and its lower quantity in molasses can reduce the yield of yeast. Malanowska *et al.*[19] stated that from molasses with K_2O content lower than 4.2%, a good yield of yeast cannot be obtained. Uhl[25] reported that molasses ought to contain not less than 4.0% K_2O based on dry substance. He also noted that potassium may be replaced by ammonium.

Magnesium is an important compound of molasses, particularly in the case of production of yeast with higher concentration of dry substance.[12,26] The deficiency of magnesium has to be supplemented, otherwise a normal yield of yeast[4,12,26,27] cannot be obtained.

Calcium content in molasses undergoes a large variation depending on the quality of processed sugar beets and on the technological conditions in the sugar factory.[4,12,14,19,24,28] Higher calcium content in molasses indicates its lower quality and usefulness for fermenting purposes.[6,7,10,24]

Microelements in molasses are very important to the growth of yeast, and their absence in the cultural medium may cause lowering of biomass.[19,23,29] Chryczeva,[30] investigating Russian molasses, noted inadequate amounts of microelements such as Mn, Mo, Fe and Co, to which Pis[18] added also Cu and Zn. The complex of microelements added to the fermenting wort increased the yield of yeast.[13]

Growth substances contained in beet molasses are an important group of organic substances because as constituents of enzymes they catalyse biochemical processes of the yeast. Those most frequently mentioned are biotin, pantothenic acid and inositol.[1,4,5,8,11,14,18,19,31–34] Their content in molasses varies over a large range. Table 2 presents the growth stimulants in molasses originating from different European countries and also their demand for receipt of the highest yield of yeast. Cane molasses is richer in biotin than beet, and the latter is higher in pantothenic acid.[4,23] Many authors reported various amounts of growth substances needed by yeasts for their normal living processes.[1,4,8,23,31,32] Olbrich[11,35] suggested mixing beet molasses with cane for levelling stimulant substances in cultural worts either by adding pure biotin or D,L-desthiobiotin. Stuhlik[12] suggested adding the corn steep-water concentrate instead of pure growth substances. Malanowska *et al.*[19] reported that addition of biotin into wort increased the yield of yeast from 8% to 14% independently of assimilable nitrogen content in molasses. Recently, in some countries, investigations have been conducted to replace pure growth substances with various organic preparations and water extracts from different waste products of the food industry such as malt sprouts,[36–38] rye sprouts,[38] mud after filtration of protein hydrolysates,[39] and hydrolysates from meat wastes.[40] In addition, investigations were carried out on the use of unsaturated fatty acids,[41] vitamin D_2[42] and oxytetracycline[43] as growth substances. The authors of these investigations stated that the

TABLE 2

Growth substances content of beet molasses and quantities needed for the highest yields of baker's yeast

Molasses and season	Biotin (μg/100 g)	Pantothenic acid (mg/100 g)	Inositol (mg/100 g)
German 1963–4[33]	6·1	0·22	120
Polish 1964–5[29]	1·7–6·4	0·06–2·3	72–340
Polish 1966–7[34]	1·0–3·7	0·12–1·2	—
German 1970–1[5]	17·7–21·8	2·3–7·0	69–183
Various[23]	4–13	5–11	570–800
Cane	100–188	1·6	250
Amounts of growth materials required for maximum yeast yields[4]	29	5·0	120
Estimated by White and Munns[64]	25	4·4	100

above-mentioned supplements raised the yield of yeast from a few to several percentage points and/or improved its quality and durability. Apart from the previously mentioned growth substances, molasses contains other growth stimulants needed by yeast such as thiamin, riboflavin, nicotinamide and folic acid. Vitamin C is not present in molasses.[4,22]

Organic acids in molasses form a large group of non-nitrogenous substances. They are degradation products of sucrose at high temperature and alkalinity, of disinfecting chemicals and of microbial processes applied in a sugar factory.[2–5,44,45]

Volatile acids, such as acetic, formic, butyric, propionic and valeric, belong to the group of substances harmful to yeast. Considerable quantities of these acids affect the growth of the yeast unfavourably or may even stop it completely. This was confirmed by several investigators.[4,46–50] Schiweck *et al.*[5] noted that acetic acid is assimilated by the yeast while formic acid in a concentration of 0·46% in the substrate did not reduce growth of the yeast. Organic acids such as lactic, citric and malic are assimilated by yeast. Schiweck *et al.*[5] and Bergander[44] reported that smaller amounts of these acids in German molasses in current production are the reason for lower yield of the yeast. Osovik *et al.*[51] confirmed this suggestion, and reported better yields of feed yeast when larger amounts of lactic and glycolic acids and glycerin were found in the medium.

Substances Harmful to Yeast

Micro-organisms originating from beet roots and the air penetrate into juices and molasses during its storage. Molasses have been graded into three classes with respect to their quality, rated according to the content of micro-organisms[49] (*see* Table 3). Molasses strongly

TABLE 3
Quality grading of molasses according to micro-organism content[4,49]

Quality grades	Number of micro-organisms/g beet molasses	Processing to pressed yeast
I	Up to 100 000	Simple and easy
II	Up to 1 million	Special pre-treatment
III	Up to 5 million	No normal yield of a full-value yeast

infected with microflora reveals such properties as dry substance below 75%, pH below 7·0 and high invert content.[9,48,50,52] The bacteriological infections of molasses and worts have been studied by many authors in the last few years. The same authors also tested various chemicals such as disinfectants.[53–56]

Colloids and suspended materials, colouring matters, sulphurous acid, and nitrates and nitrites in molasses are also harmful substances to yeast.[4,6,9,11,19,29] Larger amounts of these components in worts may lower the yield, durability and other properties of the manufactured yeast.[4,9,29] Volatile acids as harmful substances were discussed above.

Plant protection substances are more and more often mentioned in publications devoted to investigations of molasses quality.[5,57-59] Pesticides are applied in cultivation of sugar beets and during their storage before processing. Schiweck *et al.*[5] and Drescher *et al.*[59] found metabolite B of 'Pirazon' in German molasses but its amount was not harmful to the yeast. Pis[27] reported finding in Czechoslovak molasses from campaign 1971–2 residues of insecticides α, γ and δ-HCH, p,p'-DDT and p,p'-DDE in amounts which may cause lower yields of yeast.

The results presented above show that chemical composition and physical and fermentable properties of produced molasses undergo continuous deterioration of their quality as a raw material for manufacturing of baker's yeast.[5,14,18,19,57-61] They also prove that molasses have a certain number of properties, not yet identified, which may cause various technological difficulties in the production of the yeast. On the basis of a great number of investigations, the most important properties and components of molasses, which characterise their utility for the manufacture of baker's yeast, have been determined. These are given in Table 4.

The analytical data presented in Table 4 do not give full information about the quality of molasses and this is why different authors require the adaptation of some biological method to estimate the utility of molasses for the fermentation industry.[6,9,16,18,19]

SOME TECHNOLOGICAL PROBLEMS IN THE PRODUCTION OF BAKER'S YEAST

The present level of the machine and electronic industry has also affected the progress of baker's and feed yeast production and technology. Automation and regulation may be applied not only to particular stages but also over the entire process of yeast production. The introduction of modern techniques to all yeast plants depends only on economical and technological factors. High-quality molasses, carefully prepared cultural wort, selected strain of seed yeast and properly applied technology are of decisive importance in achieving good yeast yield.

Preparation of Molasses

The aim of the introductory treatment of molasses is the improvement of its fermentable features by means of homogenisation and the

TABLE 4

Quality requirements of molasses designed for baker's yeast production, obligatory in some countries

Constituent	Polish standard PN-68 R–64772	German Democratic Republic[6]	German Federal Republic[11] Before	German Federal Republic[11] At present	Austria, estimated by Vogelbusch[6]
Dry substance (refr.), wt % not less than	75	75	73·6	76·5	75
Sugar (polarimetric), wt % not less than	47	47	47	48	48
pH, in range or not less than	7·2–9·0	7·5	6·8	7·0	6·0–7·5
Invert sugar, wt % not more than	1·0	—	0·25	2·0	—
Total nitrogen, wt % not less than	1·7	—	—	—	1·2
Volatile acids as acetic acid, wt % not more than	1·4	—	—	—	—
Purity coefficient, %	55–63	—	—	—	60
Calcium and magnesium salts as CaO, wt %	1·5	0·4	—	—	—
SO₂, wt % not more than	0·1	0·1	0·15	0·15	0·25

removal of suspended matter, colloids, colour substances, volatile acids, nitrites and sulphites.[1,4,23,24,29] The next stage of the treatment of molasses is its sterilisation in order to reduce or eliminate the micro-organisms. There are physical, chemical and mechanical methods used for the clarification and disinfection of molasses. Detailed information concerned with these methods may be found in the appropriate literature.[4,12,22,29,62-64] This introductory preparation as a whole ought to be carried out in such a way as to avoid losses of sugar and formation of substances harmful to yeast.[11,65]

Yeast

The selection of proper strains of baker's and feed yeasts affects industrial utility. The yeast ought to possess good physiological features, capacity for quick multiplication, growth and assimilation of nutrients, osmotic tolerance and good adaptation to oxygen conditions.[1,12,22,23,29,64] The quality of seed yeast is very important in the cultivation of commercial yeast on wort with high concentration of dry substances or with recirculation of wort.[12,21,66]

The improvement of the yeast properties by means of various methods such as hybridisation,[67-69] mutation caused by chemicals and temperature[70] and radioactivity[71] is a subject of great interest to many authors. The laboratory of every plant has to cultivate its own pure cultures of the yeast adapted to its own conditions. Such a method ensures the reaching of high yields and quality of yeast.

Yeast Fermentation

The production of commercial baker's yeast may be carried out by different methods depending on conditions in a given plant. The methods used are feed-batch process, semi-continuous and continuous processes. This last method has several advantages, such as increase of productive capacity on the volume unit of the fermenter, decrease of working power and energy for 1 t pressed yeast produced, and the possibility of maintenance of yeast in good physiological condition.[29,63] The continuous fermentation requires securing sterility of wort, nutrients and air, programming and automation of the total process. All the above-mentioned methods of yeast cultivation permit one to obtain high yields when there are proper conditions, such as balancing nutrients added to the wort according to the needs of the yeast, proper physiological state and amount of yeast, maintenance of proper pH and temperature, providing sufficient amount of oxygen, and others, depending on the variables of a given plant. In the literature there are many publications devoted to the functioning of different yeast fermentation systems,[12,26,72] their optimisation[73–75] and intensification,[58] and to the theoretical and technical problems connected with them.[76–78]

There are also interesting experiments on yeast fermentation with limiting small amounts of sugar[79] or alcohol.[80]

The modern direction in development of baker's yeast production leads to a final dilution of molasses with water in the ratio 1:5 instead of 1:30. Initially it was applied as a combined method of alcohol and yeast production[29,64] whereas at present it is used for production of baker's yeast without formation of alcohol under the name 'MX'.[29,63] This method gives some economical and technological advantages and is therefore of interest to many authors.[12,29,63,64,81]

The continuous process of yeast cultivation, as well as cultivation with a high concentration of dry substances, requires bringing to the fermenting worts large amounts of air, and utilisation of oxygen from this to the highest degree. The problems connected with aeration of the cultural medium have been the subject of consideration by many authors. These include the influence of aeration on growth, energetic and biochemical processes in yeast,[76,82] intensification of oxygen dilution in worts[83,84] and transfer of oxygen from air to the yeast cell.[76,85,86]

The technical equipment applied in the production of baker's yeast is a separate problem, which is not discussed within the scope of this paper.

Yeast recovered in the molasses distillery is a by-product of alcohol fermentation. It occupies an important position in production of the biomass used as a component of feed or as a baker's yeast. Properly arranged technology of the distillery assures a good yield of alcohol and baker's yeast.[87]

Feed yeasts are produced from the molasses distiller's stillage, from molasses and from other raw materials. The utility of stillage for feed yeast production is dependent on the quality of molasses and of the technology applied in the distillery.[29,51] The production of feed yeast has many features in common with production of baker's yeast.

CONCLUSION

The problems discussed above have not covered all scientific and technical achievements in the range of baker's yeast which have been

presented in the world literature in the past few years. The vast
number of published works concerned with these problems demon-
strates an enormous interest by the scientific and technical world in
an area which still preserves many unsolved questions.

REFERENCES

1. Borrows, S. (1970). *The Yeast*, Vol. 3: *Yeast Technology*, ed. A. H.
   Rose and J. S. Harrison, Academic Press, London and New York,
   p. 349.
2. Silin, P. M. (1958). *Technołogija swiekłosacharnogo proizwodztwa*,
   Piszczepromizdat, Moskwa, pp. 109, 391–2, 448–57, 469–71.
3. Schapper, M. H. (1968). *Technologie des Zuckers*, Vereinder Zucker-
   industrie, F. Schneider Verlag, Hannover, pp. 2–67, 977–1015.
4. Olbrich, H. (1963). 'Molasses', in: *Principles of Sugar Technology*, ed.
   P. Honig, Elsevier, Amsterdam, p. 511.
5. Schiweck, H. and Haberl, L. (1973). *Zucker*, 26(7), p. 347.
6. Ginterova, A. and Huncikova, S. (1972). *Kvasny Prum.*, 18(1), p. 10.
7. Ginterova, A. (1973). *Kvasny Prum.*, 19(2), p. 37.
8. Stros, F. and Syhorova, V. (1965). *Listy Cukrov.*, 81(6), p. 265.
9. Soczynski, S. (1958). *Przem. Spoż.*, 12(1), p. 3.
10. Sobkowicz, G. (1962). *Przem. Ferm.*, 6(3), p. 70; 6(4), p. 93.
11. Olbrich, H. (1973). *Branntweinwirtsch.*, 113(4), p. 53.
12. Stuhlik, V. (1974). *Branntweinwirtsch.*, 114(4), p. 73.
13. Chryczeva, A. J., Palagina, N. K. and Rozmanova, N. W. (1974).
    Chleb. Kond. Prom., No. 3, p. 28.
14. Malanowska, J., Gluzinska, W. and Łabendzinski, S. (1969). *Prace
    Inst. Lab. Bad. Przem. Spoż.*, 19, p. 265.
15. Sobkowicz, G. (1960). *Zeszyty Nauk. WSR we Wrocławiu. Roln. XI*,
    No. 32, p. 3.
16. Sobkowicz, G. (1969). *Zeszyty Nauk. WSR we Wrocławiu. Roln.
    XXVI*, No. 83, p. 113.
17. Kowalenko, A. D. (1974). *Ferm. Spirt. Prom.*, No. 5, p. 27.
18. Pis, E. (1974). *Kvasny Prum.*, 20(7), p. 153.
19. Malanowska, J. and Łabendzinski, S. (1969). *Prace Inst. i Lab. Bad.
    Przem. Spoż.*, 19, p. 27.
20. Classen, H. (1926). *Z. Ver. Dtsch. Zuckerind.*, 76, p. 349.
21. Stuhlik, V., Pasteka, L. and Trieb, M. (1951). *Prum. Potravin*, 2(8),
    p. 348.
22. Underkofler, L. A. and Hickey, R. J. (1954). *Industrial Fermentations*,
    Vol. I, Chemical Publ. Co. Inc., New York, p. 237.
23. White, J. (1954). *Yeast Technology*, Chapman & Hall, London, p. 232.
24. Sobkowicz, G. (1970). *Mat. I Sesji Nauk. Komitetu Techn. Chem.
    Zywn. PAN* (Kraków, 26–27 Jan. 1970), Warszawa, p. 167.
25. Uhl, A. (1960). *Die Hefen*, Bd. 1, Verlag H. Carl. Nürnberg, p. 236.
26. Kobr, V. and Gregr, V. (1972). *Sbornik Vys. Sk. Chem. Technol.
    Praha*, E30, p. 127.

27. Pis, E. (1974). *Kvasny Prum.*, **20**(9), p. 200; **20**(10), p. 221.
28. Palagina, N. K. (1967). *Izw. Ws. Ucz. Z. Piszcz. Technol.*, No. 6, p. 59.
29. *Postep techniczny w przemyśle spirytusowym i drożdżowym* (1971), WNT, Warszawa, p. 141.
30. Chryczeva, A. J., Palagina, N. K., Czernysz, W. G. and Stafiejeva, I. A. (1971). *Chleb. Kond. Prom.*, No. 9, p. 24.
31. Malanowska, J. (1970). *Przem. Ferm. Roln.*, **14**(11), p. 32.
32. Kautzmann, R. (1969). *Branntweinwirtsch.*, **109**, p. 333.
33. Herbst, A. M. (1964). *Branntweinwirtsch.*, **104**(6), p. 132.
34. Gluzinska, W. (1972). *Roczn. Techn. Chem. Zywn.*, **22**(2), p. 197.
35. Olbrich, H. (1973). *Branntweinwirtsch.*, **113**(11), p. 270.
36. Lavrentieva, E. A. and Fertman, G. I. (1972). *Chleb. Kond. Prom.*, No. 10, p. 27; No. 4, p. 26.
37. Zahra, M. K., Gadjeva, L. A., Veselov, A. I. and Uvarov, I. P. (1974). *Prikl. Bioch. Mikrob.*, **10**(1), p. 158.
38. Jaworowska, J., Łabendzinski, S., Zoltowska, Z. and Jarosz, M. (1975). *Mat. VI Sesji Nauk. Komitetu Techn. Chemi. Zywn. PAN*, Olsztyn, 24–26 Jan., p. 87.
39. Łabendzinski, S., Zołtowska, J., Jarosz, M. and Kubacka, W. (1975). *Mat. VI Sesji Nauk. Komitetu Techn. Chem. Zywn. PAN*, Olsztyn, 24–26 Jan., p. 83.
40. Notkina, L. G., Zapara, E. M. and Balyberdina, L. M. (1971). *Chleb. Kon. Prom.*, No. 7, p. 24.
41. Barber, E. D. and Lands, W. E. M. (1973). *J. Bacteriol.*, **115**, p. 543.
42. Gongadze, N. W., Darcziana, T. J. and Czitiaszwili, N. W. (1971). *Trudy Gruz. Naucz. Isled. Inst. Piszcz. Prom.*, No. 5, p. 224.
43. Majchrzak, E., Sobczak, E. and Komorowska, Z. (1973). *Przem. Ferm. Roln.*, **17**(5), p. 1.
44. Bergander, E. (1969). *Lebensmettelind.*, **16**, p. 219.
45. Oldfield, J. F. T., Dutton, J. V. and Shore, M. (1974). *Int. Sugar J.*, **76**(909), p. 260; **76**(910), p. 301.
46. Andersen, E. (1956). *Int. Sugar J.*, **58**(689), p. 133.
47. Dierssen, G. A., Holtegeard, K., Jensen, B. and Rozen, K. (1956). *Int. Sugar J.*, **58**(686), p. 35.
48. Sobkowicz, G. and Kapusta, F. (1967). *Zesz. Nauk. WSR we Wrocławiu, Roln. XX*, No. 65, p. 99.
49. Karczewska, H. (1951). *Lebensmittelind.*, p. 70.
50. Łabendzinski, S. and Kozłowska, E. (1967). *Przem. Spoż.*, **22**(11), p. 22.
51. Osovik, A. N., Zabrodskij, A. G., Gridina, L. E., Szevczuk, Z. S. and Meszenko, W. J. (1974). *Ferm. Spirt. Prom.*, No. 7, p. 28.
52. Malanowska, J. and Korycka, W. (1968). *Przem. Ferm. Roln.*, **12**(4), p. 15.
53. Ilina, L. D., Jewnickaja, G. S. and Liszko, P. B. (1972). *Ferm. Spirt. Prom.*, No. 1, p. 21.
54. Kobrina, Ju. P. and Kozłowa, M. A. (1973). *Chleb. Kond. Prom.*, No. 6, p. 29.

56   G. Sobkowicz

55. Witkiewicz, E. (1972). *Trudy Ukr. Naucz. Isled. Inst. Spirt. Likier.*
    Prom., wyp. XIII, p. 8.
56. Kobrina, Ju. P. and Kozłowa, M. A. (1973). *Chleb. Kond. Prom.,* No.
    10, p. 27.
57. Stuhlik, V. (1971). *Kvasny Prum.,* **17**(11), p. 246.
58. Pis, E. and Pasteka, L. (1973). *Kvasny Prum.,* **19**(8), p. 176.
59. Drescher, N. and Schiweck, H. (1971). *Zucker,* **24**(16), p. 500.
60. Klaushofer, H. (1974). *Z. Zuckerind.,* **24**(4), p. 173.
61. Frago, A., Gottlasz, O., Pandi, F. and Todh, J. (1973). *Szeszipar,*
    21(1), p. 20.
62. Olbrich, H. (1973). *Branntweinwirtsch.,* **113**(16), p. 388.
63. Skiba, M. (1970). *Przem. Spoż.,* **24**(11), p. 477.
64. Butschek, G. and Kautzmann, R. (1962). *Die Hefen,* Bd. 2, Verlag
    H. Carl, Nürnberg, pp. 520–30, 565–7.
65. Szvec, W. N., Slusarenko, T. P., Kravjec, V. J. and Romanjukow,
    G. W. (1972). *Izw. Vys. Ucz. Zaw. Piszcz. Technol.,* No. 3, p. 89.
66. Skiba, J. and Ilnicka-Olejniczak, O. (1969). *Prace Inst. Lab. Bad.*
    Przem. Spoż., **19**(4), p. 637.
67. Lodder, J., Kudokormov, W. and Łangejan, A. (1969). III Internatio-
    nal Symposium on Yeast, Delft, The Netherlands, cited by Małagina,
    H. W. (1970). *Chleb. Kond. Prom.,* No. 3, p. 42.
68. Szopa, J. (1975). *Mat. VI Sesji Nauk. Komitetu Technol. Chem. Zywn.*
    PAN, Olsztyn, 24–26 Jan., p. 168.
69. Kirova, K. A. and Szevczenko, A. M. (1972). *Ferm. Spirt. Prom.,* No.
    5, p. 38.
70. Oberman, H., Renisz, W. and Pietka, M. (1975). *Mat. VI Sesji Nauk.*
    Komitetu Technol. Chem. Zywn., PAN, Olsztyn, 24–26 Jan., p. 169.
71. Vlad, E., Marsen, P. and Berbiuschi, D. (1972). *Luct. Cerc. Inst.*
    Cercsi Project Alim., **9,** p. 151.
72. Kalunyants, N. P., Ochnera, I. N. and Solomatina, L. M. (1974).
    Prikł. Bioch. Mikrob., **10**(1), p. 18.
73. Zabrodskij, A. G., Osovik, A. N., Poljanskaja, S. A. and Strizenjuk,
    E. W. (1973). *Ferm. Spirt. Prom.,* No. 1, p. 40.
74. Stoica, M. (1972). *Ind. Alim.,* No. 23, p. 134.
75. Zmarjeva, A. D. (1971). *Chleb. Kond. Prom.,* No. 11, p. 40.
76. Sokolenko, A. J. and Gandzjuk, M. P. (1972). *Ferm. Spirt. Prom.,* No.
    8, p. 36.
77. Nikołajev, P. J., Rylkin, S. S., Sokołov, D. P., Kubasov, A. V.,
    Gurina, L. V. and Bierova, L. A. (1973). *Mikrob. Prom.,* **9,** p. 1.
78. Lefrançois, L. and Revuz, B. (1973). *Ind. Alim. Agric.,* **90**(7–8),
    p. 989.
79. Miskiewicz, T., Lesniak, W. and Ziobrowski, J. (1975). *Mat. VI*
    Sesji Nauk. Komitetu Technol. Chem. Zywn., PAN, Olsztyn, 24–26
    Jan., p. 167.
80. Nagai, S., Niskizava, J. and Aiba, S. (1973). *J. Gen. Appl. Microbiol.,*
    19(3), p. 221.
81. Pis, E. (1966). *Kvasny Prum.,* **12**(2), p. 37.
82. Oura, E. (1974). *Branntweinwirtsch.,* **114**(20), p. 429.

83. Sokolenko, A. J., Gandzjuk, M. P. and Marder, A. C. (1972). *Chleb. Kond. Prom.*, No. 7, p. 35.
84. Chryczeva, A. J. (1973). *Chleb. Kond. Prom.*, No. 6, p. 37.
85. Aunicky, Z., Stros, F. and Zabojnik, R. (1971). *Kvasny Prum.*, **17**(4), p. 84.
86. Teruhiko, A. (1972). *Ferm. Technol.*, **50**(6), p. 411.
87. Kovalenko, A. D., Aszkinuzi, E. K., Orłovskij, J. K., Chil, G. N., Mariuczenko, V. A., Vasiljew, J. W., Kramarskij, N. A., Czubon, A. M. and Skripka, V. A. (1970). *Ferm. Spirt. Prom.*, No. 7, p. 33.

DISCUSSION

Edelman: Do you have a programme of production of food yeast in Poland?

Sobkowicz: Yes, we have, but not from molasses—only from stillages and other sources.

Edelman: And this is produced for human food?

Sobkowicz: Very little—mainly as feed for animals.

Russell Eggitt: The Professor has mentioned the importance of selecting the strain of yeast to make the maximum use of the nutrients in molasses, but there is also the necessity of picking the best strain of yeast to work best in the bread afterwards. Which is given precedence in Poland— selection of the maximum utilisation of the molasses or the subsequent performance of the yeast in its use in baking?

Sobkowicz: We have the yeast selected by the Micro-organism Museum in the Institute of Fermentation in Warsaw, and they carry out investigations on the different species of yeast and select from them the best for the production of baker's yeast. They are mainly from the Russian strains and from the Austrian and Yugoslav and other strains. They are then given to the industrial plant for use.

Edelman: Thank you—you really have said that the final uses are more important.

5

The Upgrading of Agricultural Wastes by Thermophilic Fungi

K. J. Seal and H. O. W. Eggins

*Biodeterioration Information Centre,
Department of Biological Sciences, University of Aston in
Birmingham, Birmingham, England*

ABSTRACT

The problems of agricultural waste management have increased over the last 25 years with an increase in the efficiency of farm husbandry. Both animal and crop production in Great Britain have been intensified to varying degrees to provide the increased demand for a good and constant quality product. The greater the crop yield or numbers of animals reared per area of land, the greater the amount of waste produced, either as straw in the case of cereals, or as manures in the case of animals. When produced in amounts greater than natural recycling processes can cope with, accumulation can occur making land more difficult to reuse or, if the waste is removed, creating storage problems. A large proportion of these wastes are cellulosic in composition together with varying proportions of nitrogen. This means that they can act, and do act under natural conditions, as a carbon and nitrogen source for cellulolytic micro-organisms. Investigations at the Biodeterioration Information Centre have shown that an indigenous flora of thermophilic fungi can be encouraged to utilise the cellulose and nitrogen in these wastes to produce fungal protein and hence an upgraded product.

Work has been concentrated on the upgrading of intensively produced pig manure and waste straw. Using thermophilic fungi an 'on farm' pilot-scale process has been devised to treat pig manure. The following problems, common to intensive animal waste management, were overcome using thermophilic temperatures of between 50° and 60°C. These were: separation of solid and liquid wastes, odour production, public health hazard, pathogen problem and the high polluting ability of the wastes. The solid product after treatment with thermophilic fungi for 14 days was enhanced in its total protein content from 5% up to between 10% and 13% and was reduced in cellulose content by about 30%. The product was also easier to handle and could be dried and stored until required.

INTRODUCTION

All processes, whether physical, chemical or biological, produce by-products or wastes. The natural processes involving the flora and fauna of the soil and water recycle these wastes by means of the carbon, nitrogen and other elemental cycles, so that very little recalcitrant accumulation occurs. The nutrients in the waste are thus recycled through the food chains to be incorporated into plant and animal structures where they are released back into the cycle. Why should it be necessary then to introduce man-made upgrading processes to channel the nutrients in other directions and deprive the natural cycles of their full complement of nutrients? The answer lies with man's ability to control and accelerate natural processes, such as food production, to increase their efficiency. This may increase the by-product quantities to such an extent that Nature's cycles are unable to treat them at the rate at which they are produced. As these by-products become more concentrated the cycles may become attenuated owing to the inhibitory nature of one stage, unable to cope with very high concentrations of waste, on later stages in the cycle.

It is well documented that industrial pollution of rivers and waterways has been due to the concentration of industrial processes and the inability of natural breakdown and recycling processes to keep track of the amount of waste being introduced into the cycles. Toxic substances have also in the past been discharged into watercourses completely arresting microbial activity and thus breaking the cycles. This will lead to a build-up in waste material. In the United Kingdom rigid legislation controlling industrial waste removal to rivers has reversed the pollution process. In parallel with the industrial waste problems, but occurring more recently, is the increased production of agricultural wastes due to the intensification of crop and animal production. Although the waste products of these industries are not classed as toxic in the normal sense of the word, when in high accumulations they can result in the same problems of water pollution encountered with factory pollution. Symptoms of this pollution are already appearing near to high-density animal stocking areas. For example, lakes and inland waterways have been subject to large-scale eutrophication[1] caused by animal manures trickling from the land which has been both biologically and physically overloaded. The by-products from cereal production are also causing a pollution problem. The straw stem left after removal of the grain must be lifted from the ground to prevent fouling of the soil for the next crop. Most of the straw produced in the United Kingdom is burnt in the field causing smoke and fire hazards and ecological problems. Removal of the straw from the field is costly and is only justified where it is to be put to use as bedding or for non-agricultural uses.

The development of upgrading methods for the recycling of animal and other agricultural wastes as an animal feed component could help to alleviate the waste problems of high-density stocking and cropping provided that any process developed was quick and economically viable.

AGRICULTURAL WASTE PROBLEMS: AN IMBALANCE OF NUTRIENTS

Wherever farm animals have been kept a variety of waste products—either direct or indirect animal by-products—have accumulated. Because systems of husbandry include the grazing of animals on open land, their wastes can be passively absorbed into the soil. Here they undergo the natural breakdown and recycling processes in conjunction with the large amounts of plant waste also deposited in the soil. The wastes are deposited in relatively low concentrations over the land. This means that the animals provide a cheap and convenient method of waste removal and disposal and, because of the low concentrations, the soil structure and its general condition are not affected. The presence of plant material provides a balance of nutrients in the animal waste so that the soil flora and fauna are able to recycle the elements for fertility at a rate equal to or greater than their deposition as the wastes.

The application of straw-based manures is still considered to be important for the improvement of soils. In addition to providing a balanced nitrogen and carbon source for plant growth, the manures are degraded in the soil to form a fine black acidic material known as humus. This is very important in maintaining soil structure, good aeration and water-holding capacity.[2] It is thus important that manures should be applied to the land wherever possible, and a British Government report[3] on waste disposal has advocated this.

However, there is an ever increasing trend towards artificial fertilisers which have the advantages of ease of handling, known chemical composition and the constant quality which they can provide. The Ministry of Agriculture, Fisheries and Food's statistics (Table 1) show that, based upon the quantity of nitrogen in artificial compound fertilisers, the use of these has nearly trebled in the period 1952–70.[4]

TABLE 1
Artificial fertiliser consumption by farmers in Great Britain based upon nitrogen subsidies

Nitrogen content (tons)		
1952–3[a]	1960–1	1969–70
125 228	272 488	359 521

[a] The year runs from 1 June to 31 May.

Thus, although animal wastes are not put back into the soil as much as they should or could be, they do not under normal spreading conditions cause ill-effects to the land. As, however, the concentration of livestock increases, as does the efficiency of crop production, then imbalances to the natural cycles can occur due to the concentration of certain nutrients in small distinct areas. For example, the eastern side of Great Britain produces 29·7% of the total wheat, barley and oats.[5] In the midland and western regions cereal production is reduced. In parallel with this, intensification of animals has taken place primarily in the midland and western areas of Great Britain. Thus, there is a vast store of carbon-rich by-products in the eastern area and a corresponding concentration of nitrogen-rich material in the midland and western areas from the animals. Although this is an over-simplification of the situation it does illustrate the present and potential waste problem which has resulted from mono-culture farming. Direct application of either the carbon- or nitrogen-rich by-products (straw in the case of cereal production and animal slurries in the case of animal production) to the land can result in an overloading problem causing the effects outlined in the introduction.

During the growth of plant crops, there is usually a concentration of useful nutrients in certain parts of the plant, which are then harvested leaving a waste for disposal. A particular example of this problem occurs in cereal production. Of the total dry weight of a cereal plant, the grain represents at most 50%, containing up to

10% protein and large quantities of easily assimilable starches[6] (about 60%). The remainder of the plant, the straw, has less than 1% protein and any potential utilisable carbohydrate is in the form of cellulose and hemicelluloses. This is considered to be a waste product, more so recently, since in Great Britain the trend in animal systems is away from the use of straw bedding and the traditional manure which results from it. However, it does contain valuable carbon which could be used to correct the imbalance within animal waste management. In 1974 nearly 60% of the straw produced in the eastern region of Great Britain was burnt in the fields[7]—a terrible waste of energy and an incomplete, albeit cheap, solution. In the same region 23% was used as bedding and 0·1% ploughed in. The ploughing-in of straw is mechanically difficult, needing power and labour, and does not cause it to decompose very quickly. This may be due to the low nitrogen available to the flora and fauna present or may be due to the mechanical resistance of the ligno-cellulose complex in the straw.

This, then, outlines the problems which agricultural waste management faces. If one considers the by-products not as wastes but as nutrients which other groups of organisms are able to utilise, then it is possible to devise processes to encourage these organisms to treat or upgrade the wastes to a product which could be almost immediately available for animal nutrition.

THE ROLE OF MICRO-ORGANISMS

The role of micro-organisms in correcting the imbalances described above, and providing upgrading processes for agricultural wastes, is very important. Where such wastes are produced in excess of the soil's ability to cope, systems must be designed which involve the soil flora, whether or not breakdown is to be carried out in the soil. Man, having increased waste production in selected localities above the level at which it can be economically disposed of, must help Nature to recycle her fixed nutrient resources at a rate equivalent to the intensive unit requirements to prevent by-product accumulation.

The involvement of micro-organisms, both naturally and artificially, in the recycling of waste nutrients from agricultural wastes can be seen in the flow diagram (Fig. 1). Here a comparison is made with the natural system involving plant and animal waste. The use of micro-organisms can by-pass photosynthesis, thus shortening the time for the flow of nutrients back to the animal. The growth of plants for feed purposes is seasonal and the nutrient from the previous year's crop must lay dormant in the soil until the next growing season. During this period the use of micro-organisms to process the waste and keep the nutrients flowing through the food chains could help to alleviate the fluctuating plant carbohydrate and protein availability situation. In such a system using micro-organisms it can be seen from the flow diagram that photosynthesis would still

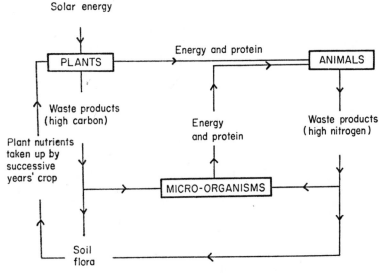

FIG. 1.   Flow diagram to show micro-organism involvement (natural and induced) in the recycling of animal and plant wastes.

be required to produce a crop and that micro-organisms could not completely replace green plants. However, the waste from the crop together with the continuously produced animal wastes could be put to good use outside the growing season in producing nutrients for animal growth.

One aspect of the work at the Biodeterioration Information Centre (BIC) has been directed towards creating processes in which plant and animal wastes are brought together and enhanced in their value. Such upgrading processes have been defined as being bio-degradative processes. Biodegradation may be defined[8] as the useful and desirable microbial upgrading of a waste material to give a product which is enhanced in its economic or aesthetic value above that of the original material. The enhancement may be in the form of increased availability for nutritional needs, increase in protein, decrease in odour, polluting ability, bulk, or simply more pleasant to handle or look at.

The traditional farmyard manure is an excellent example of the bringing together of a plant and animal waste and serves as a very good means by which ecological, physiological and indigenous species studies can be made. Many workers[9-11] have indeed investigated the characteristics of manures, providing us with valuable information in assessing their potential for thermophilic upgrading processes. Investigations have been carried out at the BIC using the composting process as a guideline in order to develop an upgrading process for the production of an animal feed component. Composting has been adequately reviewed[12-14] and need not be described here. The work has been centred around the use of a small group of fungi which are tolerant to high temperatures (40–50°C) or have their optimum activities at about 50°C. The latter group have been called the thermophilic fungi[15] and the former group the thermotolerant fungi. Since the groups were first recognised at the beginning of this century over forty years lapsed before more work was carried out.[16] Since then the groups have been characterised and their habitats, such as composts[17-19] and other self-heating piles,[20] have been thoroughly investigated. These fungi are able to grow over a wide range of temperatures and have certain selective advantages over other fungi. The fungi as a group, and the thermophiles in particular, were chosen for the following reasons:

1. There are many cellulolytic species able to use the large amounts of cellulose in plant waste as an energy source.
2. They occur naturally in animal and plant wastes.
3. They are obligate aerobes and do not produce the unpleasant odours usually associated with anaerobiosis.
4. Their pH optima tend to discourage bacteria which contain pathogenic groups.
5. They are good sources of protein, being low in nucleic acid levels.
6. Their mycelial habit gives them a colonising advantage in that they can spread over solid substrates and penetrate intact tissue without any pretreatment.[21]

7. In the thermophilic ranges the species are reduced to about 15 in number which have been well characterised in their biochemical and physiological activities.[15] Thus conditions can be created to selectively optimise their activities.

8. The thermotolerant species are active over a wide spectrum of temperatures from below 20°C up to 50°C.

9. Viable animal parasites and non-spore-forming bacterial animal pathogens can be inactivated in the thermophilic ranges.

10. Thermophilic breakdown appears to work at a greater rate than mesophilic breakdown.[4]

A series of investigations was carried out by the BIC to determine how well the thermophiles were able to biodegrade straw and animal slurry mixtures under accelerated conditions.[4] Conditions were provided on a laboratory scale to raise the temperature of a mixture of barley straw and pig slurry (carbon to nitrogen ratio about 40:1) up to 50°C in less than 24 h. It was then kept at this temperature for the duration of each experiment. The first investigation involved determining the breakdown rate of cellulose at varying temperatures. The graph (Fig. 2) shows that up to 50°C there is an increase in cellulose degradation. Above 50°C the rate decreases, probably because the large majority of thermophiles have passed their optimum growth and enzyme activities.

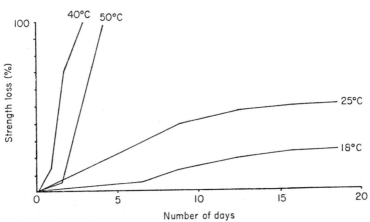

FIG. 2.   Graph to show effect of temperature on cellulolytic activity in pig slurry/straw mixture measured as strength loss of filter paper strips placed in mixtures and screened according to Eggins and Lloyd.[22]

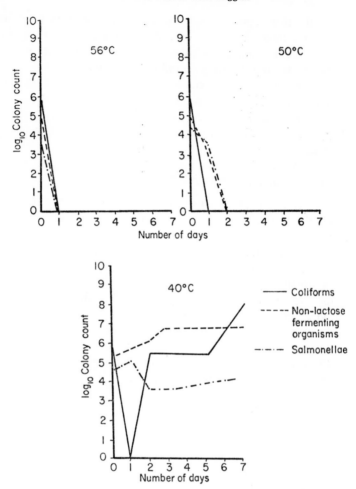

Fig. 3. Graphs to show effects of temperature on pathogenic bacteria present in pig slurry/straw mixtures.

An investigation into the pathogen resistance in the wastes as they were processed was carried out at three temperatures: 40°, 50° and 56°C. The graph (Fig. 3) shows that inactivity was complete at 50° and 56°C after 3 days but not at 40°C. This point is very important when considering the product as a potential food. Another important consideration was the suppression of fungal pathogens. The use of the high temperature excluded the mesophilic fungi which include

TABLE 2
*The frequency of occurrence of thermophilic fungi isolated from pig manure
at a variety of pH's on Eggins and Pugh cellulose agar*[23]

Fungal species	pH	% frequency of occurrence	
		40°C	48°C
Aspergillus fumigatus	4·0	0	20
	5·6	100	20
	6·6	60	—
	7·4	40	—
	8·2	10	—
Chaetomium thermophile	4·0	—	—
	5·6	60	100
	6·6	—	20
	7·4	—	40
	8·2	—	80
Humicola insolens	4·0	—	—
	5·6	100	20
	6·6	—	—
	7·4	100	—
	8·2	—	—
Humicola lanuginosa	4·0	—	—
	5·6	20	60
	6·6	100	20
	7·4	—	50
	8·2	100	100
Mucor pusillus	4·0	60	—
	5·6	30	20
	6·6	30	50
	7·4	—	—
	8·2	—	—
Stilbella thermophila	4·0	—	—
	5·6	100	—
	6·6	30	—
	7·4	—	—
	8·2	30	—
Torula thermophila	4·0	—	—
	5·6	30	20
	6·6	20	90
	7·4	100	20
	8·2	100	100

— = no growth.

the majority of pathogenic species. However, two important thermotolerant species are able to survive—*Aspergillus fumigatus*, which can
cause lung infections,[15] and *Mucor pusillus*, associated with a variety
of infections of animals and man.[24] A study of the temperature and
pH requirements of these fungi revealed that their pH optima were
well into the acid ranges (4–5) and that they were more abundant at
40°C than at 50°C (Table 2). The other thermophilic species had pH
optima in the alkaline range (7–8) and grew better at 50°C. Thus a
simple control method was to maintain the mixture at 50°C and
keep the pH slightly alkaline. Isolations from such conditions
revealed the absence of both *A. fumigatus* and *M. pusillus*.

A pilot-scale plant was constructed to test the laboratory-scale
results.[25] The plant consisted of a tower 3 m high and 1·6 m square,
containing four platforms equal distances apart (*see* Fig. 4). The

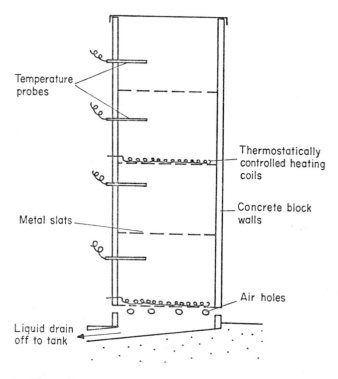

FIG. 4.   Pilot-scale tower for thermophilic biodegradation of pig slurry/straw
mixtures.

mixtures of straw and slurry were placed on the platforms and heating was applied by means of an electric soil-warming cable. In this way the mixture rose to 50°C within 24 h and was controlled at this temperature by means of thermostats and air holes in the base of the tower. Samples were removed at intervals for analysis and the tower was run for 14 days. The final product was removed and air dried. It was found that very similar conditions occurred on the larger scale and it was decided to subject the material to a nutritional analysis (*see* next section). Apart from a study of its nutritional potential the product was found to be much reduced in its bulk and could be handled more easily. There was also no obnoxious smell, this having been replaced by a pleasant earthy smell which disappeared on drying.

THE NUTRITIONAL VALUE OF UPGRADED AGRICULTURAL WASTES

It has long been recognised by farmers that pigs kept on straw bedding seem to thrive better than those allowed to roam free. This is thought to be due to the increase in nutritive value of the straw, which the pigs eat, as a result of fungal and bacterial upgrading; the micro-organisms being able to provide certain proteins and vitamins which the pigs find useful. The upgrading of the straw is aided by the deposition of the pigs' waste which provides a nitrogen source and moisture. The depth of bedding may also provide insulation for the encouragement of thermophilic conditions.

Research workers studying ways in which animal wastes might be treated and disposed of, arising from a need to combat the problems of intensive waste management, have found that these wastes have a varying nutrient composition. This ranges from the high amino acid and mineral content of poultry wastes[26] to the lower contents of pig[27] and cow wastes[28] (Table 3). Thus, as far as animal wastes are concerned, upgrading processes must be selective in the type of waste utilised and its value as a nutrient source without processing. For example, although the availability of poultry nutrients to animals is not fully known, it is usual practice simply to dry the waste and incorporate it direct into a feedstuff. Were this to be done using pig waste the lower concentration of nutrients and the higher water content would make the process uneconomic. In this case it would be worthwhile studying the possibilities to see whether a substantial increase in protein and vitamins could be achieved by fungal upgrading.

The situation with straw is different in that the carbohydrate energy source is present in the structure but its availability for utilisation by ruminants is limited. Thus any upgrading process needs to increase that availability without utilising the carbohydrate. There are several techniques in current use which achieve this but they have

TABLE 3
A comparison of the amino acid contents of various animal wastes

Amino acid	Poultry[26] (g/100 g protein)	Cattle[28] (% dry wt)	Pig[27] (% dry wt)
Aspartic acid	3·29	—	1·28
Threonine	1·92	0·74	0·67
Serine	1·85	—	0·57
Glutamic acid	4·18	—	1·59
Proline	0·63	—	0·61
Glycine	2·68	—	0·86
Alanine	2·34	—	0·98
Valine	4·04	1·00	0·75
Methionine	0·88	0·38	0·22
Isoleucine	2·72	0·84	0·51
Leucine	2·99	1·22	0·92
Tyrosine	1·36	—	0·56
Phenylalanine	1·79	0·74	0·72
Lysine	1·89	1·46	0·72
Histidine	0·72	0·48	0·28
Arginine	1·56	0·39	0·74
Ammonia	—	—	—

certain disadvantages. The mechanical grinding of straw increases the efficiency of utilisation by the rumen, but the equipment needed for the process can have a high capital and running cost. The chemical treatment of straw[29] using sodium hydroxide, and known as the Beckman process, is able to increase the availability of the carbohydrate considerably. However, this chemical is very caustic and would need very rigorous supervision were it to be used on a farm. Off-farm centralised treatment plants are a possibility, but the capital and running costs do not look economically promising at the moment. All these methods simply increase the availability of the energy source to the ruminant without adding any other nutrients. A third method, again chemical, is able to increase both the availability and the nitrogen content of the straw. This is by the use of gaseous ammonia,[30] which has been shown to be successful in adding non-protein nitrogen to the product.

TABLE 4
Amino acid content of fungal-treated pig waste
after 14 days at 50°C
(% of total dry weight)

Amino acid	Day 0	Day 14
Tyrosine	—	0·033
Lysine	0·036	0·090
Histidine	0·016	0·024
Ammonia	0·007	1·273
Arginine	—	0·057
Aspartic acid	0·049	0·217
Threonine	0·027	0·106
Serine	0·038	0·109
Glutamic acid	0·059	0·279
Proline	—	—
Glycine	0·028	0·149
Alamine	0·019	0·143
Cystine	1·20	2·58
Valine	0·04	0·143
Methionine	—	0·012 5
Isoleucine	0·014	0·077 7
Leucine	0·031	0·143

The addition of the straw to the animal waste provides the microorganisms with a carbon and nitrogen source so that the straw can be broken down and the animal waste converted into protein and vitamin. At the BIC an amino acid analysis was carried out on some product from the pilot-scale operation described in a previous section. It was found (Table 4) that the amino acids had increased over 14 days. In comparison with the amino acid contents in the previous table these are low. However, it is very difficult to compare products when the composition of the diet may vary considerably, affecting the composition of the untreated waste.[31] The product was then fed to rabbits to test for gross toxicity and palatability. The rabbits accepted the food and showed no ill-effects.

Two other groups of workers have studied the upgrading possibilities of agricultural wastes. Anthony[32] has developed his system of 'wastelage' which involves the mixing of fresh cow manure with ground grass hay in the ratio of 57:43 and then storing the mixture in a silo until fed. An amino acid analysis of the wastelage in comparison with a control diet has shown it to contain about 20% more than the total amino acid content of the control diet, making it a potential protein source for animal rations. The nutritive value of pig waste has received less attention in the past, possibly because of its high strength and handling problems. However, Harmon *et al.*[33] have studied the nutritive value of the solid residue from an oxidation ditch on rats. They found that this solid residue mixed with corn could replace between one-half and one-third of the protein of the soya bean control meal and that the feed intake was not affected, showing that the material was palatable. The addition of 1% lysine and 0·1% tryptophan together in the experimental feed significantly increased the rate of gain of the animals, showing that these amino acids were limiting in the waste.

The total amino acid content although indicative of the upgrading of a waste material, does not predict the nutritive value to the animal. Not all the amino acid content will be digestible and not all the digestible amino acid will be available. The digestible fraction is that portion which is absorbed by the gut and the available part is that actually used by the animal to produce protein. As most work investigating the nutritive value of upgraded agricultural wastes is still in its infancy, these particular points have yet to be considered.

CONCLUSIONS

Under certain circumstances, *i.e.* where the amount of agricultural waste exceeds the soil's ability to recycle it efficiently there is a need for alternative treatment methods to be devised. Animal and cereal wastes contain large amounts of nutrients which are available for microbial conversion. The storing of untreated wastes represents a holding-up of potentially recyclable nutrient, and the use of microorganisms to achieve a quick recycling could be useful in alleviating the pollution problem caused when wastes are stored or overloaded on to the land. Or it could provide a cheap source of protein to be incorporated into the animal rations.

The use of fungi as the upgrading agents offers many advantages over other micro-organisms and the thermophiles are particularly important in speeding up the process and removing potential pathogens. It has been seen that the process is able to increase the amino acid composition of the product and it has been fed to rabbits with no gross toxic effects.

It is very important in the present climate of spiralling food costs, and a realisation that there are limited resources available, that a careful study of how agricultural wastes are managed be undertaken. The possibility of their use as upgraded feed components is only one line of study. The use of wastes direct, or plant nutrients extracted from the wastes as fertilisers, is another important study which should be considered in the light of the much increased costs of manufactured or imported nitrogen and phosphorus.

ACKNOWLEDGEMENT

We thank Ciba-Geigy (Basle, Switzerland) for a grant to carry out this work, in particular to enable one of us (K.J.S.) to work for the degree of Doctor of Philosophy.

REFERENCES

1. Hetling, L. J. and Sykes, R. M. (1973). *J. Wat. Pollut. Contr. Fedn.*, **45**(1), p. 145.
2. Millar, C. E., Turk, L. M. and Foth, H. D. (1958). *Fundamentals of Soil Science*, 3rd ed., Wiley, New York.
3. *Taken for Granted* (1970). Report of the Working Party on Sewage Disposal, HMSO, London.
4. Seal, K. J. (1973). 'Aspects of the fungal degradation of intensively produced farm animal manures', Ph.D. Thesis. University of Aston in Birmingham.
5. National Farmers Union (1973). *Report on the Use and Disposal of Straw*, NFU Working Party on Straw Disposal.
6. Kent-Jones, D. W. and Amos, A. J. (1967). *Cereal Chemistry*, Food Trade Press, London.

7. *Report on Straw Disposal* (1973). Advisory Council for Agriculture and Horticulture in England and Wales.
8. Seal, K. J. and Eggins, H. O. W. (1972). *Int. Biodetn. Bull.*, 8(3), p. 95.
9. Fergus, C. L. (1964). *Mycologia*, 56, p. 267.
10. Hayes, W. A. (1969). *Mushroom Sci.*, 8, p. 173.
11. Waksman, S. A. and Cordon, T. C. (1939). *Soil Sci.*, 47, p. 217.
12. Gray, K. R., Sherman, K. and Biddlestone, A. J. (1971). *Process Biochem.*, 6(6), p. 32.
13. Kershaw, M. A. (1968). *Process Biochem.*, 3(5), p. 53.
14. Wylie, J. C. (1960). In: *Waste Treatment—A Symposium*, ed. P. C. G. Isaac, Pergamon Press, Oxford, p. 349.
15. Cooney, D. G. and Emerson, R. (1964). *Thermophilic Fungi: An Account of their Biology, Activities and Classification*, W. H. Freeman & Co., San Francisco and London.
16. Cooney, D. G. (1952). 'Morphology and taxonomy of the thermophilic fungi', Ph.D. Thesis, University of California, Berkeley.
17. Chang, Y. and Hudson, H. J. (1967). *Trans. Br. Mycol. Soc.*, 50(4), p. 649.
18. Chang, Y. (1967). *Trans. Br. Mycol. Soc.*, 50(4), p. 667.
19. Mills, J. (1973). 'The biodegradation of certain components of town waste by thermophilic fungi', Ph.D. Thesis, University of Aston in Birmingham.
20. Shields, J. K. (1969). *Mycologia*, 61(6), p. 1165.
21. Hudson, H. J. (1972). *Fungal Saprophytism*, Studies in Biology No. 32, Edward Arnold, London.
22. Eggins, H. O. W. and Lloyd, A. O. (1968). *Experientia*, 24, p. 749.
23. Eggins, H. O. W. and Pugh, G. J. F. (1962). *Nature*, 193(4810), p. 94.
24. Emmons, C. W., Binford, C. H. and Utz, J. P. (1963). *Medical Mycology*, Henry Kimpton, London.
25. Ciba-Geigy, provisional patent (filed May 1974).
26. Evans, R. A., Evans, W. C., Axford, R. F. E., Chamberlain, A. G. and Morgan, D. E. (1968). In: *Proceedings of Poultry Waste Conference*, Sunningdale Park, 29 April–1 May, MAAF (NAAS), p. 52.
27. Harmon, B. G. and Day, D. L. (1973). *Illinois Research*, 15(3), p. 14.
28. Anthony, W. B. (1966). In: *Proceedings of Symposium on Management of Farm Animal Wastes*, American Society of Agricultural Engineers, St Joseph, Michigan, Publication No. SP-0366, p. 109.
29. Carmona, J. F. and Greenhalgh, J. F. D. (1972). *J. Agric. Sci., Camb.*, 78, p. 477.
30. Waiss, A. C., Guggolz, J., Kohler, G. O., Walker, H. G. and Garrett, W. N. (1972). *J. Anim. Sci.*, 35(1), p. 109.
31. O'Callaghan, J. R., Dodd, V. A., O'Donoghue, P. A. J. and Pollock, K. A. (1971). *J. Agric. Eng. Res.*, 16(4), p. 399.
32. Anthony, W. B. (1969). In: *Proceedings of Conference on Animal Waste Management*, Cornell University, Ithaca, NY, 13–15 Jan., p. 105.
33. Harmon, B. G., Day, D. L., Jensen, A. H. and Baker, D. H. (1972). *J. Anim. Sci.*, 34, p. 403.

DISCUSSION

Garrett: The ideas which you advanced were, of course, very attractive, but as you said yourself the sources of straw and slurry are separated. I wonder if you have considered the value added to your straw in relation to the transport costs and other costs which are involved in the process.

Seal: We have considered this, and this is one of the problems. I have not personally carried out an economic evaluation of this, but Willetts at Surrey University has done some work on the correcting of the imbalance of these nutrients over the country, and he feels it could be, if it was managed properly, economic to redistribute various nutrients. But I would agree with you in that one has to consider transport costs and this is why one does get the problems of animal waste pollution in the first case, because people are not prepared to transport their wastes far enough to spread them on the land. There is enough land available in Great Britain to spread all the animal waste, but because of the situation of these intensive units it is very difficult to get to the land because of the transport costs.

Bu'lock: (i) What happens to the copper content of the pig manure?

(ii) If you are using straw you are using a relatively clean waste, but you are mixing it with what from the point of pathogens is a dirty waste as your nitrogen source. Have you any experience of running this kind of process combining a clean waste like straw with a synthetic nitrogen?

Seal: The answer to the first question is yes, copper is a problem. We found in our waste that particularly from pig units the product contains up to 200 ppm, which is just about acceptable for inclusion in pig rations, but it couldn't be used for other animals, such as cattle. This is if you are to use it pure, of course. If you are diluting it then you decrease your problem, and this has led on to us considering other ways of utilising the nutrients in the waste by actually extracting them from the waste and getting rid of the pathogen and heavy metal carryover. We have considered using other forms of nitrogen with the straw. We did some work some time ago. We first started doing some work on urea and this seemed to work quite well in organic sources, but the problems here were the cost of the urea. When we were using urea originally it was quite cheap and then it suddenly increased in price, but I do agree that one could look at other cleaner wastes to see how they would react with the straw, but one would then probably have to use some sort of inoculant. We have used various inoculant organisms which are able to utilise the straw quite quickly but they have varying degrees of success on these different types of nitrogen sources.

Chubb: May I make a comment on the use of poultry waste in cattle foods. First of all, poultry manure contains about 30% nitrogen in the form of uric acid, and one has to be a bit careful because occasionally the farmer will feed silage as well which also has an additional source of non-protein nitrogen. There is also an increase in the usage of urea in cattle feeds, and I think one has to remember that cattle are sensitive to certain levels of non-protein nitrogen and it can cause toxic problems. One has to be a little bit careful of the facile assumption that you can use dried poultry waste in cattle foods.

Emery: Dr Seal has talked specifically about the on-farm situation, but I think one should bear in mind that the farmer is a farmer and not a chemist, and one of the reasons for the relatively small application of ensilage is that the efficient ensilement of the grasses requires a fairly highly developed testing and blending capability. What I am asking is how much flexibility have you in your composting situation? Can you rely on a man who is either going to heap the stuff in with a fork or use a mechanical disperser, or does it have to be metered in very closely, knowing what the moisture limits of the straw are, and knowing exactly what the COD of the slurries are?

Seal: This is still in its developmental stage of course, and we ran it for less than a year when we were doing the work. We operated it as an on-farm process at a farm, we used local farm labour and we found that it was quite flexible. In fact, the whole system was as I said. We used the straw filters which we placed in the slurry pit underneath the pig and the animal dunged on to the straw filter and the filters were found to last between six and eight weeks, in fact the time that it took from weaning until they were used for pork. Then we removed the filters and put them into the tower and we found that it seemed to work quite well. The main problems that have arisen, and we have realised them and tried to modify our processes now, lie in the quality of the product and problems of pathogens. Although I did say that we get rid of three groups of them there are many other pathogens of course that could be present, and there is also the heavy metal problem. So we did find that there was a fair amount of flexibility but I can't quantify it, it is very difficult to do. But we did find it worked quite well. There are a lot of problems we still haven't sorted out, but we have gone over now to trying to extract nutrients from the waste and then subjecting what is left to a normal farm treatment system, because there are plenty of good treatment systems available for the farmer to use.

Stanton: What was the age of the chicken manure used in your analysis, because we have found that keeping chicken manure moist for a period alters considerably the total true protein value and of course the amino acid composition. We followed this up by looking at what micro-organisms could use uric acid as the nitrogen source, and we found that in fact using pure uric acid there are a surprising number of fungi which will actively utilise high concentrations. And this is the advantage from a theoretical point of view of some of the highly available sources of nitrogen that occur in solid fermentations. It does give a steady release of the nitrogen. I was wondering whether this has been taken into account.

Seal: Those results were not my analysis, but were extracted from a paper— I can send you the paper if you require it—and I think it does mention how the waste was treated.

Bookey: In answering one of the previous questions, the speaker said that the work veered towards the extraction of nutrients rather than trying to produce a feeding stuff. When you say 'nutrients', do you mean NPK nutrients or feeding stuffs?

Seal: Basically yes—basic building blocks that micro-organisms could use for conversion.

Clift: Two questions. First of all on the question of copper. In general there is a closed circuit—you are feeding the waste product to the animal and then recycling it back to the same animal. Have you got any data on the gradual concentration, not only of heavy metals but also of pesticides?

Secondly, what information is available on the availability of the amino acids present in the modified waste to the digestive system of the cow?

Seal: The answer to the first question is that we haven't carried out any work on the accumulation of copper and pesticides, but I believe there is some work available on this.

On the second question, we haven't actually done any work on feeding trials—you are worried about the value of amino acids?

Clift: I don't know too much about the way a cow's stomach works, but I understand it works basically on the principle of breaking down cellulose. If you are using micro-organisms to break down the cellulose, is the material still then available to the digestive system of the cow, can it in fact absorb the amino acids you produce, and would it be better feeding that material to perhaps an animal of a lower nutritional plane?

Seal: This is true, and we have modified our thinking as a result of this; the fact is that it is a waste of energy to break down, as you state, cellulose. If you are going to feed it to a ruminant you might as well just increase the availability of the cellulose. I'm not particularly well qualified to answer questions on the utilisation of amino acids but I believe they are all broken down to ammonia and then re-synthesised anyway. So if you give it a fairly simple nitrogen source it is more efficient in utilising it than it would be say in a complex protein, but I'm not really qualified to discuss this.

Satchell: I understand the original problem was primarily of disposal of pig slurry which the farmer cannot get on to the land during the winter when it is wet, and this technique that you have of composting in this way leads to the result that he has a solid stackable waste which he can then store and dispose of when the soil conditions allow him to do so. Would you say that this is a fair assessment of the real value and orientation of this work rather than any connection with feeding stuff?

Seal: This is true, yes. Our main aim is to treat the waste to reduce the polluting problems and to reduce the handling problems for the farmer. As an added bonus, it might be possible in certain situations to produce some sort of livestock feed.

Russell Eggitt: Referring to the added bonus, it is very reassuring that the temperatures of fermentation are so high that the pathogens can be inhibited, but what work is being done to ensure that the thermophilic organisms themselves are not producing any toxic metabolites?

Seal: This again is something which we did not go into too deeply, but we did do some what we call gross toxicity trials. We had some rabbits and we fed them on this product—and added sugar to make them accept it, and they didn't die. They seemed quite happy. We just didn't have the facilities to do a nutrition analysis at the time, but we can do this now.

Zadrazil: Have you studied the biotechnological parameter during experiments—for example, how much air is necessary on the first, second and third days? That is the first question, and secondly, if you have studied this biotechnological parameter, for example aeration and so on, how will this change the quality of the product?

Seal: We found we didn't need any active aeration for the process. The straw seemed to form—when it was mixed with the slurry—a fairly aerated mixture with lots of air spaces in between the waste.

Zadrazil: This was under thermophilic conditions, I presume. How much CO_2 was produced?

Seal: I don't know, we didn't measure CO_2 concentrations but we found that all we needed to do was to provide air in the bottom of the tower and its convection currents seemed to be sufficient.

6

Production of Microbial Protein from Carbohydrate Wastes in Developing Countries

F. K. E. IMRIE and R. C. RIGHELATO

Tate & Lyle Ltd, Philip Lyle Memorial Research Laboratory,
University of Reading, Reading, England

ABSTRACT

Recent forecasts of rates of population increase and of world food production have led to increasingly gloomy prognostications of widespread famine in the next decade. Data of this kind have led to a considerable number of research projects into new methods for increasing world food production. This paper deals with one of these solutions. Methods will be described for the steps required in establishing a microbial protein process within the economic and social environment of developing countries. Special emphasis will be made of the step-by-step requirements for establishing a successful process and this will be illustrated by practical examples from various parts of the world.

INTRODUCTION

Most crops are grown for only a small part of their bulk and so during harvesting and processing various parts of the plant are discarded. Part is simply ploughed back into the land and makes a valuable contribution to the structure and fertility of the soil. Another part, notably straw and dry leaves, is often burnt on the fields because collection and redistribution is too costly. There remains, collected at farms and food processing plants, many hundreds of millions of tons per annum of very low value material. Steffgen[1] quoted for the USA alone 400 million tons per annum of solid waste from the agricultural and allied industries. To this must be added many millions of tons of BOD in liquid effluents, and so for every ton of food produced a similar quantity of carbohydrate waste is collected and subsequently disposed of, often by burning or oxidation in effluent treatment plants.

The production of microbial protein from wastes of the agricultural industries has received attention in recent years with two main objectives in view—firstly upgrading the feed value of solid wastes, and secondly removing the BOD from liquid wastes with a bonus in the form of high-protein animal feed supplement. These processes face a number of economic and technical problems. The economic problems stem from the distribution of agricultural wastes. They are produced worldwide but in relatively small quantities at individual sites and often for only a small part of the year (Table 1). A plant

TABLE 1
Scale and seasonality of waste production

	Papaya	Olive	Palm oil
Average processing plant waste (tons/ year dry solids)	2 000	300	7 000
Season	10/12	4/12	11/12
Estimate of SCP production (tons/year)	500	100	1 000

built to take advantage of a fruit cull, for instance, would have a throughput of at best a few tens of thousands of tons of fruit, yielding probably less than a thousand tons of single cell protein. The factory would be inoperative for part of the year or would have to operate on a different waste. Effluents from, for instance, olive processing plants pose similar problems of low throughput and seasonality. These factors make for high amortisation costs, so the technology must be such that the capital cost of plant is minimised for an economically viable operation. Plants that operate all year round and on a larger scale, such as corn and palm oil processing plants, present less of a problem but still require a simple technology to be commercially viable.

The technical problems of microbial protein production stem from the chemical composition and physical form of the wastes. In general the solid organic material is mostly carbohydrate at least half of which is cellulose (Table 2). Starches, pectins and sugars form the remainder. If the sugars of the carbohydrate polymers can be mobilised they can form the basis of processes such as recovery of sugars or fermentation for ethanol or single-cell protein production. Cellulose, particularly lignified cellulose, is an intransigent polymer whose hydrolysis has been the subject of extensive studies and

TABLE 2
Composition of Agricultural wastes

	Bagasse	Papaya	Palm oil sludge	Potato Process water
Total solids %	49	13	5	0·7
Carbohydrate % of dry solids	82	80	40	75
Fibre	94	9	20	20
Pectins	0	7	NT	NT
Starches	0	NT	NT	60
Oligosaccharides and monosaccharides	4·5	67	NT	NT
Protein	0	5	0·4	8
Lipid	0	5	10	NT
Ash	0·7	6	NT	NT

NT = Not tested.

several processes are now operating at pilot scale in the USA, and SCP plants based on lumbering wastes and corn and sunflower trash are in production in Russia. Cellulose is often obtained in a relatively pure form, as a dry solid in quite large quantities. By contrast, carbohydrates other than cellulose are usually found as complex mixtures and in much smaller quantities. They are usually wet, often in large volumes of water. In recent years Tate & Lyle along with other groups[2-6] has developed processes for dealing with such non-cellulosic carbohydrate mixtures. It has been our intention to use as simple a technology as possible to enable application to small quantities of material, particularly in developing countries. The basis of the processes is the fermentation of the carbohydrate, or other organic materials, to yield single-cell protein or, in special circumstances, ethanol plus SCP. We present below the general features of the processes, their application to two types of waste, and the economics and the logistics of such processes.

GENERAL FEATURES OF LOW-TECHNOLOGY SCP FERMENTATIONS

The organisms used for simple recovery of biomass from wastes must have a number of special properties (Table 3). They must be capable of growth on a wide range of carbon sources, preferably simultaneously; have high growth rates to minimise the size of the fermentation system; and have a high efficiency of conversion of the substrate to biomass. The last point restricts the choice to aerobic microbes since in anaerobic growth several times more carbohydrate is consumed to obtain the necessary energy. The organisms that grow on the waste in nature may fulfil these criteria and could be used for

TABLE 3

Properties of microbes for waste utilisation

Broad substrate specifity
High growth rate
High carbohydrate conversion efficiency
Growth at high temperatures ($>35°C$)
Growth at extremes of pH
Simple recovery from fermentation
High protein content
Non-toxic

SCP production. However, they present certain drawbacks; they are usually mixed cultures of a wide range of microbes whose ratios may vary widely with small changes in waste composition or the physical environment. The organisms may therefore vary seasonally or be influenced by small upstream process changes. This may result in harvesting problems and considerable variability in the product specification.

An alternative approach is to use a micro-organism which has the required characters grown under conditions that favour its growth against that of other microbes. Filamentous moulds have been used because they can be harvested easily by filtration, and some species can be grown at low pH and high temperatures that inhibit the growth of contaminating bacteria and yeasts.

A strain of *Aspergillus niger* designated M1 has been isolated from naturally rotting material and found to conform to most of the criteria listed above.[3,4] More recently a *Fusarium* sp. has been studied in our laboratories and found to have an unusually high protein content. Both species grow on a wide range of carbohydrate-containing substrates (Table 4). Glucose, the most common constituent of carbohydrates, is rapidly assimilated by most microbes. The glucose dimer maltose and the polymer amylose were almost as readily utilised by both the *Aspergillus* and the *Fusarium*. Growth on pullulan indicates the ability to cleave the $\alpha(1-6)$ glycosidic links that form the branch points in starches. Pectin is a polygalacturonic acid present in many fruits and pectinolytic activity was found in both strains. However, neither were able to use cellulose as the carbon source. Amino acids, proteins and lipids which are present in small amounts in most biological waste materials were used by the

TABLE 4

Growth of Aspergillus niger *(M1) and* Fusarium *sp. (M4) on single carbon sources*

Substrate	M1	M4
Glucose	+	+
Maltose	+	+
Lactose	+	+
Cellulose (Whatman Cellulose powder CC41)	−	−
Rhamnose	+	+
Cellobiose	+	+
Xylose	+	+
Glycerol	+	+
Pullulan	+	+
Galacturonic acid	+	+
Soya oil	−	±
Pectin (apple)	+	+
Glutamic acid	+	+
Casein	+	+
Acetic acid	−	−
Amylose	+	+
None	−	−

Fusarium. Clearly these mould strains, whose natural habitat is rotting fruit, etc., have a very broad substrate specificity. In nature substrates are normally found in complex mixtures which may also contain compounds inhibitory to microbial growth. Growth tests using a wide range of waste materials showed that in most cases the moulds grow well (Table 5).

Having established that the moulds were capable of growth on a wide range of substrates, fermentation conditions were devised under which high yields of protein could be obtained. The carbohydrate conversion efficiencies and the growth rates were measured in 5 litre batch cultures in aseptic laboratory fermenters. Oxygen was supplied in excess as measured by *in situ* membrane electrode, *i.e.* the oxygen concentration was greater than 0·2 bar. pH was controlled to ± 0.2 unit by automatic addition of sodium hydroxide or hydrochloric acid. Temperature was controlled to within 0·5°C of the set value.

TABLE 5
Growth of two moulds on agricultural wastes

Substrate	*A. niger* (M1)	*Fusarium* sp. (M4)
Carob extract	+ +	+ +
Sulphite waste liquor	−	−
Molasses	+ +	+ +
Olive blackwater	+ +	+ +
Cassava flour	NT	+ +
Papaya slurry	+ +	+ +
Citrus waste	+	+

+ + good growth; + poor growth; − no growth.
NT = not tested.
Scoring refers to a combination of colony radial growth and density on agar plate cultures.

pH had little effect on the conversion efficiency or growth rate over the range 3·0–6·0 (Fig. 1). Below pH 4·0 the growth rate fell but the conversion efficiency was almost unchanged. The ability to grow at pH 2–3 is a valuable feature since most saprophytic bacteria and yeasts grow poorly or not at all at acid pH. Repeated open cultures in the pH range 2–4 have not shown gross contamination by extraneous micro-organisms. Aseptic precautions, which are expensive on a production scale, are therefore unnecessary.

The optimum growth temperature for *Fusarium* sp. (M4) was 35°C (Fig. 2), growth almost stopping at 40°C at pH 4. At lower pH the growth rate was higher at 40°C but stopped at 42°C. The ability to grow over a wide range of temperatures is important since heating and cooling facilities must be avoided to minimise the cost of fermentation. The conversion efficiencies found here are close to the maximum growth efficiencies reported for filamentous moulds.[7,8]

The effects of pH and temperature on growth rates and carbohydrate conversion efficiencies were established in the presence of excess oxygen. The oxygen demand of rapidly growing cultures of a mould at 10–20 g/litre dry weight is in the range 100–200 mmol/litre/h. To satisfy this demand requires the use of high-powered aeration and

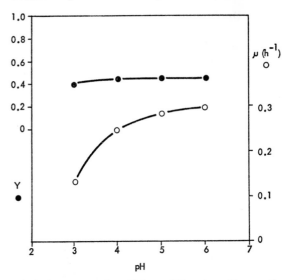

FIG. 1. Carbohydrate conversion efficiency (Y) and specific growth rate (μ) of *Fusarium* sp. (M4) in batch cultures: effect of pH. Carbohydrate: sucrose, 40 g/litre. Temperature 30°C.

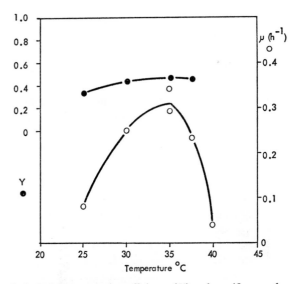

FIG. 2. Carbohydrate conversion efficiency (Y) and specific growth rate (μ) of *Fusarium* sp. (M4) in batch cultures: effect of temperature. Carbohydrate: sucrose, 40 g/litre. pH 4·0.

mixing systems. But to install such systems would be inefficient since the peak oxygen demand occurs for only a few hours in a batch fermentation cycle of 20 h. Lower power inputs which would cause oxygen-limitation of growth would extend the fermentation cycle but would consume less power overall. However, during oxygen-limited growth many organisms exhibit mechanisms for gaining energy which give a low conversion efficiency of carbohydrate to biomass and leave a residue of organic material in the process water. When the *Fusarium* sp. (M4) was grown under oxygen-limited growth conditions the growth rate was lower, but the oxygen respired and carbohydrate efficiency was unchanged, and extracellular organic compounds did not accumulate (Table 6). Thus oxygen-limited growth conditions may be used to control the rate of growth and to save power costs.

TABLE 6
Effect of oxygen-limitation of growth on carbohydrate conversion efficiency of Fusarium *sp.* (M4)

	Oxygen excess	Oxygen-limited
Maximum O_2 transfer rate (mol/litre/h)	0·100	0·025
Oxygen consumed (mol/litre)	0·56	0·53
Biomass produced (g/litre)	17·0	16·3
Carbohydrate yield constant	0·43	0·41
Time to reach max. biomass (h)	12·0	20·0

Inoculum, 2 g biomass/litre; pH 4·0; temperature 35°C; 40 g/litre sucrose.

The product of this fermentation is a mass of fine filaments, or hyphae, which make up the fungal mycelium. The crude protein content of the dry mycelium was in the range 25–35% for *A. niger* (M1) and 41–51% for *Fusarium* sp. (M4). The actual protein content calculated from the amino acid composition was 70% of the crude protein for *A. niger* (M1) and 80–90% of the crude protein for *Fusarium* sp. (M4). The amino acid profiles (Fig. 3) are similar to soya meal. They compare favourably with the FAO reference except that they have a low methionine content, like many microbial proteins. Feeding trials with chickens and pigs have shown the material for strain M1 to be non-toxic. It was a good substitute for part of the soya bean meal in feeds with pigs. The results of chick growth trials varied with the waste used for the preparation of the SCP and further tests are in progress to elaborate upon the results.

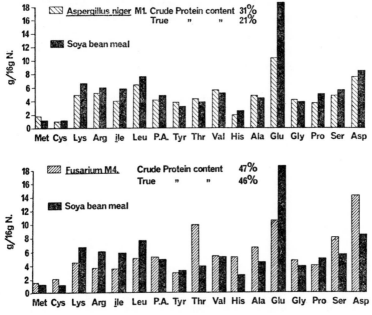

FIG. 3.   Amino acid content of mycelium.

PROCESS DESCRIPTION

Waste materials suitable for the growth of the microbes described above can be classified broadly into two categories. These are the solid or semi-solid wastes such as spoilt fruit, carob pods, date waste and molasses, and low-concentration wastes which are usually pollution hazards, such as olive and palm oil process water, corn steep water and canning waste water. Carob pods and spoilt papaya have been studied in our laboratories (Table 7). The carob tree is found in the Mediterranean countries. Its bean is collected for a valuable gum. The pod has a high sucrose content and has long been used in cottage industries for making syrup and sweets. The papaya is a soft-fleshed tropical fruit which has a substantial local consumption and is also packed for expensive markets in the USA and the Caribbean.

A waste such as papaya cullage may be slurried with water or in the case of the carob pod a hot-water extract made. The concentration is adjusted to give approximately 4% fermentable carbohydrate and the media fermented to give approximately 2% fungal biomass. If the whole waste is slurried and fermented the result is an increase of the protein content of the dry material to 15–25%. If an extract of fermentable carbohydrates is made the dry product contains 30–50% protein, depending on the fungus used.

TABLE 7
Analysis of carob and papaya waste

Waste	Carob pod	Papaya cull
% dry matter	70	13
Composition % of dry matter:		
Fibre	5·8	9
Sugars	54·9	67
Pectin	—	7
Protein	4·5	5
Lipid	0·5	—
Ash	3·0	6
Dry SCP production (kg) per ton fresh waste	250	60

The simplest apparatus for treatment of solid wastes consists of a tank in which the slurry or extract is prepared, a fermenter equipped with a stirrer and an air compressor, and a rotary vacuum filter. The total power consumption is about 1·0 kWh/kg biomass at 25% solids. A plant of this type will be installed in Belize in the near future. It will produce about 100 tons/year of single-cell protein from a variety of waste materials. For plants much larger than 100 tons/year a cooling system is required to remove the heat of fermentation. If possible the wet cake should be fed, after pasteurisation, directly to animals, thereby avoiding the expensive drying step. If dried, the material can be bagged and is stable for months.

Microbiologically the process is a simple batch fermentation. The waste is prepared and a small quantity of diammonium phosphate or other ammonium salt is added, to give sufficient anions to produce a low pH as the ammonium is assimilated. The fermenter is inoculated with a large number of spores of the mould which germinate and grow as long-branched filaments. During growth the pH falls rapidly and the growth of contaminant microbes is inhibited. After about 20 h the fermentable carbohydrate is exhausted and growth stops. 90% of the culture is harvested by filtration and the remaining 10% is left as inoculum for the next batch of medium.

TABLE 8

Microbial protein production from solid agricultural waste: capital costs

SCP production (300 day operation)	100 tons/year ($'000)	500 tons/year ($'000)
Material preparation	7	12
Fermenter	5	14
Aeration	6	16
Cooling	—	6
Filtration	11	41
Water filters	3	9
Installation	9	23
Buildings	5	14
Drier	10	30
Total	56	165

The capital cost of equipment is low, $56 000 for the smallest plant envisaged, 100 tons/year (Table 8). However, the operating costs per ton of product are high on such a small scale (Table 9). In this example the cost of skilled labour in Belize and an arbitrarily chosen five-year amortisation period was used. The process could be economic on the 100 tons/year scale only in countries with cheap labour since labour contributes over half the cost. As the scale of operation is increased, the unit price, of course, decreases.

The treatment of watery effluents from agricultural processing plants differs in several respects from that of solid wastes. Effluents are often produced 24 h per day and for much of the year. The

TABLE 9

Microbial protein production from solid agricultural waste: operating costs

SCP production (300 day operation)	100 tons/year ($'000)	500 tons/year ($'000)
Raw materials	2·7	13
Power (150–700 MWh)	3·0	15
Labour	20·0	30
(Direct costs)	(25·7)	(58)
Amortisation (5 years)	11·2	35
Total	36·9	93
Unit cost	$369/ton	$190/ton

concentration of substrates for fermentation is low, as high as 25 g/litre in palm oil process water, more normally less than 5 g/litre in the wastes from the canning industry and from starch processing (Table 10). In these cases the reduction of the biological oxygen demand (BOD) may be more important than the production of single-cell protein. At least three fungal processes are already in operation for simultaneous BOD reduction and SCP production.

TABLE 10
Analysis of potato and palm oil process effluents

	Potato process water	Palm oil process water
Solids %	0·7	5·0
Carbohydrate % dry solids	80	40
Fibre	20	20
Pectin	+	+
Reducing sugars	+	+
Starches	60	—
Protein	8	0·4
Lipid	+	10
Ash	< 10	c. 5
BOD$_5$ (mg/litre)	400	22 000
Volume of effluent (m³/h)	80	20
Potential SCP production (tons/year)	180	c. 1 500

The 'Symba' process, using an *Endomycopsis* to hydrolyse starch in wastes followed by *Torula* yeast growth on the sugar, was developed in Sweden many years ago.[6] The Pekilo process for starch wastes and sulphite waste liquor uses conventional aseptic continuous culture in stirred fermenters.[5] The lagooning process described by Church *et al.*[2] for corn processing wastes is reported to have turned effluent treatment into a profitable operation. Work in our own laboratories, and in conjunction with Dr R. N. Greenshields at Aston University, has centred on the use of unstirred tower fermenters.[9] The process water, after addition of inorganic salts, is percolated up a column-shaped fermenter. Aeration is accomplished by sparging air through a perforated base plate. The mould grows in this column and is retained in the fermenter by means of a stagnant zone at the top which causes the mycelium to settle back into the fermenter whilst the water flows off. Thus high concentrations of mould are held in the fermenter

TABLE 11
*Microbial protein production from process
effluents: capital costs*

	$'000
Fermenters (4 × 10 m³)	55
Air compressor (20 m³/min)	18
Filtration	46
Drier and bagger	60
Installation	30
Buildings	25
Total	234
Land area required approx. 3 000 ft²	

Effluent: 20 m³/h; 22 000 mg/litre BOD_5; 300
days/year; 1500 tons/year SCP.

to permit rapid processing of the waste in relatively low fermenter
capacities. The form of the mycelium is important in such fermenters;
it must be as tightly branched tiny pellets, giving a macroscopic
appearance of sand grains, to enable efficient aeration and sedimentation. In other aspects the process is similar to that for solid wastes.
Costings made on the basis of a very high BOD material, palm oil
waste, from a typical factory, show the process to have a capital cost
of less than $250 000 for a plant processing over 10^5 gal/day (Table
11). The process appears to be profitable using UK labour costs when
the product is sold at the UK soya meal price (Table 12).

TABLE 12
*Microbial protein production from process
effluents: operating costs*

	$'000	
Raw materials per annum	40	
Power (1 200 MWh)	24	
Labour	125	
(Direct costs)	(189)	
Amortisation (5 years)	47	
Total	236	
BOD cost	7·4 c/kg	
SCP cost	16·0 c/kg	
SCP sale at UK soya price	20·0 c/kg	
Net profit	2·0 c/kg BOD	

MASS AND ENERGY BALANCE

It can be argued that in a world with limited material resources, and in particular energy, processes should be subjected to analyses of conservation, mass and energy as well as conventional costing procedures. The process can then be compared with others which use the same raw material or produce the same product and an assessment made of its relative efficiency. The practical value of such analyses depends on a knowledge of the factor limiting agricultural productivity, for instance supply of energy or provision of protein or of calorific food intake. This in turn depends on the social and political priorities set by the community. Here we have made a restricted analysis of the mass and energy balances for SCP production from wastes, without the knowledge of what limits overall agricultural productivity.

TABLE 13

Carbon and nitrogen balance

Carbohydrate + Oxygen →	SCP	+ CO_2	+ 2 700 kcal
1 kg C 1·3 kg	0·5 kg C	1·8 kg	
$(NH_4)_2HPO_4$ →	SCP	+ Effluent	
1 kg N	0·9 kg N	0·1 kg N	

The substrate mass balances for SCP production (Table 13) show that most of the nitrogen is retained in the product, but half of the carbohydrate is lost, used for energy for the synthesis of the highly ordered biological macromolecules. However, if the materials would otherwise be burnt, buried or discharged to the rivers and seas, the recovery of 50% of the carbon represents a net increase in carbon available to the food system, gained at the expense of a small quantity of fixed nitrogen. Similarly a summation of the energy inputs to the process can be made and compared with the energy content of the SCP recovered. The power consumption of the plant plus the energy content of the ammonium salt is the input, equivalent to c. 3000 kcal/ kg dry SCP. The energy recovered as SCP is c. 5500 kcal/kg.[10] Thus, ignoring the energy tied up as plant and the energy used as manual labour, there is a net gain of 2500 kcal/kg.

CONCLUSION

The partial recovery of agricultural wastes as single-cell protein could make a contribution to conservation of the fixed carbon resources produced on the land. Wastes can, in certain circumstances, be recovered by commercially viable processes, particularly where an expensive alternative disposal method is necessary. Even operating scales as low as a few hundred tons/year can be made economic if the process can be used for most of the year and the labour costs are low, conditions which can be met in many developing countries.

ACKNOWLEDGEMENTS

The authors thank the directors of Tate & Lyle Ltd., for permission to publish this paper.

Our thanks are also due to S. A. Campbell and G. G. Morris for their assistance in this work.

REFERENCES

1. Steffgen, F. W. (1972). *Project Rescue: Energy from Solid Wastes*, Pittsburg Energy Research Center, US Bureau of Mines, Pittsburg, Oct.
2. Church, B. D., Nash, H. A. and Brosz, W. (1972). *Developments in Industrial Microbiology*, **13**, p. 30.
3. Imrie, F. K. E. and Vlitos, A. J. (1973). 'Production of fungal protein from carob', *Proceedings of 2nd Int. Symp. on SCP*, MIT, Cambridge, Mass., 29–31 May.
4. Morris, G. G., Imrie, F. K. E. and Phillips, K. C. (1973). 'The production of animal feedstuffs by the submerged culture of fungi on agricultural wastes', *Proceedings of 4th Int. Conf. on Global Impacts of Applied Microbiology*, São Paulo, Brazil, 23–28 July.
5. Romanschut, P. (1975). 'The Pekilo process', in: *SCP II*, ed. S. R. Tannenbaum and D. I. C. Wang, MIT Press, Cambridge, Mass.
6. Jarl, K. (1969). *Food Technology*, **23**, p. 1009.
7. Righelato, R. C., Trinci, A. P. J., Pirt, S. J. and Peat, A. (1968). *J. Gen. Microbiol.*, **50**, p. 399.
8. Carter, B. L. A., Bull, A. T., Pirt, S. J. and Rowley, B. I. (1971). *J. Bacteriol.*, **108**, p. 309.
9. Imrie, F. K. E. and Greenshields, R. N. (1973). 'The tubular reactor as a simplified fermenter', *Proceedings of 4th Int. Conf. on Global Impacts of Applied Microbiology*, São Paulo, Brazil, 23–28 July.
10. Prochazka, G. J., Payne, W. J. and Mayberry, W. R. (1973). *Biotech. Bioeng.*, **15**, p. 1007.

DISCUSSION

Phillips: Was the cost of $190 per ton for the protein based on dry powder?
Righelato: Yes.

Russell Eggitt: I would like to be assured in this very important work that adequate research is also going on into the possible production of mycotoxins in these biomasses. It seems to me that relatively short-term feeding experience could just not be adequate. This has got to be longer term and we must look at some of the more insidious results of these mycotoxins. Are any tests being done?

Righelato: We recognise that the toxicity can be a major problem—it is difficult to test for this when you are using waste materials, often a series of different waste materials, in one and the same plant. One is not producing a standard product, so I don't really think that in this type of technology a really comprehensive testing scheme is possible. If one went into a thorough testing scheme, on economic grounds one wouldn't be able to carry out the same process. However, there are, in our labs at least, ongoing toxicity and feeding trials. We are doing these at the same time both here and in Central America.

Nelson: Have you considered the chance of contamination of the *Aspergillus niger* with other toxin-producing *Aspergillus* species such as *Aspergillus flavus*? Does your process inhibit the growth of these other species? I am particularly concerned with the chance contamination of the system you describe.

Righelato: We have run open cultures, as I mentioned, and plating out from them shows no other organism than the *Aspergillus* we put in to start with. We haven't deliberately inoculated with pathogenic moulds, and I think this is something we must go ahead and do to reassure ourselves on that basis.

Edelman: May I just make a comment. I know that Dr Russell Eggitt has mentioned several times the problems of mycotoxins and that is just a small aspect of toxicology. There are other toxicological problems and I should just like to spend a moment on the control problems that one has in a programme of this sort, so that people here don't feel that all you have to do is just find some convenient fermentation system and launch the product on to the public. The Protein Advisory Group of the United Nations and the FDA of the United States, which are the leaders in the regulations for this sort of work, have laid down very stringent requirements before you can use the material for human food and they are becoming more and more stringent in the consideration of using it for an animal feed. Just to give you an example, if you want to do a full-scale toxicological study with one animal species, say a rat, it is liable to run you into anything between £150 000 and £250 000. Now the PAG and the FDA require you to use at least two species for testing, and in addition to this of course you have to have acceptability trials with animals, or even more particularly with human beings. This sort of work is going to take at least three or four years, because the requirement for the animal testing is that you have to do a full lifetime study and rats unfortunately cannot be accelerated in their death rate. You have to run through at least three generations to make sure that the foetus is not in any way affected. The cost is enormous and with interest rates running at around 10–15%, you can never make a profit from your R & D. The fact that it costs £250 000 for even one lifetime study implies that you need to make some gigantic profit in the future in order to pay for the process. The toxicology of the situation is going to be the tail that wags the dog in all these programmes. Now that is a slight hobby-horse of mine because I am faced with situations of this sort, but this doesn't mean to say that we do not, in fact, do work of this sort which is of such overwhelming importance.

Righelato: If we have to go through the recommendations of the PAG for our small-scale animal feed production, we just wouldn't have such processes.

Edelman: I would just make one other point about that, and that is we have got to be very careful that the bureaucrats don't kill us all stone dead with starvation while saving us from dying from food poisoning!

Davidson: Can you advise me as to how frequently a continuous processing unit should be sterilised in order to be assured that no pathogenic organism is in fact generated through the processing, which would in any case invalidate all your previous testing, or is this catered for?

Righelato: It depends how bad your plant is. I don't think one can give a straight answer to that. In many cases people find that they have to sterilise their equipment every time they set up a fermentation, and even if they do that there still might be contamination at the end of the run, because the equipment has not been designed for totally aseptic operation. The sort of processes that I was talking about don't rely on enforced asepsis but on asepsis produced by the conditions that the organism grows under, and no sterilisation is carried out.

Edelman: You are caught here between having the lower cost of a non-aseptic system which might be acceptable for animal feed, and all the other attendant problems that come with it, and the higher cost of having a totally aseptic system so that you can have a mono-culture. This is probably not justified for animal feed; it is difficult to know. Certainly for human food you would have to have this. You could not possibly have a human food plant using material which could conceivably be contaminated, and it is easy to discover whether you are contaminated or not, for if you are running an aseptic plant then once you get it contaminated you shut the plant down, clean it out and start up again. You can run these continuous aseptic plants for as many as thousands of hours without getting contamination, and thousands of hours is months, so if you've got your system right you don't need to clean down, but for the other system you certainly do have an attendant problem.

Gould: The speaker and the Chairman seem to have discounted somewhat the advice of the PAG and the FDA in that they have indicated that we in industry or the universities in the UK may be throttled by these bodies. I would recommend that since these bodies have vast experience in this type of screening, we ought to take their recommendations seriously. I would go on to say that although the larger industries doing this type of

SCP production have been accused of indulging in high technology, this is not really so. As a member of BP, possibly the leading company in SCP production, certainly one of the leaders anyway, I would refute the statement that we have indulged in high technology. We have used the lowest technology that we possibly can to have a satisfactory process giving a satisfactory product, and the reason why we have used the lowest technology possible is because, as has been indicated, it is so expensive to use higher technology than is needed. We do not wish to build in costs to our products because this makes them less competitive. We are doing so as a result of our experience over many years in this particular game, and I feel that anyone who wishes to embark on the loosely called low technology in this particular type of work may find themselves in difficulties, because the technology we are using is really the lowest. Perhaps I could emphasise these remarks that I have made by taking a few comments made this morning. The opening remarks indicated that unrealised mutation in the organism could be disastrous. Another speaker said that we must remove the pathogens from waste, and many of these wastes, carbohydrate wastes, could be subject to mycotoxin contamination. Although the fermentation conditions would inhibit growth, I have not heard yet that all organisms able to get into the fermentation will be made non-viable. They will be inhibited perhaps, but not definitely killed. We heard from our speaker from Poland that even molasses give problems in yeast production, and I would suggest that molasses is a well-used material, and if that is going to give problems others will too. We have heard that silage making will be used more if the technology was not so high. Now, I do not really think this is high technology, but it shows that people have doubts about what we would call low technology. Finally, I would say that in our particular process we have realised that much of the contamination, unless we are extremely careful, comes in after the fermentation, in the actual separating and the standing and possibly the drying process. Having made these remarks a plea for as low a technology as we can, but not the lowest, so that we run into trouble, could I ask, is it unwise to sell such units if they can't be controlled once they leave the premises from which they are sold?

Righelato: It would be unwise to sell them if it were not possible to exercise some sort of control, and the problems of operating this sort of thing, particularly in the countries in the developing world, must not be underestimated. The way we are going about it is putting up a plant of our own in Central America and we will see how we can make it work using local labour but overseeing it ourselves. Referring to your comments on contamination, I think if we are going to make use of waste, or even the mycelium waste which is produced by many of the antibiotic manufacturers, we have to accept that there is a slight risk. It has been done for years by certain antibiotic manufacturers who sell off the mycelium without the sort of controls that you are talking about, and no problems have arisen so far as I am aware, thus there is some precedent.

Wimpenny: Can I go another step, then, and say that to go to the other extreme the ensilaging process is a natural process from which you get natural organisms operating. You feed these to animals without any particular worry, so somewhere in between the two extremes there must be a happy medium where you can say the process will operate successfully. After all, there are many natural processes from which you get organisms selected that operate perfectly well without any fear of toxicity. It obviously has to be tested, but I think that is taking the opposite point of view to that which was made just now by Dr Gould. It just needs to be moderated.

Bu'lock: I think that if we followed the BP line there would be no butter, no cheese, no eggs, no meat or potatoes, because the production of all these is carried out under very unhygienic conditions, except when they have been processed by a multi-million international company. As the previous comment was made, there is an intermediate level here which has to be aimed at, but could I come back to the animal feed situation and the question particularly of mycotoxins. The thing which concerns me is that it is one thing to test a product—I think this is a very reasonable thing to do—but mycotoxins are produced by specific fungi and are not the general phenomena some people seem to imagine. Mycotoxins are produced by fungi which are genetically capable of producing those mycotoxins under the right environmental conditions. Now one of the great hopes, of course, is that by growing the organism at maximum growth rate and under a particular set of conditions it will not produce toxins which it might well produce under other circumstances. I personally think that this is one of the more hazardous situations because it is an organism which is only being prevented by your phenotypic controls from producing the mycotoxin which it is genetically capable of making, and this is why I am very worried about *Fusaria*. One would like to know not merely whether these *Fusaria* have been tested as an SCP product but whether they have been screened under conditions which will be optimal for toxin production, which are not the same as SCP biomass-producing conditions. This is why I am even more scared about *Trichoderma* because this is the key organism in one process which is actually being operated, and while we are scratching our heads about whether we ought to do this or that or the other with a perfectly harmless organism like *Aspergillus oryzae*, there are people in the USA who are busy selling sackfuls of *Trichoderma* mycelium which I would have thought was an extremely hazardous procedure. There has to be a middle line somewhere along the way.

7

Microbial Production of Oils and Fats

C. RATLEDGE

Department of Biochemistry,
University of Hull, Hull, England

ABSTRACT

The demand for oils and fats, like all our requirements for basic commodities, is increasing annually. The price of these materials, again like all others, has more than doubled in the last two years. The United Kingdom and the rest of Western Europe relies heavily on imported oils and fats—over 1 million tons are imported annually into Great Britain. The uses for oils and fats, however, are very diverse: about 40% of the total is destined for food, the rest is used in a wide range of products from soaps and detergents to paints and varnishes.

With the increasing technological developments in the fermentation industry it now becomes practicable to consider the production of a 'single-cell oil' in the same way as we currently consider 'single-cell protein' production. If it is economic to produce SCP to compete with soya beans at £140/ton, with a 45% protein content, then it should be economic to produce an SCO to compete with soya bean oil which currently costs about £400/ton. The microbial production of fat is, however, a slower process than protein production and requires the careful selection of fat-accumulating species as not all micro-organisms have this ability. Appropriate organisms, usually yeasts or moulds, can, however, be grown under continuous culture conditions to yield high concentrations of fat. Some of the advances in this direction are described as this method of culture has only recently been recognised as being feasible.

The choice of growth substrate, as well as growth conditions, is of utmost importance. The substrate must, of course, be cheap and abundant. Almost all the substrates, including hydrocarbons, starch, lactose, etc., which are currently being considered or used for SCP production can be successfully and efficiently used by fat-accumulating yeasts and fungi. However, the nature of the carbon substrate as well as the growth conditions can greatly influence the relative proportions of the fatty acids being synthesised. It is therefore up to the microbiologist to optimise these conditions so that the maximum amount of high-quality fat is produced in the shortest possible time.

INTRODUCTION

Fat, or more correctly lipid, is an intrinsic part of most foods. Unlike protein, however, fat is not an essential component of our diet save for the few milligrams of polyunsaturated fatty acids needed each day. Fat, however, contributes many characteristics which are important to food and throughout the world considerable quantities are consumed each year. About 16 million tons, derived mainly from plant sources such as soya bean oil, palm oil, groundnut oil, etc., are eaten either directly or after incorporation into foods such as margarines and salad creams. How much 'unseen' fat, *i.e.* fat directly associated with meats and other foods, is eaten is not certain. The demand for edible fat is continuing to increase, particularly in those countries which previously have had inadequate supplies of this commodity. This demand is exacerbated by the requirements of industry for fat for technical purposes such as in the manufacture of paints, varnishes, detergents, soaps, polishes, etc. In all about 45 million tons of 'visible' oils and fats are produced each year at a total value probably in excess of £10^{10}. In the UK this obviously places a large strain on our balance of payments as we import about 1·2 million tons of oils and fats each year and it is therefore important that all alternative sources are carefully evaluated.

Micro-organisms are well known to be able to produce fat; in Germany, during both World Wars, commercial processes were designed to effect such conversions. Micro-organisms might therefore be considered as a reasonable alternative source for these commodities, but unfortunately, during times of normal commerce such microbial processes are found to be uneconomical. Whether this will always be so is uncertain because of the rapid and dramatic changes which can take place in world politics. Developing countries which produce much of the world's edible oil will probably be dissatisfied to continue in their role of producer/exporter of the unprocessed oilseed and may well wish to begin their own extraction and refining programmes. Such events will automatically lead to higher prices being paid by the consumers, and should prices escalate unilaterally then microbial fat will surely become an economic proposition.

THE NATURE OF MICROBIAL FATS AND OILS

Yeasts and moulds rather than bacteria or algae are usually considered the most appropriate from which to choose suitable species for fat production.[1-3] Table 1 lists some of the more prolific fat producers along with the relative proportions of fatty acids extracted

TABLE 1

Fat contents and fatty acids of some oleaginous yeasts and moulds

Organism	Fat content (% w/w)	Fat coeff.[a]	Relative % (w/w) of principal fatty acids in lipid						Ref.
			16:0	16:1	18:0	18:1	18:2	18:3	
Candida 107	42	22	37	1	14	36	8	—	4, 5
Crytococcus terricolus	65	21			Not given				6
Lipomyces lipofer	38	—	17	4	10	48	16	3	7
Lipomyces starkeyi	38	15	40	6	5	44	4	—	8
Rhodotorula gracilis	64	15	20	2	1	42	21	8	9
Aspergillus terreus	57	13	23	tr	tr	14	40	21	10, 11
Chaetomium globosum	54	—	58	3	8	27	—	—	12, 13
Gibberella fujikuroi	45	8			Not given				14
Mucor circinelloides	65	14			Not given				15
Pythium ultimum	48	—	23	9	7	22	15	2	16

[a] Fat coefficient = g total fat formed/100 g substrate utilised.

COMPONENT GLYCERIDES OF FATS

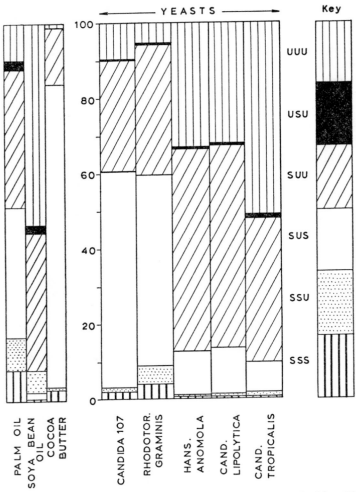

FIG. 1. Distribution of fatty acids upon the glycerol moiety of triglycerides isolated from the lipids of various yeasts. S = any saturated acid (mainly palmitic and stearic acids), U = any unsaturated acid (mainly oleic and linoleic acids). Sequence of acids on the glycerol (*i.e.* positions 1, 2 and 3) is as specified. (From Thorpe and Ratledge.[4])

from their lipids. The fat content clearly must be as high a percentage of the cell dry weight as possible, but because the ultimate price commanded by the fat depends upon its fatty acid composition, considerable emphasis has to be given to this latter aspect.

As far as the rather meagre amount of analytic data on the fatty acids of oleaginous micro-organisms allows us to make comparisons, the fat obtained from micro-organisms is in no way inferior to that obtained from plants. The fatty acids are the same (*see* Table 1) and show similar variations in their relative proportions, as do different species of plant; hydroxy or methyl-branched acids are usually absent;[9,17] and the distribution of these acids upon the triglyceride moiety is the same as that in plants.[4] This latter point is illustrated in Fig. 1. The predominating type is usually l-oleyl-(or palmityl)-2-oleyl-3-palmityl-(or oleyl)-glycerol, *i.e.* SUU, UUS or SUS type (where S = any saturated acid and U = any unsaturated acid). Complete triglyceride analysis of microbial fat has in fact only been worked out in one or two instances.[4,8,18] The amount of triglyceride within the crude fat extracted from micro-organisms varies from over 90% to being less than 30% according to the species.[4,6,13] Clearly for an edible microbial fat to be satisfactory the content of the triglycerides should be as high as possible, for this is the form of over 95% of the oil or fat extracted from most oilseeds. Phospholipids, sterols and sterol esters are therefore concomitantly very low. This criterion does not apply should the microbial fat be destined for technical use: here it is the content of fatty acids *per se* which must be at a maximum, but this aspect of microbial fats is outside the scope of this chapter.

CULTIVATION OF OLEAGINOUS MICRO-ORGANISMS

Whichever organism, because of the quality and quantity of its fat, is selected for fat production, it must obviously be able to grow at a reasonable rate in submerged culture, preferably but not necessarily in continuous culture. It also must be able to grow on a cheap form of carbon and this point is discussed later. With regard to the method of cultivation, fat formation usually occurs after growth of the organism has ceased. The pattern which is usually seen in batch culture is illustrated in Fig. 2. The limiting nutrient is usually the nitrogen supply[1,3,9] but HPO_4^{2-} or Mg^{2+} can sometimes be the nutrient which limits cell proliferation.[3] In the fat production phase, the lipid is stored within the microbial cell in the form of discrete droplets which facilitates subsequent extraction.

Most studies on fat accumulation have examined cultures growing in batch culture, but recently we have investigated this process in continuous culture which offers a clear economic advantage over batch culture methods if large-scale production were to be undertaken.

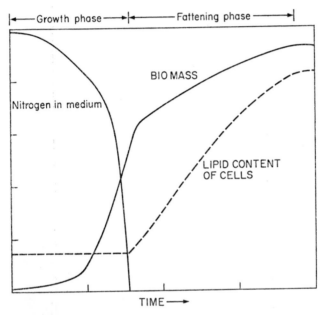

Fig. 2. Idealised diagram showing course of lipid formation in an oleaginous micro-organism growing in batch culture. A nutrient, such as nitrogen, is allowed to become exhausted and the excess carbon is then converted to fat.

Although we have so far only examined the capabilities of one particular yeast, *Candida* 107, our results probably have a general applicability as other workers[19] have simultaneously established that continuous culture affords a method of achieving high fat synthesis in other yeasts.

The course of fat formation in *Candida* 107 grown in continuous culture on nitrogen-limiting medium at various dilution rates is shown in Fig. 3. (The dilution rate, or throughput, of such a system governs the growth rate of the organism: the faster the dilution rate, the faster the organism grows up to its maximum capability; after this point wash-out from the fermenter begins.) Accumulation of fat was achieved by allowing the yeast to have a fairly long residence time in the fermenter. If the yeast was grown at too low a dilution rate, too much of the substrate was used up for maintaining the basal

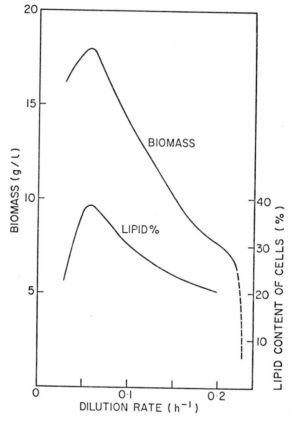

Fig. 3. Lipid formation in *Candida* 107 growing in nitrogen-limited medium in continuous culture. (From Gill.[5])

energy requirements of the organism so that the amount of fat formed was depleted. The amount of fat in these cells (40%) was the same as that achieved in batch culture[20] and was of the same composition.[5] Interestingly the conversion of substrate to fat was one of the highest reported for fat production, indicating that continuous culture is probably the most efficient means for the culture of oleaginous organisms.

There is thus every reason to hope that the advantages which continuous culture has conferred upon single-cell protein production processes will therefore be applicable for 'single-cell oil' production. Clearly, however, the increased residence time of organisms in a fermenter lowers the output rate (*i.e.* g product/litre of medium/h) from that fermenter, but this may be offset by being able to work at higher cell densities than are normally considered optimum for protein production. Thus if a cell density of say 60 g/litre could be sustained in continuous culture for fat production, this would be equivalent in output rate to a yeast at 20 g/litre growing three times more quickly and being used for SCP production. The effectiveness of micro-organisms as fat producers will therefore depend primarily (a) on the quality of fat being produced and (b) on the cost and efficiency of conversion of the substrate.

The assessment of the 'quality' of a fat, or the price it is likely to command on an open market, is not an easy task. A knowledge is needed of the current price structure of the major oil and fat commodities as well as information of their properties (*i.e.* fatty acid/triglyceride composition) and applications. Some of this information has already been presented elsewhere,[1,3] but suffice to say that, in general, polyunsaturated acids, especially linoleic acid (18:2), are at a premium and any oil containing more than 50% of linoleic acid usually commands a price of about £400–£450/ton. An oil such as that from *Aspergillus terreus* (Table 1) is therefore more desirable than that from *Candida* 107 or *Lipomyces starkeyi* whose fatty acid profiles approximate to that given by palm oil[1] and which commands a price of only £300/ton. However, some manipulation of the fatty acids of micro-organisms is possible by changing the culture conditions or by a change of substrate. Effects of different aeration rates, temperature and pH have all been examined with respect to lipid composition (*see* Tables 2, 3 and 4 and references therein for examples). In general, changes in temperature seem to produce larger changes in lipid composition than either of the other two parameters. It is apparent from the data given in Table 2 that different organisms can give quite different responses and that in most cases these changes are difficult to interpret. Lower growth temperatures usually seem to lead to an increase in the fluidity of the fat being produced;[24] that is, either the fat becomes more unsaturated or higher proportions of

TABLE 2

Effect of temperature on fatty acid composition of micro-organisms

Temperature	Relative % of main fatty acids						% Unsaturateds	% Poly-unsaturateds
	16:0	18:0	18:1	16:1	18:2	18:3		
Candida utilis[21]								
30°	12	1	34		48	3	88	51
20°	11	0	27		43	12	89	55
15°	16	0	26		33	17	84	50
Penicillium soppii[22]								
34°	18	4	18		43	14	77	57
25°	20	5	8		48	15	73	63
15°	21	5	4		51	16	73	67
Rhodotorula gracilis[23]								
35°	21	10	45	7	18	2	66	20
27°	14	12	53	10	12	4	71	16
20°	22	8	53		10	3	68	13

Candida tropicalis on *n*-alkanes[24]	10:0	13:0	15:0	16:0	17:0	17:1	18:0	18:1	% Unsaturateds
40°	—	1	16	31	17	15	4	3	25
30°	3	8	10	22	12	14	10	3	27

Cultures were grown in batch culture, except *C. utilis* which was grown in continuous culture under glucose limitation.

TABLE 3
Effect of pH on fatty acid composition of yeasts

Rhodotorula gracilis[9]

pH of growth	Relative % of major fatty acids					% Unsaturateds
	16:0	18:0	18:1	18:2	18:3	
3·0	19	6	35	21	13	69
4·5	15	4	51	21	6	78
6·0	26	1	41	24	7	72

Candida lipolytica grown on *n*-alkanes[25]

pH of growth	Relative % of major fatty acids						% Unsaturateds
	15:0	16:0	17:0	17:1	18:1	18:2	
2·5–3·0	6	18	8	35	18	7	63
4·0–4·5	9	27	15	23	11	5	43
6·0–7·0	9	24	13	28	13	3	49

Both yeasts were grown in batch culture; in neither case was cell yield significantly changed by change in pH.

TABLE 4
Effect of oxygen tension on fatty acid composition of yeasts

Organism	Condition of growth	Relative % of main fatty acids					% Unsaturateds
		16:0	18:0	18:1	18:2	18:3	
C. utilis[21]	High O₂ tension	18	—	42	34	0	76
	Low O₂ tension	15	—	29	45	0	74
C. utilis[26]	High O₂ tension	11	—	24	39	25	88
	Low O₂ tension	11	—	36	46	4	86
Candida 107[27]	High O₂ tension	24	6	45	15	3	63
	Low O₂ tension	31	8	42	9	2	53

All organisms grown in continuous culture under nitrogen-limited conditions.

shorter chains are synthesised. Changes in fatty acid composition
can also be brought about by changes in the nutrients, besides
carbon, being supplied to the cultures,[10,28] but accurate data related
to oleaginous organisms grown under carefully controlled conditions
are, however, lacking at the moment.

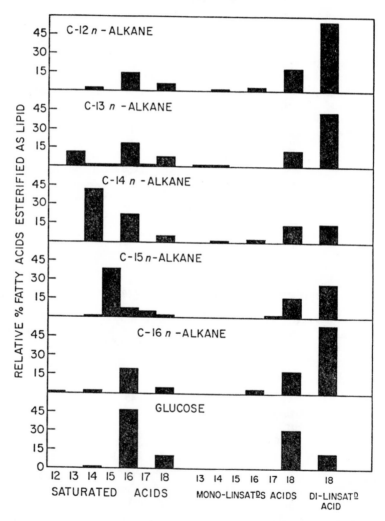

FIG. 4.   Changes in fatty acid composition of *Candida* 107 growing on various
n-alkanes. (From Thorpe and Ratledge.[4])

The limits to which the fatty acids of micro-organisms may be varied are much greater than would perhaps be deduced by inspection of Tables 2, 3 and 4. These limits are best shown when micro-organisms are grown on n-alkanes. Here the alkane is oxidised to the corresponding fatty acid which is then incorporated either as such or after chain elongation. Such changes are illustrated in Fig. 4 for *Candida* 107 growing on alkanes from C_{12} to C_{16}. Unfortunately alkanes, even mixtures or fractions of alkanes, are now relatively expensive. Moreover, as alkanes are readily absorbed into the fat droplets of micro-organisms (unchanged alkanes can always be recovered from the lipids of organisms grown on these materials), they are not really suitable for production of an edible single-cell oil. But by using alkanes we can see the extent to which micro-organisms can be made to shift their lipid constitution and it is therefore up to the microbiologist to see how such changes may be brought about without recourse to using alkanes as a growth substrate.

ECONOMICS OF MICROBIAL FAT PRODUCTION

It has been calculated[1,3] that if a suitable oleaginous organism was grown on molasses as carbon source, then given a conversion of 22% of carbon to fat (*see* Table 1) and molasses costing about £86/ton of fermentable carbohydrate, a 'single-cell oil' would ultimately cost between £500 and £600/ton, this value including all fermentation costs. Similar costs can be calculated for n-alkanes as substrate where although the conversion of substrate to fat may now be as much as 30%, this is offset by alkanes costing about £130/ton.

The calculation of exact costs is always difficult, however, and it may be more appropriate to compare single-cell oil production with what is known about the economics of single-cell protein production.[29,30] If single-cell protein is to compete against more conventional sources of protein such as from soya bean or fishmeal it should cost about the same as these materials. As 1 ton of protein derived either from soya bean or fishmeal currently sells at about £300–£310/ton, yeast grown for single-cell protein must cost no more than £180/ton to produce if it contains 60% protein. This, in fact, is close to the current price (£160–£170/ton) for baker's yeast cultivated on molasses. If a different yeast, say *Rhodotorula gracilis*, were now grown for single-cell oil production under similar conditions it too should cost £180/ton plus probably another 25–40% to allow for the cost of extra substrate which is consumed during fat accumulation. Thus, if this yeast had a fat content of 60%, the final cost of the single-cell oil would be £385 to £420. This may therefore be a more realistic estimate of the likely cost of a process, as any company indulging in such a scheme would probably not be buying its substrate on an open market but would, either through price concessions or control over the source of the substrate, be able to obtain the material at considerably less. This is obviously no different from what occurs in those industries currently concerned with single-cell protein manufacture.

Thus by comparison it seems that microbial oils and fats might be able to achieve economical parity with conventional sources of oils and fats. If cheaper sources of carbon than either molasses or alkanes were to be available in suitable quantities, then it is almost certain that a single-cell oil would be a feasible and economic proposition. Such substrates which are readily utilised by oleaginous organisms include starch, lactose (from whey) and pentoses (from wood pulp manufacture). Information regarding the availability of these materials is given elsewhere in this book.[31–33]

CONCLUSIONS

One can argue that if production of microbial protein from waste materials is considered to be a profitable venture, then production of microbial oils and fats should also be so. The feasibility of being able to produce a cheap microbial fat is now quite evident. It is pertinent to point out, however, that microbial protein, being aimed primarily at the animal feed market, may have less exacting standards of acceptability than a single-cell oil which is primarily destined for human food. A microbial oil will probably, therefore, have to undergo very stringent testing before being accepted on an equal footing with plant oils. An exception to this would obviously be if the microbial oil was to be used for technical purposes.

REFERENCES

1. Whitworth, D. A. and Ratledge, C. (1974). *Process Biochem.*, **9**(9), p. 14.
2. Woodbine, M. (1959). *Prog. Indust. Microbiol.*, **1**, p. 179.

3. Ratledge, C. (1975). In: *Economic Microbiology*, Vol. 2, ed. A. H. Rose, Academic Press, London.
4. Thorpe, R. F. and Ratledge, C. (1972). *J. Gen. Microbiol.*, **72**, p. 151.
5. Gill, C. O. (1973). Ph.D. Thesis, University of Hull.
6. Pedersen, T. A. (1962). *Acta Chem. Scand.*, **16**, p. 1015.
7. McElroy, F. A. and Stewart, H. B. (1967). *Canad. J. Biochem.*, **45**, p. 171.
8. Suzuki, T. and Hasegawa, K. (1974). *Agric. Biol. Chem.*, **38**, p. 1371.
9. Kessell, R. H. J. (1968). *J. Appl. Bact.*, **31**, p. 220.
10. Singh, J. and Sood, M. G. (1972). *J. Sci. Fd. Agric.*, **23**, p. 1113.
11. Singh, J. and Sood, M. G. (1973). *J. Amer. Oil Chem. Ass.*, **50**, p. 485.
12. Mumma, R. O., Fergus, C. L. and Sekura, R. D. (1970). *Lipids*, **5**, p. 100.
13. Mumma, R. O., Sekura, R. D. and Fergus, C. L. (1971). *Lipids*, **6**, p. 584.
14. Borrow, A., Jeffreys, E. G., Kessell, R. H. J., Lloyd, E. C., Lloyd, P. B. and Nixon, I. S. (1961). *Canad. J. Microbiol.*, **7**, p. 227.
15. Bernhauer, K. and Rauch. J. (1948). *Biochem. Z.*, **319**, p. 101.
16. Bowman, R. D. and Mumma, R. O. (1967). *Biochim. Biophys. Acta*, **144**, p. 501.
17. Harries, P. C. and Ratledge, C. (1969). *Chemy. Ind.*, p. 582.
18. Haley, J. E. and Jack, R. C. M. (1974). *Lipids*, **9**, p. 679.
19. Krumpphanzl, V., Gregr, V., Pelechova, J. and Uher, J. (1973). In: *Adv. Microbial Engineering* (Part I), ed. B. Sikyta, A. Prokop and M. Novak, Wiley, New York, p. 245.
20. Ratledge, C. (1968). *Biotech. Bioeng.*, **10**, p. 511.
21. Brown, C. M. and Rose, A. H. (1969). *J. Bact.*, **99**, p. 371.
22. Salmonowicz, J. and Niewiadomski, H. (1965). *Rev. Franc. Corps Gras*, **12**, p. 309.
23. Enebo, L. and Iwamoto, H. (1966). *Acta Chem. Scand.*, **20**, p. 439.
24. Thorpe, R. F. and Ratledge, C. (1973). *J. Gen. Microbiol.*, **78**, p. 203.
25. Dyatlovikskaya, E. V., Greshnykh, K. P., Zhdannikova, E., Kozlova, L. I. and Bergelson, L. P. (1969). *Prikl. Biokhim. Mikrobiol.*, **5**, p. 511.
26. Babij, T., Moss, F. T. and Ralph, B. J. (1969). *Biotech. Bioeng.*, **11**, p. 593.
27. Ratledge, C. and Hall, M. J. Unpublished work.
28. Bhatia, I. S., Raheja, R. K. and Chahal, D. S. (1972). *J. Sci. Fd. Agric.*, **23**, p. 1197.
29. Ratledge, C. (1974). In: *Projects and Prospects in Industrial Fermentation*, Octagon Papers No. 1, ed. A. J. Powell and J. D. Bu'lock, Manchester University, p. 41.
30. Ratledge, C. (1975). *J. Appl. Chem. Biotech.* (in press).
31. Imrie, F. K. E. and Righelato, R. C. (1975). 'Production of microbial protein from carbohydrate wastes in developing countries', this volume, p. 79.
32. Oosten, B. J. (1975). 'Protein from potato starch mill effluent', this volume, p. 196.
33. Coton, S. G. (1975). 'Recovery of dairy waste', this volume, p. 221.

DISCUSSION

Righelato: (i) What basis did you use for calculating the economic productivity of fat of 2·5 g/litre/h as a rate of producing lipid?

(ii) Could you go a bit further into the technology of recovery of fat from yeasts?

Ratledge: (i) If one does calculations for protein output in single-cell protein production one can arrive at figures of about, let us say, 5 g protein/litre/h. Judging the difficulty of the process and the fact that it has to go slower with a fat-producing process, we thought about half that rate of protein would be what was needed for an ideal process. In other words, if one is going to produce 20 000 tons of fat a year one doesn't want to have to build fermenters of the size of supertankers, one wants to keep this within the bounds of reason and 2·5 is about the rate that you have to aim at to break even if you are going to do it on a large scale.

(ii) The second point was fat recovery. At the moment, working on a small scale, fat recovery is only done by solvent extraction. If we dry the yeast by freeze drying it does prove very easy to get it out by solvent recovery. We have had talks with people who extracted fat from Russian yeast grown on hydrocarbons and they say that it can be done by conventional processes. There doesn't seem to be any objection from the mechanical point of view of getting the fat out of the yeast at the end of the day.

Wilbey: Would the defatted yeast be suitable for use in animal feed?

Ratledge: Yes, it would. It does not contain a high concentration of protein. If you take one of the classical fat-producing yeasts, this can contain about 60% fat. It will only contain about 15–20% protein, the rest being made up of carbohydrate, a few other components and some ash, so there isn't a high content of protein as such. It is unlikely that it would be suitable for calf rearing or chicks at the premium end of the market. It would perhaps be suitable for the middle range of the market. It could certainly be used for animal feeding.

Kapsiotis: The presence of odd carbon fatty acids in SCP produced on *n*-alkanes resulted in producing animal fats with these odd carbon fatty acids in them. This created apprehension to the health authority of a country where SCP is to be industrially produced. What are the physiological or toxicological implications for the consumer of such fats?

Ratledge: From what I read in the literature there should be no disadvantage in handling odd carbon chain fatty acids. Metabolism yields propionic acid instead of acetic acid. Propionic acid will then be converted into succinic acid through a sequence of reactions and should present no problem at all to any animal. However, I showed that slide with the alkanes not so much as to say let us use alkanes as a substrate, but to show that micro-organisms have a much greater capability than we might imagine for changing its fatty acid spectrum to force the organism perhaps to produce more short chain acids than we would like or we would normally get. But we never find if we use carbohydrate as the substrate anything other than very small traces of odd carbon chain fatty acids.

You can find the same amount of odd carbon chain fatty acids in any vegetable oil that you look at—1 % or 2 % of C-15 or C-17. You can find the same 1 % or 2 % in our own yeast fat and fungal fats, but I would pass the question on to someone else who might like to answer it.

Mrs Parry: What is the criterion used to define 'nutritionally adequate' in Table 1 ?

Ratledge: It is defined, I think, in terms of nutrition as a whole. What is very difficult to calculate is to know how much unseen fat people eat. It follows that if we eat a lot of meat, which we do in most of Europe and North America, we will consume a lot of fat associated with that meat. In countries such as India and Africa where there is much less dependence on meat the amount of fat coming from other sources, the unseen fat, will be much less, so they will in fact be pressed even harder to maintain an adequate level of nutrition as regards fat.

Mrs Parry: Is this serious provided their essential fatty acid requirements are met?

Ratledge: Don't forget that is only about 10 kg per person per year, which is a very small amount of fat needed, and these nutritional values have, I think, been laid down by international authorities. I have just taken their word that this is the amount of fat needed for adequate nutrition.

Burrows: Some micro-organisms produce fat extracellularly. Can this property be developed into a fat production process?

Ratledge: No. Fat produced extracellularly is first of all usually of a low concentration, and secondly it tends to be a rather unusual fat—sophorides, for example, which aren't easily digestible. The concentration in fact is usually less than 1 g/litre, whereas I am talking about fats producing 20 g/litre in a fermenter where you have a cell population of say 30 g/litre.

Hay: Do these fats have the same chemical composition as common fats?

Ratledge: As far as anyone can tell, and there has been a great deal of analytical work done, there appears to be no difference between yeast or fungal fat and the composition of a plant seed oil, like soya bean oil. The fatty acid composition is exactly the same. Triglyceride content isn't as high in micro-organisms as it is in plants. Save for that, there is no difference at all.

8

Algal Proteins

G. PRIESTLEY

*Western Biological Equipment Ltd,
Sherborne, Dorset, England*

ABSTRACT

The production of increasing amounts of waste material by rapidly expanding urban communities and as a result of more intensive agricultural practices, coupled with the need for increased amounts of high-grade protein, suggests the application of algal culture techniques for waste recycling. Lagoon culture of algae, using either sewage or nitrogen- and phosphorus-rich waste waters as primary substrate, can produce higher dry weight yields of superior protein quality than can higher plants under similar climatic conditions if the lagoon is operated on a semi-continuous basis using optimum catch techniques. Study of the engineering techniques for algal culture shows that a simple, relatively non-turbulent system relying on evaporative cooling would eliminate many of the problems which have beset algal culture since its inception due to excessive reliance on process engineering techniques and vain competition with SCP production.

The main problems encountered reside in separating the product from the culture, although the use of filamentous algae would eliminate the primary separation stage. Although crude algae can be eaten by humans, it will not be accepted on a large scale without expensive fractionation; until economic fractionation and texturisation techniques are developed, it seems likely that an extra link in the food chain, e.g. to produce beef protein, is the best way of upgrading the crude algal product into an acceptable form. Calculations on this basis demonstrate that increased yields of such an upgraded protein can be obtained compared with conventional fodder, although caution must be exercised in extrapolating laboratory yield figures of algal protein to the production scale.

INTRODUCTION

The need for alternative protein sources is universally recognised, the approximately exponential increase in population tending to outstrip the linear increase in conventional agricultural production. Concomitant with this is the increase in production of human waste materials in rapidly expanding urban areas, and those from animals

114

due to intensive agricultural techniques; this is not only a potential pollution threat (especially dangerous to water supplies) but also represents a potential substrate for protein production. This is represented in Fig. 1.

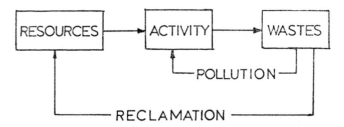

Fig. 1. Simple representation of the terrestrial ecosystem.

The use of algae in sewage oxidation has been advanced as a doubly attractive contribution to solving these manifold problems, since they can break down the organic structures and render the water potable (*e.g.* for use in irrigation or horticulture) while providing what is essentially a nutritious by-product (Fig. 2).

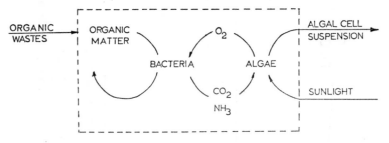

Fig. 2. Representation of controlled photosynthesis pond for processing organic wastes (after Oswald and Golueke[59]).

Mention may also be made of algal culture on reservoirs and other similar water bodies subject to NPK fertiliser run-off, again caused by intensive farming practices.

The purpose of this paper is to examine the rationale of algal protein production, essentially on an autotrophic basis. It is hoped that the problems, as well as the advantages, of this novel protein source will be equally illuminated.

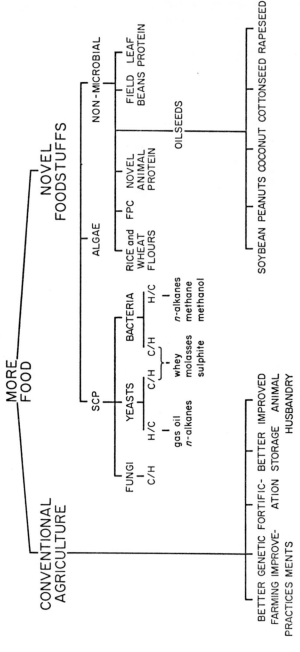

Fig. 3. Summary of techniques of increasing protein production.

METHODS OF INCREASING FOOD PRODUCTION

A summary of currently available methods is given in Fig. 3. The main purpose of this diagram is to show that algae should be compared less to single-cell protein and more to higher plants. Algae cannot be produced economically on an autotrophic basis using conventional SCP production techniques due to prohibitive energy costs (although the Japanese have grown *Chlorella* heterotrophically, the higher specific growth rates of yeasts would make better use of the equipment). Algae have an essentially similar amino acid spectrum to typical SCP microbes, and the nucleic acid content is less due to the intrinsically lower specific growth rate.[1] A less capitally intensive approach is therefore possible, which favours Third World development where neither capital investment nor the necessary level of technical expertise are usually indigenously available. Lower yields can therefore be accepted, since one does not have to justify heavy capital expenditure on the plant.

Superficially, algae have a distinct advantage over heterotrophs in that they can fix atmospheric CO_2; however, as has been pointed out elsewhere,[2] this argument is only valid economically if there is a shortage of fixed carbon on a global scale. This is recognised not to be the case; any advantage conferred on algae by autotrophy lies in the even distribution of CO_2 over the face of the Earth. In the case of bacterially produced CO_2 in sewage oxidation ponds this factor is of course irrelevant.

It is therefore natural to compare algae to higher plants; agriculture itself cannot be compared to the process engineering approach used in SCP production since the process is a batch (or at best a semi-continuous) one, with no control over important parameters such as climate. Figure 4 shows that, while the peak yields of algae and higher plants are similar (dictated by the same CO_2 supply and energy input), the intrinsically higher growth rates of algae would allow the peak population size to be achieved earlier and maintained for longer. Higher growth rates essentially mean that any product removed by harvesting would be replaced much more quickly, lending the process to a type of semi-continuous culture in which the cut is determined by optimum catch principles. It is evident that the total yield of dry matter obtained from such a system would be larger than for a conventional agricultural crop. It is, however, better to talk in terms of the rate of *protein* production per unit area, in which respect

G. Priestley

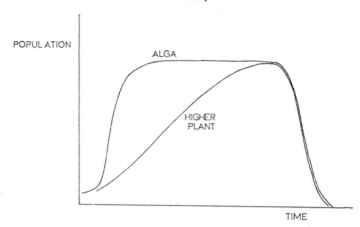

FIG. 4. Simplified representation of the effect of growth kinetics on the seasonal yields of algae and higher plants (after Vincent[2]).

algae again score over higher plants due to their higher protein content; combined with the higher seasonal dry matter production rates, this gives a far higher theoretical protein production rate than for any other plant, or animal produce (Table 1).

It should, however, be noted that the figures for *Spirulina* and *Chlorella* were obtained using fairly sophisticated equipment and CO_2 supplementation. It is tempting to use these and laboratory data, presumably obtained under ideal conditions, in extrapolations

TABLE 1
Protein productivity data for algae compared with other sources (after Vincent[2])

Protein source	Protein yield (kg dry weight/ha/year)
Spirulina platensis	24 300
Chlorella pyrenoidosa (Emerson)	15 700
Clover leaf	1 680
Grass	670
Peanuts	470
Peas	395
Wheat	300
Milk from cattle on grassland	100
Meat from cattle on grassland	60

TABLE 2

Productivity of some algae under various conditions

Alga	N source	System	%CO_2	Biomass production (g/m²/day)	% Protein	Protein production (g/m²/day)	Source
Uronema barlowi	Urea	Stagnant	0·03	0·91	34·77	0·32	Priestley (unpublished)
Hormidium flaccidum	Urea	Stagnant	0·03	0·84	31·46	0·27	
U. barlowi	Nitrate	Stagnant	0·03	1·43	51·95	0·74	
U. barlowi	Urea	Agitated	0·03	6·00	27·21	1·63	
U. barlowi	Urea	Agitated	1·00	17·20	30·14	5·06	
U. barlowi	Urea	Agitated	3·00	19·50	28·32	5·55	
U. barlowi	Urea	Agitated	5·00	20·62	28·76	5·95	
U. barlowi	Urea	Agitated	10·00	18·40	21·58	3·97	
U. barlowi	Nitrate	Agitated	0·03	9·07	27·25	2·48	
U. barlowi	Nitrate	Agitated	1·00	16·61	26·25	4·36	
U. barlowi	Nitrate	Agitated	3·00	20·90	25·20	5·25	
U. barlowi	Nitrate	Agitated	5·00	21·80	22·50	4·89	
Ulothrix sp.	Nitrate	Agitated	0·03	3·60	43·00	1·55	Ionescu[3]
Hormidium sp.	Urea	Agitated	5·00	47·80	42·70	18·70	Hindak and Pribil[4]
Ulothrix sp.	Urea	Agitated	5·00	42·80	43·00	17·60	
Uronema sp.	Urea	Agitated	5·00	39·20	42·10	16·90	
Stigeoclonium sp.	Urea	Agitated	5·00	39·00	49·00	19·10	

to the production scale, where relatively low CO_2 levels, non-ideal light regimes and temperature fluctuations will occur. Table 2 shows particularly the influence of CO_2 and agitation on production rates.

Algae as a Foodstuff

The data presented in Tables 3 and 4 show that algae have a favourable composition. However, along with other vegetable proteins, the cells must be fractionated in order to render the proteins directly available for direct human (or other non-ruminant) consumption, since the gut does not possess the enzymes to break down the cell walls. While fractionation is easily achieved in the laboratory, extension to the production scale is fraught with difficulties, not least of which is the cost (which could increase the cost of the final product on a protein basis by at least sevenfold[2]). The product will therefore stand a better chance of initial adoption if it can be tolerated by non-ruminants without fractionation.

Algae Used Directly as a Human Food

The earliest recorded feeding trial on man was performed by Jorgensen and Convit,[21] who administered an algal 'soup' to the inhabitants of a leper colony in Venezuela; the soup was readily accepted in quantities of up to 35 g/day, resulting in generally improved weight gains and general health. Powell *et al.*,[7] after feeding a mixed *Chlorella* and *Scenedesmus* product, found no pathological effects when the algae were provided in amounts up to 100 g/day, either alone or in confections; although gastrointestinal upsets occurred in the first few days, they subsided when the diet was continued. Provision of algae in excess of 100 g/day resulted in severe nausea, flatulence and other associated gastrointestinal upsets. This has been confirmed by other workers;[11] a mixture of *Chlorella pyrenoidosa* and *Scenedesmus obliquus* incorporated into a jelly was tolerated at the level of 50–100 g/day for 22 days with no side effects, but raising the level to 150 g/day induced allergic reactions in three of the five subjects.

Lee *et al.*[22] fed *Ch. pyrenoidosa* (equivalent to 6 g N/day) and other test proteins (fish flour, soya bean flour and dried whole egg), and combinations of the algal protein with the other test proteins, to human subjects, the rest of the diet containing 0·66 g N/day. A negative nitrogen balance occurred with the algal diet alone, protein

TABLE 3

Composition of some algae and algal feeds compared with egg and meat muscle
(% dry weight)

Alga	Protein	Fat	Ash	C/H	Fibre	Source
Scenedesmus obliquus	49·1	5·6	—	—	—	Miyoshi[5]
Scenedesmus obliquus	55·0	10·3	—	7·5	—	Pabst *et al.*[6]
Chlorella/*Scenedesmus*	59·0	19·0	6·0	13·0	—	Powell *et al.*[7]
Sc. obliquus	52·1	5·1	—	—	11·0	Witt and Schröder[8]
Chlorella TX 7-11-05	55·5	7·5	8·3	17.8	3·1	Lubitz[9]
Scenedesmus sp.	46·1	—	8·7	—	—	Lautner[10]
Ch. pyrenoidosa/*Sc. quadricauda*	51·2	11·5	9·0	23·1	5·0	Kondrat'ev *et al.*[11]
Ch. vulgaris	60·0	2·5	6·0	—	1·8	Groza *et al.*[12]
Ch. vulgaris	47·4	8·8	14·7	—	9·1	Bock and Wünsche[13]
Chlamydomonas rheinhardti	36·4	5·7	18·0	38·9	—	Burlacu *et al.*[14]
Hormidium sp.	44·5	2·2	2·9	—	7·0 ⎫	
Ulothrix sp.	45·1	1·1	6·9	—	11·2 ⎬ Hindak and Pribil[4]	
Uronema gigas	58·4	1·7	7·1	—	9·7 ⎭	
Egg	48·8	44·5	4·2	2·8	— ⎫	
Meat muscle	57·1	37·1	8·2	2·0	— ⎬ Miller[15]	

G. Priestley

TABLE 4

Amino acid composition of some algae compared with FAO reference and egg proteins

Alga	Lysine	Threonine	Cystine	Valine	Methionine	Isoleucine	Tyrosine	Phenylalanine	Tryptophan	Leucine	Histidine	Arginine	Aspartic acid	Serine	Glutamic acid	Proline	Glycine	Alanine
Chlorella vulgaris[16]	10·2	2·8	0·2	5·5	1·4	3·5	2·8	2·8	2·1	6·1	3·3	15·8	6·4	3·3	7·8	7·2	6·2	7·7
Chlorella pyrenoidosa[17]	2·4	1·9	—	2·7	0·6	1·7	—	2·1	0·4	1·2	0·7	2·4	—	—	—	—	2·2	—
Chlorella ellipsoida[18]	5·9	4·9	0·7	7·9	0·6	4·5	1·7	4·2	—	9·3	1·7	5·8	8·8	5·2	10·5	5·0	10·4	12·2
Ulothrix sp.[4]	1·5	1·8	—	2·6	—	0·6	2·4	3·4	—	1·4	1·4	3·2	1·4	0·7	7·8	—	1·4	5·5
Uronema gigas[4]	6·3	4·0	0·5	6·8	—	4·0	1·3	4·7	—	10·5	0·9	11·5	9·1	6·8	13·5	—	6·5	13·2
Spirulina maxima[19]	4·6	4·6	0·4	6·5	1·4	6·0	3·9	4·9	1·4	8·0	1·8	6·5	8·6	4·2	12·6	3·9	4·8	6·8
Whole egg[20]	6·6	4·8	2·3	6·1	3·3	5·0	4·0	4·8	1·9	8·2	2·3	6·4	9·7	7·1	12·6	3·7	3·1	5·5
FAO reference	4·2	2·8	2·0	4·2	2·2	4·2	4·2	2·8	2·8	1·4	4·8	—	—	—	—	—	—	—

digestibility being only 69% (cf. 71–75% when the alga was combined with other test proteins, and 77–82% for the other sources alone). The nitrogen balance was maintained with fish flour, soya bean and egg, with 1:2 mixtures of algae with these, and a 2:1 mixture of the algae with fish flour. The algae could therefore replace one-third of the fish protein and up to two-thirds of the egg protein without impairment of nitrogen retention.

Mitsuda *et al.*[23] concluded that fresh, dried or solvent-extracted *Chlorella* was digested hardly at all by humans, whereas isolated algal protein was easily digested. Even the filamentous cyanophyte *Spirulina*, used for thousands of years as a staple food in Chad and elsewhere, has been shown[19] to be nutritionally poor, giving only 76% protein digestibility.

Algae Fed Directly to Other Non-ruminants

There are more data available for non-ruminants such as rats and chicks than for humans. Supplementation with some essential amino acids can induce higher weight gains in rats; *e.g. Sc. obliquus* and *Ch. pyrenoidosa* when supplemented with lysine,[24] and *Ch. pyrenoidosa* with methionine[25] resulted in higher weight gains than with the crude dried alga alone. Nitrogen absorption has been reported[26] to be a function of the mechanical damage to which the cells have been subjected; cooked algae,[27] for example, are digested better than uncooked. Evidence of low carotenoid digestibility by chicks (manifested by an increase in the colour index of egg yolks, bills and legs) has been reported;[28–30] supplementation of the feed with glutamic acid can improve the utilisation of carotenoids and of vitamin E.[31]

Some values of protein efficiency ratios, biological values and compositions of algal feeds are given in Tables 3, 5 and 6.

Thus, in general, it appears that unfractionated protein is not efficiently utilised by non-ruminants, although it can be tolerated without any really harmful effects. There is evidence to suggest[34] that, as one would expect, algae are digested better by ruminants (cattle) than by non-ruminants (swine). To utilise the product adequately, therefore, there are two main alternatives: fractionation of the raw material, with the attendant increase in cost price on a protein basis; or introduction of an extra link in the food chain by feeding to ruminants, which can upgrade the protein at the expense of a tenfold loss of energy for each successive link in the chain.

TABLE 5
Biological values of some algal feeds compared with other protein sources

Protein source	Test animal	BV	Source
Chlorella vulgaris	Rat	52·9	Bock and Wünsche[13]
Scenedesmus obliquus	Rat	47·0	
Brewer's yeast	Rat	84·0	
Aspergillus oryzae	Rat	44·0	Fink and Herold[32]
Mycelia from penicillin fermentation	Rat	60·0	
Casein	Rat	100·0	
Spirulina maxima	Rat	62·0	Clement *et al.*[19]

TABLE 6
Protein efficiency ratios of some algal feeds compared with other test proteins

Protein source	Test animal	PER	Source
17–18% soybean meal (+0·54% DL-methionine)	Chick	2·76	
17–18% *Scenedesmus obliquus* (+0·8% DL-methionine)	Chick	1·07	Koci and Kociova[33]
17–18% *Sc. obliquus* (+2% wheat protease)	Chick	0·55	
17–18% *Sc. obliquus*	Chick	0·95	
18% *Sc. obliquus/Ch. pyrenoidosa*	Chick/rat	1·55/1·38	
18% *Sc. obliquus/Ch. ellipsoidea*	Chick/rat	0·31/0·94	Leveille *et al.*[25]
18% *Sc. obliquus/Spongiococcum excentricum*	Chick/rat	0·43/0·34	
18% casein	Rat	2·50	
10% *Ch. pyrenoidosa* (+0·2% DL-methionine)	Rat	2·90	
10% *Ch. pyrenoidosa*	Rat	2·19	Lubitz[9]
10% casein	Rat	3·30	
10% defatted egg protein	Rat	4·01	

FRACTIONATION OF ALGAE

There have been several reviews[35,36] of methods of protein extraction from microbes in general, but few techniques which work in the laboratory have been successfully operated on the production scale. Many methods involve the degradation or denaturation of the cell proteins, which may be a disadvantage if the extracted proteins are to be textured; others, such as plasmolysis and autolysis, would probably have to be operated under aseptic conditions.

Partial disruption of the cells, *e.g.* by ball-milling, may be used to increase the available protein and thus improve digestibility, but the cell walls will still remain available to cause gastrointestinal upsets. Removal of the cell debris will be necessary if the product is to be used as a human food, and the proteins must then be rapidly stabilised; a procedure has been outlined for this,[37] whereby disruption and debris removal was followed by drying and pH or heat precipitation. It is important that the lipid fraction (*i.e.* including chlorophylls, xanthophylls and other pigments of the photosynthetic apparatus) be separated from the protein fraction to prevent fat oxidation.

The use of mutant strains with weakened cell walls would render simple mechanical disruption easier, as would the cultivation of naturally thin-walled algae such as the filamentous chlorophyte *Hormidium*.

Mechanical Methods of Disruption

Boiling, roller drying and vacuum drying have been found to increase protein availability and therefore digestibility;[26] nitrogen availability being a function of the degree of disintegration of the cell walls. This was confirmed by Hedenskog *et al.*,[37] who showed that the degree of digestibility of ball-milled cells was proportional to the number of broken cells.

Homogenisation is an attractive technique in that the cell proteins can be released without excessive protein hydrolysis; this is important if the proteins are to be textured. Other techniques, such as ultrasonic probes[38] and colloid mills,[39] are likely to be confined to pilot scale at the most; in general it appears that most totally mechanical methods are likely to remain expensive in terms of capital investment and running costs.

Chemical Methods of Disruption

Various techniques involving chemical alteration of the cell wall have been tried, *e.g.* butanol-induced autolysis[40] and hydrogen-bond breaking agents such as phenol,[41] formic acid[42] and urea.[23] The latter seems the most attractive for food use. The major problems of these techniques lie in the recovery of the chemical (for economic reasons) and ensuring that the final product is not rendered toxic by its application. The attraction of urea, as has been stressed elsewhere,[2] lies in the possibility of direct texturisation of the protein on precipitation by pH change, dilution or by heating; the textured product could then be washed free of urea and the urea recycled.

Of the other available treatments, hydrogen peroxide has been tried unsuccessfully;[37] alkaline hydrolysis causes protein degradation,[40] whereas acid hydrolysis (usually by HCl) results in high residual salt concentrations in the finished product.

Enzymic Methods of Disruption

These are becoming increasingly attractive economically, especially in view of the recent advances in immobilised enzyme technology. As yet, no enzyme appears to have been found for breaking down whole algal cells, although isolated cell walls can be lysed by the gastric juice of the snail.[43] Other methods have been suggested,[2] including *in vitro* lysis of cells by extracellular enzymes of microbes grown specifically for the purpose; alternatively, fermentation of algae with microbes[37,44] in a similar way to fermentation of milk and cassava could be used, with a concomitant improvement in flavour.

Fat Removal and Decolorisation

It is essential that, for human use, the algal material must not contain the lipids, especially pigments, which give crude algal protein its characteristic 'fishy' taste and render it susceptible to bacterial attack and oxidation (which induce the equally characteristic 'off' flavour and odour). Solvent extraction is the obvious method of lipid removal, and has been discussed elsewhere.[45] An interesting technique, although uneconomical, has been described[46] in which *Ch. pyrenoidosa* was bleached using high light intensity at high oxygen partial pressures in the absence of CO_2. Although the energy cost of this particular system is high, it does suggest that other techniques of oxidation, possibly by H_2O_2, could be acceptable.

Texturisation and Presentation

Even if a food is nutritious, it must look, feel and taste like food before it will be accepted on a large scale. This may suggest that, at least initially, algal protein should be incorporated as a protein additive to an existing product rather than as the sole basis of a new textured protein product. The algal protein need not be purified to the extent (about 80%) required for say a spinning process, and the taste could be disguised.

Techniques for producing meat analogues have been described,[47,48] using either spinning or extrusion procedures. Extrusion, in which a slurry of the protein complex in water accompanied by a binding agent (*e.g.* wheat starch, gluten or egg white) is heated until plasticised and then passed through heated dies, is the cheaper process since a less refined protein stock can be used (which need not be completely soluble). The product appears as a finely celled foam, although the binding agents may also modify the rheology of the 'dough' to improve the extrusion procedure and the final product structure. Spinning, using techniques similar to those in use in the textile industry, is a far more expensive process than is extrusion, involving isolation of the protein in alkaline solution to which small amounts of gelifiants such as alginates and carrageenins have been added. The fibres may then be spun and coagulated in acid solution (sometimes with the addition of Ca^{2+}). The cost of such a process cannot be justified for algal protein; if the protein is to be textured at all, then the technique of Mitsuda *et al.*,[23] already referred to, appears to be the most promising.

ALGAE USED DIRECTLY AS ANIMAL FEED

Inclusion of ruminants in the food chain would remove the need for fractionation, but at the expense of a loss of total energy of about one order of magnitude for each food chain link. There would be no need for cell disruption or essential amino acid (mainly methionine) supplementation, although some initial pretreatment of the feed would be necessary, if only for storage purposes, *e.g.* compression into cakes, with addition of roughage (possibly sawdust), trace minerals and possibly an additional nitrogen source such as urea. Rough calculations, presented in Table 7, show that a distinct improvement in the yield of beef protein can be obtained using algae as the primary protein source, even taking very low figures for algal protein production yields.

This form of upgrading of algal protein must be the most attractive in the short term, until economic techniques for fractionation have been devised. The data, especially for *Spirulina*, indicate the potential of algal protein as a feedstock, although it should be remembered that the alga was grown in a fairly sophisticated system with CO_2 supplementation. The figure for *Ulothrix*, which should be fairly typical of the yield from relatively unmanaged fresh waters subject to NPK fertiliser run-off, is inserted as a cautionary note to show that so much depends upon the degree of sophistication of the culture system. It is worth, therefore, examining the logistics of approach of system design in some detail.

TABLE 7
Theoretical beef protein yields on algal feedstocks compared with grass

Primary protein source	Yield of protein (kg/ha/year)	Yield of beef protein[a] (kg/ha/year)
[b]Filamentous algae[4]	20 000	2 000
Spirulina platensis[19]	24 300	2 430
Chlorella pyrenoidosa[45] (Emerson)	15 700	1 570
Ulothrix sp.[3]	1 660	166
Grass	670	67

[a] Assuming an approximate conversion factor of 0·10.
[b] Extrapolations from laboratory data.

THE ENGINEERING OF ALGAL CULTURE

Basic Kinetics

At low cell densities and low light intensities, the behaviour of the whole culture can be expressed in terms of the individual cell, *i.e.* the overall culture growth rate can be represented by the specific growth rate of the cell:

$$dN/dt = kN$$

where N is the population density.

The culture is light-dependent at low values of light intensity (I) and cell density (N), but as I increases to a value I_s (the saturation intensity) with corresponding cell density N_s, the culture becomes

independent of light intensity. The two phenomena of light dependence and saturation may be expressed as in Fig. 5. I_b is the compensation intensity at which gains of photosynthate are just balanced by
losses due to respiration.

A cell at an intensity lower than I_s will operate metabolically at a
rate governed by I_s provided the light intensity is not sufficiently
high to induce photo-oxidation or chlorosis.

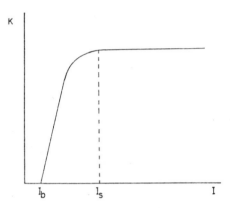

FIG. 5. *K-I* plot showing dependence of growth rate on light intensity.

As the population density increases so does mutual shading; the
growth rate curve becomes linear with time, and Einstein's Law of
Photochemical Equivalence applies, *i.e.* the rate of product formation
(gain of photosynthate) is proportional only to incident energy at a
given temperature:

$$dN/dt = kI$$

All commercially operated cultures must, for economic reasons,
operate at such a culture density as to be in the linear phase of
growth.

As the culture density increases, the value of I_s decreases and the
compensation intensity I_b becomes the stronger parameter; the
growth rate decreases with increasing cell density N, until the culture
enters the stationary phase (*i.e.* $I_s = I_b$).

The Large-scale Culture of Algae

Large-scale culture began in the early 1950s,[21,49,50] cultures varying from 1 to 1000 litres capacity. During 1951 the A.D. Little Co.[51]

experimented with *Chlorella* cultures varying from 2000 to 5000 litres, and by 1953 culture systems of 10 000 litres were being operated at the University of California.[52] Since that time the average size of culture system has been increasing rapidly. By 1955 Tamiya[53] reported the development of a 100 000 litre unit, and a 2 million litre system had been constructed at the University of California. A 40 000 litre unit has been installed at Trebon, Czechoslovakia,[54] accompanied by smaller units of a similar type at Rupite, Bulgaria, and Tylicz, Poland.[55] Units of similar size have been reported at Leningrad, USSR,[56] while the development of algal mass culture systems in Italy has been described.[57] A system was developed in the south of France for the filamentous cyanophyte *Spirulina*, utilising combustion gases as the CO_2 source.[58]

The trend, as pointed out by Oswald and Golueke,[59] is that the total capacity of algal mass culture systems is increasing logarithmically with time. Although the paper by Oswald and Golueke was written only in 1968, when the total volume was estimated at 10^7 litres, it is difficult to estimate in 1975 whether the projected total volume (about 10^{10} litres) has in fact been realised. If the continuing interest in algal mass culture for water clarification is maintained, extrapolation shows that by 1989 the total volume of 10^{15} litres could supply the feedstock for the total world protein requirement to be fulfilled by animal protein.

Design Considerations for Large-scale Units

In the development of any system for algal mass culture there are three fundamental approaches, each with a different economic rationale:

1. Bioregenerative systems such as photosynthetic gas exchangers for life support systems in space and in submarines must operate at the maximum possible efficiency and be of small overall volume; rigorous costing procedures are not applied, and sophisticated automative techniques may be used.
2. Even if algae grown in symbiosis with bacteria on sewage oxidation ponds are regarded as a by-product only, economy of cultivation is still an important factor.
3. Algae grown autotrophically as a foodstuff must be subject to stringent cost minimisation on a protein produced per unit area basis if the process is to be commercially viable.

If we can accept lower yields, a lower capital investment on plant is required; if a simple separation technique is used, the overall cost can be reduced and the whole system can be operated by unskilled personnel. The latter point is of vital importance in Third World areas, and also renders the final product more acceptable to the indigenous population.

Logistics of Approach

On an economic basis alone the system must be open, *i.e.* the surface of the culture must be exposed to the ambient environment. Although closed systems offer a greater CO_2 economy, in that CO_2 lost from the culture surface by transpiration can be recycled, this is only an advantage if supplementary CO_2 is being added.

It has been shown[60] that the cooling of the culture through heat exchangers accounted for 30% of the total budget in the A.D. Little plant (a closed system); it should be remembered that any radiation incident on a culture which is not actually used in photosynthesis or lost by reflection appears as heat. Closed systems tend to remain at a higher temperature than open ones, due to the greenhouse effect and the absence of evaporative cooling; this may be an advantage at some times of the year when the temperature is too low for efficient photosynthesis in an open system, but is far outweighed by the extra cooling costs incurred. Evaporative cooling in an open system, growing algae with progressive temperature optima to follow the seasonal trend, appears to be the most economical solution.

Geometry

In order for a mass culture system to operate efficiently the algae must absorb the maximum amount of light at a suitable intensity, *i.e.* without being subject to photo-oxidation. This implies the need for a high surface to volume ratio, since the maximum capacity of any photoreacting system is proportional to the area of irradiated surface. Beer's Law suggests that high absorbence of incident light can be achieved by varying the depth of the absorbing layer and the concentration of the absorbing substance; in the latter case this is the concentration of biomass in the system or, more accurately, that of the chlorophyll in the chloroplasts. As the photosynthetic efficiency of the chloroplasts decreases with increasing light intensity, elevated efficiencies in the macrosystem can only be achieved at high radiation intensities if the light absorption by the chloroplasts does not exceed the maximum rate of the dark reactions possible at a given temperature. This suggests the need for three-dimensional structures which can dilute the incident radiation to mean values at which the system can function more efficiently by reducing saturation losses. Higher plants have evolved such a 'dispersion in space' mechanism in which the leaves form an internal receiving surface, effectively increasing the available surface area to a value much greater than the boundary area of the plants. Various analogous techniques have been tried with algal cultures, ranging from light-diffusing cones[61,62] to water sprays;[54] the first of these may be ruled out on economic grounds alone on a large scale, as may the use of dentate or corrugated surfaces, while the second can be eliminated due to the high cost of pumping, complex lighting pattern and high transpiration rates of water and CO_2.

The easiest way of creating the degree of light dilution required is to utilise the light–dark effect by imposing turbulence on the system ('dispersion in time'). The random nature of turbulence precludes the subjection of all the cells in suspension to the same pattern of movement between the irradiated and dark regions necessary for the desired intermittency effect; although a suitable mean periodicity may be achieved, the variation from the mean value is so large that the requisite light–dark cycle may be experienced by only a small fraction of the algae present in suspension. The acceptability of turbulence will therefore depend upon the rigidity with which the desired intermittency must be experienced; it has been demonstrated that under certain conditions a perceptible increase in efficiency can be achieved,[63] even if it is less than with a non-random mixing pattern.

Thickness of the Culture Layer

The total weight of algae in a mass culture system is an area-dependent term; thus if the algal content is to be economic the remaining important parameters are the depth and density of suspension. Separation and circulation costs decrease with increasing culture density, whereas the linear growth rate is inversely proportional to culture thickness. Factors militating against excessive reduction of culture depth include variations in the medium due to transpiration of water and CO_2, and a lower heat inertia with associated thermal instability.

Slope of the Culture System

Many of the early culture units had a slope of 2–3% in order to improve circulation and prevent cell sedimentation.[64] The angle and degree of slope are also of importance if the maximum amount of sunlight is to be absorbed. At equinox the angle of light incidence is similar to the degree of latitude, whereas at solstice it is about 15° less; in temperate northern climates a slope of about 40° would therefore be the most efficient over the whole of the growth season. The difficulties of keeping a suspension on a slope of this magnitude, plus high pumping costs, render such a slope impracticable.

The relative amount of radiation incident on a suitably sloping surface should increase with increase in latitude, but in fact the amount of light lost by scattering is similarly related; typical figures for the net incidence of light are given in Table 8.

TABLE 8

The effect of latitude on seasonal radiation (after Telkes[65])

°N	kcal/m²/day		
	June	December	Average
18	5 425	4 176	5 253
21	6 512	3 939	5 156
25	5 974	2 992	4 068
33	5 156	2 172	4 176
36	7 599	1 518	4 671

Supply of CO_2

Although various techniques have been used for enriching the growth medium with CO_2, this is generally uneconomical and will not be discussed here. If there is a cheap supply of CO_2 available, e.g. from stack gases or fermentation processes, it should be introduced at a rate calculated to keep the average rate of dissolved CO_2 constant; in a circulating system there is inevitably a concentration gradient as the gas is metabolised by the algae and lost in desorption from the surface; the latter effect is particularly great in the case of strongly agitated open cultures due to the rapid rate of surface renewal.

METHODS OF SEPARATION

Separation can be divided into three main stages: primary, secondary (dewatering) and tertiary (drying).

Primary-Separation

Filtration. The high resistance of an algal filter cake renders filtration very difficult; vacuum filtration, while considerably easier, is uneconomical at low inlet concentrations, and so a preliminary concentration stage would be necessary in this case.

Centrifugation. Although centrifugation is the most efficient means of separation, the economics are based on underflow rate rather than on solids removed; an initial algal concentration of 200 mg/litre would require the removal of one million gallons of liquid per ton of centrifugate. Although the economics would be more favourable if the operating density of the suspension were increased, the latter is governed by factors such as light, nutrient, detention time, optimum catch and suspended solids in the medium. Since an increase in detention period increases land requirements, the saving in power costs resulting from increased residence time may be offset by increased land costs.

Flocculation. The coagulation of algal suspensions with filter alum, lime or organic cationic flocculants has the advantage of requiring little power; power is only needed for rapid mixing after addition of the flocculating agent, followed by gentle stirring to allow the development of floc particles of the requisite size. The disadvantage of the technique is the physico-chemical or chemical change induced in the medium due to pH effects, thus necessitating treatment of the medium before recycling. The harvested product also tends to contain aluminium or calcium.

Autoflocculation[66] would overcome the problem of supernatant recycling. The phenomenon usually occurs in the afternoons of sunny days, and is manifested by the clumping of cells. The disadvantages of the technique are unreliability and the need for separate ponds to allow the culture to be run off. It is of possible use as a standby treatment if land is readily available.

The use of filamentous algae, which can be raked from the surface with relative ease, eliminates the need for the primary separation and therefore offers a more economical solution.

Secondary Separation

The dewatering stage is necessary to the preparation of the slurry prior to the tertiary (drying) stage. Although centrifugation and gravity filtration have been used for the purpose, the best method is probably sandbed percolation which has the advantage of combining the dewatering and drying steps.

Tertiary Separation

Mechanical (drum) drying has been found to be successful, as has sun drying; as mentioned above, sandbeds appear to be the best alternative. An open sandpit about 3–5 in deep has been used to dry the slurry from the primary (centrifuged) separation in 3–5 days using a sandbed area of 10–15% of the total growth area.[66] The dried product can then be raked from the beds as flaky chips. Disadvantages of the technique include the contamination of the product by sand, and possible vitamin loss due to the combination of slow drying and long exposure to heat and light.

The relative costs of the main separation techniques are given in Table 9.

TABLE 9

Summary and relative costs of separation processes (based on data of Golueke et al.[66])

		Approx. cost ($/ton)
Primary separation	Centrifugation	10–20
	Flocculation, followed by sedimentation or flotation:	
	(i) alum	20–25
	(ii) lime	15–20
	(iii) cationic polymers	20–40
	(iv) autoflocculation	Land costs
Secondary separation	Centrifugation (solid bowl)	7–20
	Gravity filtration	15–20
Tertiary separation	Drum drying	20–40 (incl. labour)
	Sun drying	8–20
	Sandbeds	14–20

REFERENCES

1. Maynard Smith, J. (1969). In: *Proc. 19th Symposium of the Society for General Microbiology*, Cambridge University Press, p. 1.
2. Vincent, W. A. (1971). In: *Proc. 21st Symposium of the Society for General Microbiology*, Cambridge University Press, p. 47.

136   G. Priestley

3. Ionescu, A. (1970). *Rev. Roum. Biol. Ser. Bot.*, **15**, p. 103.
4. Hindak, F. and Pribil, S. (1968). *Biologia Plantarum*, **10**(3), p. 234.
5. Miyoshi, T. (1960). *Shikoku Acta Med.*, **16**, p. 76.
6. Pabst, W., Jekat, F. and Rolle, I. (1964). *Nutritio et Dieta*, **6**, p. 279.
7. Powell, R. C., Nevels, E. M. and McDowell, M. E. (1961). *J. Nutr.*, **75**, p. 7.
8. Witt, M. and Schröder, J. (1967). *Landwirtsch. Forsch.*, **20**, p. 148.
9. Lubitz, J. A. (1963). *J. Fd. Sci.*, **28**, p. 229.
10. Lautner, V. (1966). *Biol. Chem. Vyz. Zvirat.*, **2**, p. 371.
11. Kondrat'ev, J. I., Byckov, V. P., Usakov, A. S., Bojko, N. N., Klyskina, N. S., Abaturova, E. A., Korneeva, N. A., Terpilovsky, A. M., Belyakova, M. I. and Kasatina, A. G. (1966). *Vop. Pitan.*, **25**(6), pp. 9, 14.
12. Groza, I., Boldijar, A. and Vlad, G. (1966). *Rev. Zooteh. Med. Vet.*, No. 7, p. 24.
13. Bock, H. D. and Wünsche, J. (1967). *Jährbuch Tiernährung Fütterung*, **6**, p. 544.
14. Burlacu, G., Salageanu, N., Baltac, M., Marinescu, A. G. and Ionila, D. (1968). *Studii Cercet. Biol. Ser. Zool.*, **20**, p. 397.
15. Miller, S. A. (1968). In: *Single-Cell Protein*, ed. R. I. Mateles and S. R. Tannenbaum, MIT Press, Cambridge, Mass., p. 79.
16. Fowden, L. A. (1954). *Ann. Bot.*, **18**, p. 257.
17. Combs, G. F. (1952). *Science*, **116**, p. 453.
18. Uesaka, S. (1965). *World Rev. Animal Protein*, **4**, p. 11.
19. Clement, G., Giddey, C. and Menzi, R. (1967). *J. Sci. Fd. Agric.*, **18**, p. 497.
20. Mauron, J. (1968). In: *Evaluation of Novel Protein Sources*, Proc. IBP Wenner-Gren Symposium, Stockholm, p. 211.
21. Harvey, D. (1970). *Tables of Amino Acids in Foods and Feeding Stuffs*, Commonwealth Agricultural Bureau, Farnham Royal, Bucks., England.
22. Lee, S. K., Fox, H. M., Kies, C. and Dam, R. (1967). *J. Nutr.*, **92**, p. 281.
23. Mitsuda, H., Yasumoto, K. and Nakamura, H. (1969). In: *Engineering of Unconventional Protein Production*, Chem. Eng. Progr. Symposium Ser., **65**(93).
24. Hundley, J. M., Ing, R. B. and Krauss, R. W. (1956). *Science*, **124**, p. 556.
25. Leveille, G. A., Sauberlich, H. E. and Shockley, J. W. (1962). *J. Nutr.*, **76**, p. 423.
26. Meffert, M.-E. and Pabst, W. (1963). *Nitritio et Dieta*, **5**, p. 235.
27. Cook, B. B., Lau, E. W. and Bailey, B. M. (1963). *J. Nutr.*, **81**, p. 243.
28. Prokes, B. and Bauer, B. (1970). In: *Ann. Rep. Algolab. Trebon for 1969*, ed. J. Necas and O. Lhotsky, Czechoslovak Acad. Sci., Trebon, p. 190.
29. Madiedo, G. and Sunde, M. L. (1964). *Poultry Sci.*, **43**, p. 1065.
30. Lautner, V. and Nevole, J. (1964). *Zivoc. Vyr.*, **9**, p. 513.

31. Lautner, V. (1965). *Biol. Chem. Vyz. Zvirat.*, **1**, p. 265.
32. Fink, H. and Herold, E. (1956). *Hoppe-Seylers Zeitschr.*, **305**, p. 183.
33. Koci, S. and Kociova, E. (1965). *Zivoc. Vyr.*, **10**, p. 733.
34. Hintz, H. F., Heitman, H., Weir, W. C., Torrell, D. T. and Meyer, J. H. (1966). *J. Animal Sci.*, **25**, p. 657.
35. Wimpenny, J. W. T. (1967). *Process Biochem.*, **2**(7), p. 41.
36. Tannenbaum, S. R. (1968). In *Single-Cell Protein*, ed. R. I. Mateles and S. R. Tannenbaum, MIT Press, Cambridge, Mass., p. 343.
37. Hedenskog, G., Enebo, L., Vlendova, J. and Prokes, B. (1969). *Biotechnol. Bioengng*, **11**, p. 37.
38. James, C. T., Coakley, W. T. and Hughes, D. E. (1972). *Biotechnol. Bioengng*, **14**, p. 33.
39. Garver, J. C. and Epstein, R. L. (1959). *Appl. Microbiol.*, **7**, p. 318.
40. Mitsuda, H. (1965). In: *First Int. Congr., Fd. Sci. and Technol.*, London, Vol. 2, ed. J. M. Leitch, Gordon & Breach, London and New York.
41. Westphal, O., Luderitz, O. and Bister, F. (1952). *Z. Naturforsch.*, **7b**, p. 148.
42. Lovern, J. A. (1966). In: *World Protein Resources*, ed. A. M. Altschul, American Chemical Society, Washington, DC, p. 37.
43. Northcote, D. H., Goulding, K. J. and Horne, R. W. (1958). *Biochem. J.*, **70**, p. 391.
44. Becker, M. J. and Shefner, A. M. (1963). Technical Documentary Report No. AMRL-TDR-63-115.
45. Tamiya, H. (1959). *Proc. Symposium on Algology*, New Delhi.
46. Chapman, D., Christensen, G., Pilgrim, A., Stern, J. and Zimmers, J. (1965). US Patent 3 197 309.
47. Courts, A. (1973). *Process Biochem.*, **8**(2), p. 31.
48. Boyer, R. A. (1954). US Patent 2 682 466.
49. Spoehr, H. A. and Milner, H. W. (1949). *Plant Physiol.*, **24**, p. 120.
50. Ketchum, B. H., Lillick, L. and Redfield, A. C. (1949). *J. Cell Comp. Physiol.*, **33**, p. 267.
51. Ludwig, H. F. and Oswald, W. J. (1952). *Sci. Monthly*, **74**, p. 3.
52. Gotaas, H. B., Golueke, C. G. and Oswald, W. J. (1964). Report Series 44, No. 5, Sanitary Engng. Res. Lab., University of California.
53. Tamiya, H. (1955). In: *Proc. World Symp. Appl. Solar Energy*, Stanford Res. Inst., p. 231.
54. Setlik, I., Sust, V. and Malek, I. (1970). *Algological Studies* (Trebon), **1**, p. 111.
55. Necas, J. and Lhotsky, O. (1969). *Ann. Rep. Algolab. Trebon for 1968*, Czechoslovak Acad. Sci., Trebon.
56. Pinevich, V. V. and Versilin, N. N. (1961). *Acad. Sci. USSR, Moscow*, p. 96.
57. Stagno d'Alcontres, G., Lamonica, G. and Conti, M. P. (1960). *Atti Soc. Peloritana*, **6**, p. 349.
58. Clement, G., Rebeller, M. and Trambouze, P. (1966). *Rapp. Inst. Fr. du Pétrole*, No. 13778.

59. Oswald, W. J. and Golueke, C. G. (1968). In: *Single-Cell Protein*, ed. R. I. Mateles and S. R. Tannenbaum, MIT Press, Cambridge, Mass., p. 271.
60. Fisher, A. W. (1955). *Proc. World Symp. Appl. Solar Energy*, Phoenix, Arizona, p. 243.
61. Myers, J. and Graham, J.-R. (1961). *Plant Physiol.*, **26**, p. 539.
62. Mayer, A. M., Zuri, U., Shain, Y. and Ginzburg, H. (1964). *Biotechnol. Bioengng*, **6**, p. 173.
63. Miller, R. L., Fredrickson, A. G., Brown, A. H. and Tsuchiya, H. M. (1964). *Ind. Eng. Chem. Des. Dev.*, **3**, p. 134.
64. Gummert, F., Meffert, M. E. and Stratmann, H. (1953). In: *Algal Culture from Laboratory to Pilot Plant*, ed. J. S. Burlew, Carnegie Institution of Washington, Publ. 600, p. 166.
65. Telkes, M. (1953). *Ind. Eng. Chem.*, **45**, p. 1108.
66. Golueke, C. G., Oswald, W. J. and Gee, H. K. (1968). *J. Water Pollution Control Fed.*, **37**, p. 471.

DISCUSSION

Wimpenny: Have you any comments about the use of *Spirulina maxima*? I gather it is quite digestible.

Priestley: Yes, it has been used as a material for feeding trials.

Thompson: Do your figures refer to kg of protein or cell mass?

Priestley: Protein.

Lalla: It is possible to decolorise *Spirulina maxima*. Work has been carried out successfully under UNIDO auspices by the Canadian Research and Productivity Council. The economics of this process depend on where the operation is sited.

Garrett: People regard algal culture, certainly in our climate, with great scepticism, but I should like to advance some reasons which suggest that we should redress this balance. Firstly, algal culture is one of very few potential methods for the treatment of farm effluent. Secondly, the feasibility of algal culture under temperate climatic conditions has not been precluded by any definitive study. Thirdly, the productivity of mixed algal/bacterial systems is very much higher than that of axenic systems upon which many predictions have been based. We believe that this is because the CO_2 produced by bacteria in mixed systems switches the path of carbon in the algae from the biosynthesis of glycolate, which would subsequently be excreted by the cells, through the Calvin cycle and into assimilates. Finally, the low values widely reported for digestibility of algal proteins may be attributable to the widespread occurrence in their cell walls of sporopollenin, one of the most resistant compounds known in the organic world. Future efforts should concentrate on those algae which have been shown to lack this wall component. Reasons such as these should redirect attention to waste-grown algae as protein sources.

9

Food from Waste Paper

D. E. BROWN and S. W. FITZPATRICK

Department of Chemical Engineering, University of Manchester Institute of Science and Technology, Manchester, England

ABSTRACT

Processed timber is used more and more in disposable communication and packaging materials. Until recently the disposal has been by incineration or dumping. Energy problems and conservation ideals have prompted the increased operation of recycle procedures. Fluctuations in the demand for recycled products and the accumulation of low-quality packaging materials will mean that some ultimate outlet must be available within the system.

The cellulosic content of paper and cardboard varies widely from the value associated with pure timber pulp, depending on the degree of additive and 'recycle' that it contains. The structure of the natural crystalline cellulose is that of a complex coiled polymer of 1–4 linked glucose molecules. These glucose molecules can be utilised if they can be made available by hydrolysis. The possibility of a sugar liquor industry similar to that operating on the saccharification of starch materials could be envisaged.

Two approaches to the utilisation of the glucose contained in cellulose are possible. Suitable micro-organisms containing enzymes which can degrade the cellulose can be cultured directly on the waste paper. The final outcome of such processes would be either animal feedstuffs or compost fertilisers. Alternatively the cellulose can be hydrolysed by either chemical or enzymic methods to yield a glucose liquor. This glucose liquor can then be used either as a fermentation energy source from which such products as proteins, organic acids and alcohol could be produced, or separated for direct consumption.

This paper will examine some of the problems involved in such a type of technology with particular emphasis on enzymic saccharification and fungal protein production.

INTRODUCTION

Cellulose occurs as the structural substance of most plants. It is thus present as a component in all agricultural products and arises as waste in such things as bagasse, straw, coffee grounds, etc. Timber processing generates a large amount of cellulosic waste during the

139

preparation of wooden items and pulp for the production of paper and cardboard. The possible ways in which these various cellulosic wastes might be utilised as energy sources have recently been reviewed.[1]

More specifically, large amounts of paper are used in modern communication and packaging materials. Some of this is collected and recycled into the manufacture of cardboard. Stockpiling of paper occurs within such recycle systems due to fluctuating demands within the industry. Natural decomposition of the stored paper can occur to the point where it becomes unsuitable for incorporation into cardboard, etc. Such material then becomes a discarded solid waste. Ultimately discarded paper and cardboard appears in large quantities in the municipal authorities' solid waste collections.

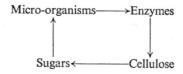

FIG. 1.   Microbial decomposition of cellulose.

Porteous[2] states that 50% of the Birmingham City refuse is composed of paper and cardboard. At the present time such solid wastes are dealt with either by dumping into land fills, composting or incinerating. With the rapid change of economic factors, other possible procedures for handling solid wastes are being considered. In particular the feasibility of utilising the cellulosic content of waste paper to produce food commodities is attracting considerable attention.

Processes have been described[1,2] in which the cellulose is hydrolysed to glucose liquor using acid digestion of the waste. Alternatively it is well known that natural decay processes attack cellulose wherever it occurs in isolation from the living plant. Biodeterioration of cotton and timber occurs continuously. Figure 1 shows a simple schematic arrangement of this natural process and this paper will be concerned with the possibility of exploiting the mechanisms operating within this cycle.

One possible method of exploitation is to operate the complete cycle. An appropriate micro-organism can be selected and cultured in a fermenter in a medium containing cellulose as the carbon source. The end-product of such a process is the biomass containing an appropriate quantity of protein together with any unconverted debris associated with the cellulose. Alternatively the cycle shown in Fig. 1 can be considered in separate pieces. If the enzymes produced by the micro-organisms can be separated from them, then they could be used in a controlled reaction to degrade cellulose to sugars. The sugar liquor could then be further used in a selected fashion as indicated in Fig. 2 in either food or fermentation processes.

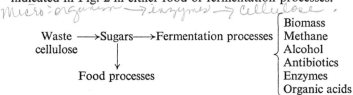

FIG. 2. Potential products from waste cellulose.

NATURE OF PAPER

Wood contains from 45% to 60% cellulose, 17% to 35% lignin (a complex polymer of phenylpropane units[3]), various hemicelluloses and inorganic ash content. Simple mechanical pulping does not change the overall analysis of the material and the resulting paper has poor strength and cannot retain a bright appearance. This type of paper is used for newspaper production. Digestion of the wood chip with alkaline sulphite solution at high temperature and pressure solubilises the lignin and hemicelluloses. The resulting fibres are high in cellulose content and form the starting material for most paper products. In the manufacture of specific paper requirements many additives are incorporated into the various formulations. Waxes and resins give strength and water resistance, clays give the opaque and smooth finish required for printing, and pigments and dyes are added for colouring.

Studies on the hydrolysis of waste paper have thus reported a value of 51% for the *Guardian* newspaper[4] using the method described by Updegraff.[5] This compares with a figure of approximately 70% available cellulose reported by Brandt *et al.*[6] for the *Boston Globe*. Products such as cardboard have the greatest proportions of the non-cellulosic additives such as clay. It is therefore doubtful whether a typical supply of waste paper material generated through separation processes on municipal refuse could exceed 50% cellulosic content.

STRUCTURE OF CELLULOSE

Cellulose is a large polymer molecule made up of D-glucose elements joined by β-1,4-glucosidic bonds[7] as indicated in Fig. 3. The extent of polymerisation varies from source to source but contains between 500 and 2000 elements in wood pulps.[8] The polymer molecule is a long thread-like structure but is variously folded and bundled and stabilised by hydrogen bonding.[9] The degree of order created within the bundle determines whether it is crystalline or amorphous cellulose. Cotton is made up of almost pure cellulose and is therefore of a relatively crystalline form termed α-cellulose. Wood on the other hand is a mixture of α-cellulose and β-cellulose which is ordered in structure and soluble in 17·5% NaOH.[1] In the natural state, the cellulose fibrils are associated with the other materials such as lignin and hemicelluloses in a complex heterogeneous structure.

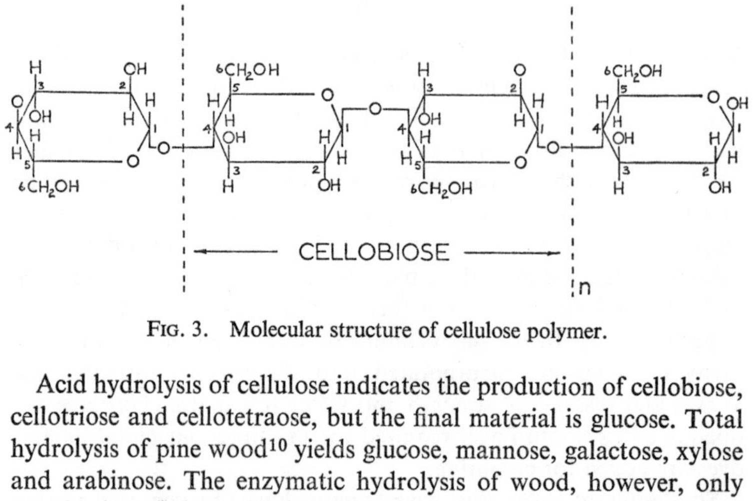

FIG. 3.   Molecular structure of cellulose polymer.

Acid hydrolysis of cellulose indicates the production of cellobiose, cellotriose and cellotetraose, but the final material is glucose. Total hydrolysis of pine wood[10] yields glucose, mannose, galactose, xylose and arabinose. The enzymatic hydrolysis of wood, however, only attacks the cellulose and the product is glucose with some cellobiose.

CELLULASE

In order that a given micro-organism might utilise natural crystalline cellulose it must produce extracellular enzymes which are able to hydrolyse the carbohydrate down to glucose. Enzymes involved in such a scheme are collectively referred to as cellulases. A simple schematic diagram of the levels of enzymatic attack is shown in Fig. 4. At the lowest level there is β-1,4-glucosidase or cellobiase which breaks cellobiose into two glucose molecules. The next group are the exo-β-1,4-glucanases which are able to hydrolyse to cellobiose and glucose any loose chain ends which may exist in the structure. Reduction of the polymer length is carried out by endo-β-1,4-glucanases which hydrolyse bonds in the middle of the polymer chain. The most difficult steps between reactive and crystalline cellulose have still not been elucidated. It has recently been proposed[11] that the opening-up of the crystalline structure might be assisted by an oxidative step which introduces carboxylic acid groups into the structure.

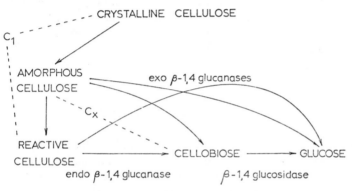

FIG. 4. Enzymatic degradation of crystalline cellulose.

The broad classification of the cellulase complex into C_1, C_x and β-1,4-glucosidase was originally made by Reese *et al.*[12] Existence of these subdivisions was based on the fact that many enzyme preparations were found to be capable of hydrolysing simple cellulosic materials such as carboxymethyl cellulose (CMC) but only a few have extra components (C_1) which could attack the native crystalline materials. These schemes have been reviewed elsewhere.[7,13–15]

The enzyme complexes produced by various micro-organisms have been purified and separated by chromatography and isoelectric focusing.[16–19] Many separate enzyme fractions can be identified in this way,[11] although it has been shown[11,20] that synergism exists between the components in that only certain combinations will give the same hydrolytic effects as the original enzyme complex. It has been observed[21,22] that end-product inhibition of the glucanases occurs as cellobiose accumulates, and this effect has been modelled.[23] Recently, von Hofsten[24] suggested that the synergism observed between components in a cellulase might simply be the repeated removal of inhibitory end-products in the degradative sequence.

The identification of the exact role of each species of enzyme within the cellulase may eventually be possible. However, specific practical applications will also always dictate that macroscopic procedures are available. Thus the assay methods for cellulase enzymes are usually based on the measurement of the quantity of reducing sugar (measured using the dinitrosalycylic acid method[25]) produced under standard conditions from a variety of substrates. Filter paper is considered to be a suitable test for C_1 type activity,[26] whereas many workers[27,28] have used carboxymethyl cellulose which will only indicate levels of C_x activity. A viscometric procedure is available[29] in the case of carboxymethyl cellulose. Other procedures using pretreated cottons have been described[19] and, most recently, tests have been carried out on the rate of release of a dye from dyed cellulosic material.[30]

CELLULASE BIOSYNTHESIS

At present only a few micro-organisms are known to synthesise the complete enzyme system capable of attacking native cellulose.[12] *Trichoderma viride* is particularly suitable in this context.[26] Medium and strain development have been carried out[31-33] and processes using strains QM6a,[34] QM9123[33] and QM9414[35] have been reported. In these processes, the micro-organism is grown on a medium containing relatively pure cellulose such as Solka Floc or Avicel as the carbohydrate source. The process usually extends over about 10 days.

Although *Trichoderma viride* can produce cellulase on a variety of carbon sources,[31] cellobiose is believed[32] to be the natural inducer. However, sophorose, a β-1,2 dimer of glucose found as an impurity in commercial glucose,[36] has been shown[37,38] to be a particularly good inducer.

Recently, Brown et al.[39] reported that acceptable yields of filter paper activity cellulase[26] could be produced by *Trichoderma viride* QM9123 in approximately 70 h. The medium was based on the recipe of Mandels and Weber[26] but replaced the cellulose with commercial glucose (containing traces of sophorose) and consisted of 5 kg/m³ glucose monohydrate, 2 kg/m³ KH_2PO_4, 1·4 kg/m³ $(NH_4)_2SO_4$,

0·3 kg/m³ MgSO₄.7H₂O, 0·4 kg/m³ CaCl₂.2H₂O, 0·3 kg/m³ urea and 1×10^{-3} m³/m³ of a trace elements mix.[26] The medium was sterilised at pH = 3·7 and then corrected to pH = 6·5 with sterile NaOH before inoculation. The fermenter was operated so that oxygen limitation did not occur and cellulase was formed if the uncontrolled pH passed through a minimum of approximately 2·8. A typical result of such a fermentation is shown in Fig. 5. It was further shown that cellulase could be produced in continuous culture using this strain and medium.

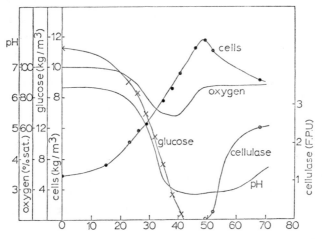

FIG. 5. Biosynthesis of cellulase by *Trichoderma viride* QM9123.

PRETREATMENT OF WASTE PAPER

The direct attack of the native material can be greatly assisted by a variety of pretreatment processes, although it is difficult to discuss their various merits outside the context of the saccharification reaction. However, whether the material is to be used directly for producing micro-organisms or to be hydrolysed to sugar liquor, the process is greatly speeded up by some form of modification.

Before any pretreatment process can be accomplished, it is necessary to reduce the paper to approximately 1 cm sized pieces in some kind of shredding machine. Mandels *et al.*[35] have used the Mighty Mac Mulcher and a JayBee disintegrator for this stage of the operation. Further reduction is variously reported using a pot ball mill,[35,40,41] Sweco Vibro Energy Mill,[6,35,40] fluid energy mill[35,40] and Waring blender.[42] The most comprehensive investigation of milling techniques is reported by Mandels et al.[35] The main conclusion is that the operation of the simple ball mill imparts an increased reactivity as well as producing interfacial area compared with the other techniques.

Heat treatment of the cellulose has been investigated[40,41] in some detail and the main conclusion is that it is beneficial. It is believed that the operation is an oxidative reaction[41] and results show that heat treatment before rather than after ball milling gives the best results. The conditions recommended are 200°C for 25 min and ideally should be carried out simultaneously with the ball-milling operation.

Various chemical processes can be applied to improve the accessibility of the cellulose. Simple wetting with water is a necessary step if the material has been dried at some stage. Swelling the fibres with mild acid or alkali treatment can be carried out. However, although such material is readily hydrolysed, only low concentrations (5% by weight) of the swollen fibres can be contained in the reactor. Complete removal of the lignin can be carried out by traditional paper-making processes. Boiling the waste paper for 1 h in 1% NaOH and then 1 h in dilute peracetic acid (1 part acetic anhydride and 5 parts 35% hydrogen peroxide) has been reported.[42] Other chemical pre-treatment processes have been examined and are described by Mandels et al.[35]

MICROBIAL GROWTH ON WASTE PAPER

Much work is proceeding on the upgrading of the protein content of many agricultural wastes such as straw, bagasse and sawdust by the direct growth of micro-organisms on the materials. Some of this work has recently been reviewed.[1,43] Clearly, the process is limited to those micro-organisms which produce a highly active cellulase system. However, it may be possible that processes containing mixed cultures will be found to be advantageous. Accessibility of the reaction sites to the enzymes is poor and so the process is relatively slow. Growth of the micro-organisms is limited by the rate at which glucose can be produced by the enzymic hydrolysis.

Very little of the effort has been specifically directed at the use of waste paper as the carbohydrate source. Updegraff[44] studied the growth of *Myrothecium verrucaria* on waste newspaper and obtained a production rate of 0·012 kg protein/m³ of fermenter volume/h. Figure 6 shows the time course of the growth of *Trichoderma viride* on the *Guardian* newspaper in a medium chosen to be optimum for the production of cellulase.[39] The solid material contained approximately 11% protein (1·8% nitrogen × 6·25) which if recovered at about 150 h would give a production rate of 0·005 kg protein/m³/h. It is most likely that this production rate could be increased to a similar value to that of Updegraff by the increase of medium constituents to the point at which oxygen limitation would occur.

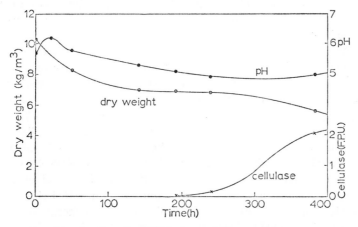

Fig. 6. Growth of *Trichoderma viride* on newspaper.

ENZYMATIC HYDROLYSIS OF WASTE PAPER

Cultures which contain cellulase in the medium can be easily separated by filtration, preferably on glass wool pads at laboratory scale. The resulting filtrate, adjusted to approximately pH = 5·0, can be stored for long periods at 2°C.[41] Such filtrates containing at least 1 unit of filter paper activity[26] are often used directly. A preservative, merthiolate at 0·005% by weight, is added[6,35] as a bacteriostat, which is very necessary during the saccharification process. If a solid product is required for prolonged storage or transportation, then the inorganic salts and the enzymes can be precipitated by addition to acetone under turbulent conditions. The ratio is 1 part filtrate to 2 parts acetone. The precipitate is dried at low temperature

(30°C) for 24 h and has been successfully stored without loss of activity for at least two years.[45] Solutions of the enzymes can be readily reproduced by dissolving the powder in water, and concentrations of solution with higher cellulase activity than the original fermentation filtrate can be produced although the activity/weight of powder relationship is non-linear. An alternative method of producing concentrated cellulase solutions is by ultrafiltration of the original liquor.[40] This will become the most convenient method as this technology develops.

The environmental conditions for maximum rate of hydrolysis have been examined and particularly for the *Trichoderma viride* cellulase a pH of 4·8 and a temperature of 50°C have been established.[41,46]

Most of the work reported to date on the saccharification of cellulose has involved the use of batch reactions and the substrates have been of a relatively pure form such as Solka Floc and filter paper. The effect of heat treatment at 100°C for 15 h on the batch hydrolysis of ball-milled *Guardian* cellulose is shown in Fig. 7. The waste paper was shredded in a hammer mill and then ball milled for 50 h until a mean size of 70 μm resulted. The cellulase solution was produced as described above using *Trichoderma viride* QM9123 and details are recorded elsewhere.[47] The theoretical yield of glucose would be $51\% \times 100 \times 1·11 = 56·5$ kg/m³ from an initial charge of 100 kg paper/m³. This process levelled off at a concentration of 12 kg/m³ presumably due to some end-product inhibition effect.[21,22] In the case of the untreated newspaper a reduction in the rate was also observed at approximately 6 kg glucose/m³. The heat treatment completely removed this phase of the process and resulted in a relatively high rate of hydrolysis until 8 kg/m³ had been produced. This effect of heating before ball milling has been observed previously using Solka Floc.[46]

A further important observation has been made[48] that the cellulase is relatively easily adsorbed on to cellulosic material. Provided unhydrolysed cellulose is present in the reactor, then the enzymes remain associated with the substrate. In practical terms this means that it is not necessary to remove sugar from the reactor using ultrafiltration techniques,[40] but that sugar liquor, free from enzymes, can be removed through a simple filter.[6] A test of this adsorption process on newspaper cellulose is shown in Fig. 8. Unheated ball-milled *Guardian* was charged to the reactor in a similar experiment to that

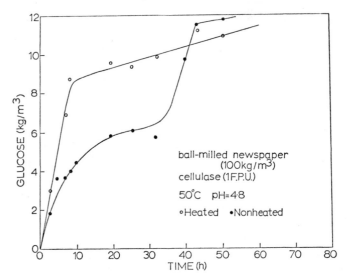

Fig. 7. The effect of heat treatment on the enzymatic hydrolysis of newspaper cellulose.

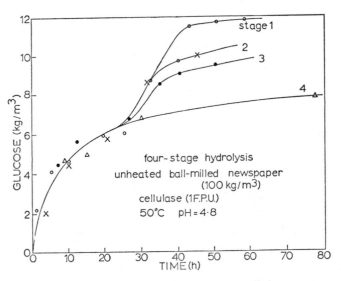

Fig. 8. Four-stage batch saccharification of ball-milled newspaper.

shown in Fig. 7. After 60 h the solids were filtered and re-suspended in buffer solution at pH = 4·8 and temperature 50°C. The cellulase which was adsorbed on the cellulose started the hydrolysis process over again in a similar manner to the first stage. Four actual periods of hydrolysis were conducted on the original charge of cellulose and enzyme. If the various concentrations of glucose are collected together, $12+10+9+7 = 38$ kg/m^3 would have been produced if one contact could have been possible. This represents 38/56·5 = 67% conversion of available cellulose, which is in good agreement with the observations made by Brandt et al.[6] The fact that the saccharification process followed the same path in each stage suggests that the inhibitory materials might be associated with the fibres at relatively high concentration compared with the bulk of the liquid. The addition of fresh buffer solution possibly washes out these materials from the fibres and allows the reaction to proceed as before.

Biomass could be produced from this sugar liquor to compare with the direct method. Assuming a yield coefficient of 0·5 kg cells/kg glucose and biomass of 35% protein, then the glucose from the four-stage process would give $38 \times 0·5 \times 0·35 = 6·7$ kg protein/m^3. The total time required would be 3 days for enzyme production + 8 days for hydrolysis + 1 day for biomass production = 12 days. The production rate on this basis would be $6·7/12 \times 24 = 0·023$ kg protein/m^3/h compared with 0·012 kg protein/m^3/h achieved by the direct route.[44] This comparison is a very crude analysis of the system but serves to indicate the potential. In reality some glucose would be needed to produce the cellulase. However, if biomass was the desired product, then the cells from the cellulase fermentation would be available. It is hoped that the enzyme will not be lost completely so that a further addition of cellulose without more enzyme would produce more glucose. Again, in reality both the hydrolysis and the biomass stages would operate continuously so that batch rates only give general indications about the relative rates of operation between different processes.

CONCLUSIONS

The various aspects of enzymatic hydrolysis of waste cellulose and the stages needed for a process route from waste paper to food products have been reviewed. A case has been presented for the operation of separate stages in order to obtain sugar liquor as a final or intermediate product. Calculations suggest that separate stages will give a higher production rate for protein compared with direct growth of biomass on the cellulose.

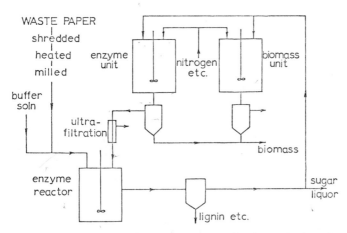

FIG. 9. Schematic arrangement of proposed plant for the production of sugar liquor or biomass from waste paper.

Figure 9 shows a schematic arrangement of a possible system for the utilisation of waste paper based on the discussion presented above. Various aspects of such a process will require further investigation before realistic economic analysis can be applied. Methods of pretreatment of the paper have not had very extensive investigation. Hydrolysis and adsorption mechanisms of the enzymes in the reactor have not been fully developed. In particular the survival of the enzyme in the process will be especially important. Further improvements in the biosynthesis of the enzymes might also be anticipated. The application of continuous operating techniques will also help to determine realistic rates of processing and perhaps solve some of the problems of the end-product inhibition.

In the current rapidly changing economic situation it is almost impossible to determine a realistic appraisal of the feasibility of such processes. In any event they will have to be associated with some centralised collecting operation and will involve large-scale process engineering installations.[49]

ACKNOWLEDGEMENT

One of the authors (S.W.F.) acknowledges the receipt of a research studentship from the Science Research Council during the period of work reported here.

REFERENCES

1. Reese, E. T., Mandels, M. and Weiss, A. H. (1972). *Adv. Biochem. Eng.*, **2**, p. 181.
2. Porteous, A. (1971). *New Scientist and Science J.*, 24 June, p. 736.
3. Forss, K. (1975). *Proc. Symp. on Enzymatic Hydrolysis of Cellulose*, Hotel Aulanko, Finland, March.
4. Halsted, D. J. (1973). Ph.D. Thesis, UMIST.
5. Updegraff, D. M. (1969). *Analytical Biochem.*, **32**, p. 420.
6. Brandt, D., Hontz, L. and Mandels, M. (1972). *A.I.Ch.E Symp. Series*, No. 133, **69**, p. 127.
7. Norkrans, B. (1967). *Adv. Appl. Microbiol.*, **9**, p. 91.
8. Kirk, R. E. and Othmer, D. F. (1964). *Encyclopaedia of Chemical Technology*, Vol. **4**, 2nd ed., Wiley, New York, p. 593.
9. Ranby, B. (1969). *Adv. in Chem. Series*, No. 95, p. 139.
10. Underkofler, L. A. and Hickey, R. J. (1954). In: *Industrial Fermentations*, Vol. **1**, Chemical Publ. Co., New York.
11. Eriksson, K.-E. (1975). *Proc. Symp. on Enzymatic Hydrolysis of Cellulose*, Hotel Aulanko, Finland, March.
12. Reese, E. T., Siu, R. G. H. and Levinson, H. S. (1950). *J. Bacteriol.*, **59**, p. 485.
13. Jurasek, L., Colvin, J. R. and Whitaker, D. R. (1967). *Adv. Appl. Microbiol.*, **9**, p. 131.
14. Reese, E. T. and Mandels, M. (1973). In: *Advances in Enzymic Hydrolysis of Celluloses and Related Materials*, ed. E. T. Reese, Pergamon Press, Oxford.
15. Pathak, A. N. and Ghose, T. K. (1973). *Process Biochem.*, **8**(4), p. 35; **8**(5), p. 20.
16. Gilligan, W. and Reese, E. T. (1954). *Can. J. Microbiol.*, **1**, p. 90.
17. Selby, K. and Maitland, C. C. (1965). *Biochem. J.*, **94**, p. 578.
18. Selby, K. and Maitland, C. C. (1967). *Biochem. J.*, **104**, p. 716.
19. Wood, T. M. and McCrae, S. I. (1972). *Biochem J.*, **128**, p. 1183.
20. Wood, T. M. (1975). *Proc. Symp. on Enzymatic Hydrolysis of Cellulose*, Hotel Aulanko, Finland, March.
21. Reese, E. T., Gilligan, W. and Norkrans, B. (1952). *Physiologia Plantarum*, **5**, p. 379.
22. Mandels, M. and Reese, E. T. (1965). *Ann. Rev. Phytopath.*, **3**, p. 85.
23. Ghose, T. K. and Das, K. (1971). *Adv. Biochem. Eng.*, **1**, p. 55.
24. von Hofsten, B. (1975). *Proc. Symp. on Enzymatic Hydrolysis of Cellulose*, Hotel Aulanko, Finland, March.

25. Sumner, J. B. and Somers, G. F. (1944). In: *Laboratory Experiments in Biological Chemistry*, Academic Press, New York.
26. Mandels, M. and Weber, J. (1969). *Adv. in Chem. Series*, No. 95, p. 391.
27. Horton, J. C. and Keen, N. T. (1966). *Can. J. Microbiol.*, **12**(2), p. 209.
28. Hulme, M. A. and Stranks, D. W. (1970). *Nature*, **226**, p. 469.
29. Almin, K. E. and Eriksson, K.-E. (1967). *Biochim. Biophys. Acta*, **139**, p. 238.
30. Linko, M. (1975). *Proc. Symp. on Enzymatic Hydrolysis of Cellulose*, Hotel Aulanko, Finland, March.
31. Mandels, M. and Reese, E. T. (1957). *J. Bacteriol.*, **73**, p. 269.
32. Mandels, M. and Reese, E. T. (1960). *J. Bacteriol.*, **79**, p. 816.
33. Mandels, M., Weber, J. and Parizek, R. (1971). *Appl. Microbiol.*, **21**, p. 152.
34. Ghose, T. K. (1969). *Biotechnol. and Bioeng.*, **11**, p. 239.
35. Mandels, M., Hontz, L. and Nystrom, J. (1974). *Biotechnol. and Bioeng.*, **16**, p. 1471.
36. Mandels, M. and Reese, E. T. (1959). *Biochem. and Biophys. Res. Commun.*, **1**, p. 338.
37. Mandels, M., Parrish, F. W. and Reese, E. T. (1962). *J. Bacteriol.*, **83**, p. 400.
38. Yamane, K., Suzuki, H., Hirotani, M., Ozawa, H. and Nisizawa, K. (1970). *J. Biochem.*, **67**(1), p. 9.
39. Brown, D. E., Halsted, D. J. and Howard, P. (1975). *Proc. Symp. on Enzymatic Hydrolysis of Cellulose*, Hotel Aulanko, Finland, March.
40. Ghose, T. K. and Kostick, J. A. (1970). *Biotechnol. and Bioeng.*, **12**, p. 921.
41. Ghose, T. K. (1969). *Biotechnol. and Bioeng.*, **11**, p. 239.
42. Toyama, N. and Ogawa, K. (1972). *Proc. 4th IFS: Ferm. Technol. Today*, p. 743.
43. Bellamy, W. D. (1974). *Biotechnol. and Bioeng.*, **16**, p. 869.
44. Updegraff, D. M. (1971). *Biotechnol. and Bioeng.*, **13**, p. 77.
45. Waliuzzaman, M. (1975). Ph.D. Thesis, UMIST.
46. Ghose, T. K. and Kostick, J. A. (1969). *Adv. in Chem. Series*, No. 95, p. 415.
47. Fitzpatrick, S. W. (1974). M.Sc. Dissertation, UMIST.
48. Mandels, M., Kostick, J. and Parizek, R. (1971). *J. Polymer Sci., C.*, **36**, p. 445.
49. Das, K. and Ghose, T. K. (1973). *J. Appl. Chem. Biotechnol.*, **23**, p. 829.

DISCUSSION

Wimpenny: You said you could get 45 units of sugar from 100 units of cellulose. I wonder what are the chances of a cellulase system producing the maximum 100% yield of sugar from cellulose?

Brown: I think they are very good. I'm not sure at this stage why these particular experiments—which were experiments carried out at a very early stage in our work—gave these sort of figures. They are the sort of figures which other people have observed when handling the natural crystalline material. Possibly it is something which is a genuine problem or it may just be the inefficiencies of our current experimental techniques. The ultimate potential might be very much higher, round about the nineties.

Selby: You talked about the cellulose system and quite interestingly about the point that the cellulase will go with the substrate. In the days when I was working on this, one of the characteristic points of the cellulose system was the synergism between what we then used to call C_1 and C_x. It seems to me that you didn't actually mention the synergistic effect, but presumably that has not been discarded, because it was a very clearly demonstrable fact.

Brown: No, and I do talk about it in my paper.

Selby: What I wanted to comment on was that if there is synergism, then to get an efficient carryover of enzymes substantive to substrate, which you are suggesting can be done, this is a means of using enzymes economically and avoiding metabolite repression. To get these effects you need to have these components carried over in proportion.

Brown: Some sort of refining process does go on.

Selby: To go back to the alternative, there is a point here which could be followed up.

Brown: Yes. It has also been suggested that the synergistic effect is possibly an interaction with the product inhibition, and that what is happening is that at any one instance one enzyme is producing inhibitor which sits there in the way, but if there is another enzyme which can immediately remove it then what you see is the overall effect. It is in fact a mutual operation keeping the product inhibition from building up. I agree with you that there is quite a lot of work going to be needed in this particular area before the reactor can be fully economically designed. I think I would make a plea as well that it should be carried out in continuous flow reactors because I think this is the only place where you get accurate steady-state information. It is a little bit like the microbiological problem. You can apparently do a lot of interesting experiments in shake flasks but you move forward far quicker in fact if you can get a continuous flow process to operate. The rates you measure are steady-state phenomena and you can make a better assessment of what has really happened.

Wood: In many cases the yields of depolymerising enzymes are greater in static culture. What is the best way this can be overcome?

Brown: You mean surface culture? This is just a matter of finding out the nutrient limitation you are undergoing. Very often the pH profile or the nutrient limitation which is required to produce a particular product happens to appear rather fortunately on your surface culture. I think that in order to make large quantities it has been demonstrated in such tradi-tional industries as the antibiotic industry that you must go forward into submerged culture for production on a large scale. It happens that a microbiologist will unravel what he observes on his surface culture and is easily able to translate it into measurable parameters.

Wood: But is it not the case that cellulase production is less in submerged culture?

Brown: I am quite sure that the micro-organisms don't know they are hanging around on cellulose in terms of their biochemistry because it is going to be a much smaller molecule which passes through their cell wall and it is up to us to find out what these molecules are. Then we can grow micro-organisms, as I have demonstrated with the experiments we did in connection with glucose, in media with no cellulose present and the micro-organism makes the same range of products.

Pace: As the economics of cellulose utilisation processes could well be governed by the pretreatment operation, which pretreatment do you think is the best in economic terms?

Brown: From what has been done to date it would seem that a heat treatment before ball milling seems to be the accepted pretreatment procedure which is going to be absolutely minimal for such waste material as sawdust and paper.

Pace: I understand in the process that over half the cost lies in ball milling.

Brown: Yes, I'm afraid it does—this is one of the problems in the economics, that ball milling does seem to give not only an increase in surface area which is obviously necessary, but it does something to the availability of the cellulosic polymer which is not found in other size reduction techniques.

10

Cultivation of a Thermotolerant Basidiomycete on Various Carbohydrates

B. VON HOFSTEN

*Institute of Biochemistry, University of Uppsala,
Uppsala, Sweden*

ABSTRACT

Only a few plant carbohydrates can be degraded in the stomachs of man and other monogastric mammals. In contrast, many of the fungi which cause wood decay or live in soil can grow on complex plant materials. This can be utilised for conversion of various agricultural products and wastes into fungal mycelia containing valuable protein, provided a source of nitrogen is added. Special demands must be made upon fungi considered for food production, and many mycelia grow too slowly to make large-scale cultivation feasible. The cell material must not only be nutritious and harmless, but it should preferably be palatable and have a good structure. Several basidiomycetes appear to fulfil at least some of these requirements, but they are often difficult to grow in submerged culture. A fungus has now been cultivated in stirred fermenters of up to 1000 litre capacity, and the results are encouraging. The fungus used causes white-rot decay in wood, and its perfect state has been classified as Phanerochaete chrysosporium. *It grows at temperatures of up to 40°C and can be cultivated on various cereal flours, brans and cellulose-containing products. The protein content of the harvested biomass varies considerably depending upon growth conditions, but it has been possible to maintain serial cultures of dispersed mycelia which contain up to 40% protein of a favourable composition. The cell material is easy to filter off and has a white colour and a weak mushroom flavour. It is necessary to optimise the medium composition and cultivation conditions for each type of substrate in order to obtain fungal biomass of good quality and to attain good utilisation of all ingredients in the medium. It is possible to recover enzymes and other compounds present in the culture filtrates.*

INTRODUCTION

Nordic mythology tells us that the Viking warriors, who had been killed in battle and then gone to the heavenly abode of Valhalla, had a pig called Saerimner. This was a marvellous beast because it was slaughtered and eaten every night and then resurrected the following morning. The myth does not say on what the pig was fed, but I

156

suppose there were agricultural and household wastes even in Valhalla.

Modern man keeps billions of pigs and chickens under factory-like conditions, and they are given a carefully balanced diet containing large amounts of valuable protein of which the larger part is wasted when it is converted to meat. This situation is not satisfactory in a world where millions of people are starving, and every effort should be made to use our food resources more efficiently. Let us therefore develop a modern version of the Viking magic by growing cultures of nutritious fungi on agricultural products. It would then be possible to obtain a continuous supply of large amounts of a meat-like product rich in protein, vitamins and minerals. Something of this philosophy is behind our project on the cultivation of higher fungi, and I sometimes like to call it 'Project Saerimner'.

CHOICE OF SUITABLE FUNGI FOR FOOD PRODUCTION

Higher fungi have the advantage over other unconventional foods that fruiting bodies of many species are widely consumed in many countries. The cultivated mushroom is not only nutritious but considered a delicacy, and large quantities of other fungi are grown and highly appreciated in oriental countries.

Many basidiomycetes can be grown in submerged liquid culture to give mycelia with mild taste and attractive texture, but yields are often low and few higher fungi grow at temperatures above 30°C.[1] A reason for poor growth under laboratory conditions is that many of the edible fungi normally form mycorrhizal associations with tree roots and therefore have rather special nutritional requirements.

A group of basidiomycetes capable of degrading a wide variety of polysaccharides is that which causes white-rot decay of wood. These fungi play an important role in the natural decomposition of plant litter, and they are usually much easier to grow in mycelial culture than are the mycorrhizal fungi. A well-known group of fungi which usually produces typical white-rot decay is the Polyporaceae family, and a strain of the common species *Polyporus squamosus* is used for food production in Bulgaria. Professor A. K. Torev of the Georgi Dimitrov Agricultural Academy, Plovdiv, has described this work which involves the current construction of a factory for an annual production of several thousand tons of mycelia. His book[2] is written in Bulgarian and is therefore, unfortunately, not yet widely known.

We have studied a white-rot fungus which has the advantage of growing at temperatures of up to 40°C. The strain with which we are working was isolated in Sweden from a pile of wood chips, but it appears to have a very wide geographical distribution. Other strains have been found in such exotic places as deserts in Arizona, vineyards in the Alma Ata region and various places in Indonesia. The exact systematic position of the fungus is still not quite certain, but it is clearly a basidiomycete.[3] We use the name *Sporotrichum pulverulentum* for its imperfect stage, which is the form in which we grow it. Burdsall and Eslyn[4] have recently given the perfect stage the name *Phanerochaete chrysosporium* (n. sp.) of the Corticiaceae family. Fruiting bodies of several related fungi are commonly eaten, and there is no evidence that these fungi form any kind of mycotoxin.

Detailed toxicological tests must of course be carried out to prove that *S. pulverulentum* mycelia are free of toxic and anti-nutritional compounds and we have initiated such studies. We have also started a screening programme in which we shall test various other thermotolerant fungi for growth on agricultural wastes, and I believe that many interesting basidiomycetes may be found in tropical countries.

SUBSTRATES FOR CULTIVATION OF FUNGI

S. pulverulentum has a wide enzymic adaptability, and many types of plant materials can be converted to fungal mycelia provided a nitrogen source is added.[5] I have grouped substrates which we have tried into three categories, but it is impossible to draw distinct borderlines between them:

(a) *High-quality substrates suitable for production of edible mycelia:*
Starch and sugar-containing hydrolysates.
Flours of cereals and other seeds.
Starchy roots and tubers.
Cheese whey, molasses, etc.

(b) *By-products of agriculture and industry which may need pre-treatment to support rapid fungal growth yielding either food or feed products:*
Brans and other seed coat materials.
Vegetable and fruit residues including maize cobs, press cakes, peels, etc.

(c) *Materials which are now used inefficiently or wasted but which could be upgraded to animal feed or possibly also to food products:*
Straw, bagasse, husks, etc.
Waste fibres from forest products and other industries.

The maximum yield of protein which can be obtained through cultivation of fungi on carbohydrates and an inorganic nitrogen source is 25–30% calculated on the amount of degraded carbohydrate.[6] This value may be apparently increased if cultures are grown in media containing amino acids. *S. pulverulentum* is proteolytic and low-quality proteins can therefore be upgraded to fungal protein of high biological value. The fungus requires thiamine for growth, but this vitamin and other factors which stimulate growth are usually present in flours and similar substrates. The composition of the medium must of course be balanced for each type of substrate to give as rapid growth and high yields as possible.

There is a loss in available food energy when cereals and similar substrates are converted to mycelia. Such a decrease in caloric content is only acceptable if it is balanced by a worthwhile increase in protein quality. What is acceptable will vary from region to region depending on the food production, distribution and consumption pattern.

Rapidly growing mycelia have a nitrogen content of 7–8%, whereas older cells or those growing under nutrient-limited conditions are highly vacuolated and may contain as little as 1–3% N. It is not possible to convert values on nitrogen content to protein by multiplying by the conventional factor of 6·25, because the fungal cell walls contain non-protein nitrogen. The cell walls of *S. pulverulentum* are very thin, but their proportion of the total cell material increases considerably in ageing cultures. The only safe way of analysing the true protein content of mycelia is therefore to carry out amino acid determinations, and we have found that the protein content varies between 25% and 40% depending on how cultures have been grown. The proportion of essential amino acids in the fungal protein varies somewhat with the culture conditions. Table 1 shows the pattern obtained on a biomass grown on barley flour, and it compares very favourably with the new FAO/WHO provisional amino acid scoring pattern.[7] The RNA content correlates with the growth rate and we have found values between 2·5% and 3·5%.

The potential for cultivation of fungal mycelia on starch-rich cereals as well as roots and tubers is enormous. A far too large proportion of these products is now utilised at low efficiency for meat production.

Brans and rice polishings are particularly interesting substrates for *S. pulverulentum* cultures because they are regularly available in very large quantities and growth is rapid on small particles.

TABLE 1
Essential amino acids in S. pulverulentum *protein*

| | mg amino acid/g protein | |
	S. pulverulentum	FAO/WHO pattern
Isoleucine	39	40
Leucine	69	70
Lysine	62	55
Phenylalanine ⎫ Tyrosine ⎭	96	60
Cystine ⎫ Methionine ⎭	44	35
Threonine	49	40
Tryptophan	15	10
Valine	50	50

Enormous quantities of more fibrous seed residues such as husks and extracted press cakes are available and we have demonstrated that the fungus can grow on such materials. It remains to be seen whether fungal cultures can compete with those naturally occurring in ruminants.

S. pulverulentum forms a range of enzymes which hydrolyse cellulose and hemicellulose, and the fungus can even degrade lignified wood fibres. It can therefore be used to upgrade waste fibres from the pulp and paper industries into a biomass which has potential application as animal feed.[8] The problem is that growth is rather slow on such fibres, and the product will contain little protein. Structural polysaccharides are well protected against degradation, and mechanical and/or chemical pretreatment will generally be necessary before fibrous substrates can be used as substrates for fungi, thus affecting the economic viability of the process. I am personally of the opinion that fibrous plant materials in most cases are more suitable for other industrial processes rather than production of protein. I have recently discussed the complex interaction between different enzymes which takes place in the microbial degradation of highly ordered polysaccharides such as cellulose, and several other authors have described current projects on the utilisation of cellulosic wastes in the proceedings from a symposium held in Aulanko, Finland, early in 1975.[9]

CULTIVATION TECHNOLOGY

The enzymic adaptability of *S. pulverulentum* indicates that it may be utilised in several protein-producing processes embracing a range of technological levels. The objective will in each case be to maximise the difference between the value added to the substrate and the costs incurred in the processing. The latter include development and capital charges (related to the complexity of the chosen process), energy input, labour cost and charges related to environmental control. The availability of raw materials and local patterns of food consumption will undoubtedly be major factors affecting the choice of process, as will be the possibility of marketing possible by-products of the cultivation.

In our development work we have cultivated the fungus on simple and complex substrates in shake flasks, air-lift fermenters and batch-stirred fermenters. We have also investigated draw-and-fill operations including replacement of 90% of the culture of each of twelve cycles. The fungus grows at temperatures of up to 40°C, and the doubling time on starchy materials in a rich medium is about 4 h at 35°C. A 2% suspension of barley flour can be completely degraded in 1–2 days depending on the inoculum size, yielding approximately 10 g of dry mycelium containing at least 35% true protein. Under pH control the cultures grow well at maintained pH values down to 4. We are at present studying growth at higher substrate concentrations and the effect of different nitrogen sources and growth factors on the yield and composition of the biomass. The main problem in this work is the high viscosity of mycelial cultures containing more than 2% dry matter, and it is also difficult to achieve a complete utilisation of the medium ingredients if the substrate concentration becomes too high.

Cultivation on valuable substrates such as flours would be appropriate for large-scale production of a high-quality food product for which it would probably be required to develop fed-batch or continuous fermenter systems. The technological advantages of the latter have been discussed elsewhere[10] as well as some of the engineering problems. For example, pretreatment of substrates may be necessary to avoid problems in the sterilisation. The large volume of process water required would also dictate a need for recycling of the aqueous streams.

A general problem in fungal cultivations is to maintain adequate mixing and oxygen transfer due to the high viscosity of mycelial suspensions. Furthermore, shearing conditions must be related to the desired morphology of the organism without affecting the metabolism. Homogeneous mycelial suspensions of *S. pulverulentum* have been maintained in stirred fermenters, whereas a pellet type of growth was obtained in air-lift fermenters.

Growth on plant materials containing structural polysaccharides is a complex process in which the enzymic hydrolysis may be rate-limiting rather than the biosynthetic capacity of the fungus. *S. pulverulentum*, when grown on suspensions of fine wheat and rice

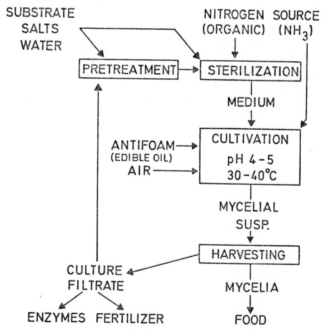

FIG. 1.　Flowsheet for production of fungal biomass.

bran and polishings, gave high yields of fungal biomass with comparable protein contents to those obtained on flours. However, complete degradation of such substrates requires cultivation times of 2–3 days unless they are pretreated, and the cost of such pretreatment must be balanced against the value of the product.

Our current development of *S. pulverulentum* cultivation is along the lines of a process as suggested in Fig. 1. The technology chosen should be appropriate to availability of raw materials and the likely scale of operation. Production of a food grade product is likely to be on a large scale (10^4–10^5 tons per annum) due to high capital and development costs. Small-scale batch processes may be more suitable where there is a greater degree of variability and/or seasonality in raw materials. We are interested in establishing co-operation with other research groups interested in the development work.

USE OF MYCELIA AND BY-PRODUCTS OF CULTIVATION

No product is food until it is eaten, and many ambitious projects on novel protein sources will probably never leave the laboratory stage. The need for extensive nutritional and toxicological testing programmes at an early stage of the development work is self-evident, but the increasing complexity and cost of the very large-scale animal tests required[11] is a matter of serious concern. The fact that people eat mushrooms and probably would like the taste and physical appearance of industrially cultivated mycelia gives us reason for optimism about our project, but we are certainly conscious of the long road to acceptability.

Harvesting of mycelial cultures is usually very simple, and the *S. pulverulentum* biomass is easy to filter off from the culture liquid, which is usually clear and has a pleasant smell reminiscent of apples. The whitish filter cake has a distinct mushroom odour and a mild taste, and the product may either be used directly or stored frozen. The mycelial mass can be dried by various conventional methods, and we are at present testing its food technological properties. Torev[2] has given a number of recipes of foods in which mycelia have been introduced in Bulgaria, and a 'mushroom sausage' has periodically been sold and well accepted on the open market.

Enzymes occurring in the filtrates of fungal cultures may be used in pretreatment of substrates or find application in other processes. An α-amylase is for example present after growth of *S. pulverulentum* on flours, and we have recovered this enzyme using either a hydrophobic gel with high capacity or precipitation with tannin. Other enzymes are also found in cultures grown on brans and similar materials containing cellulose and hemicellulose, and it should be worthwhile to recover them.

Torev[2] has shown that higher fungi have stimulating effects on the root growth of higher plants. While this effect was first observed with extracts of fungal mycelia and fruiting bodies, it has since been demonstrated (Torev, personal communication) that filtrates of basidiomycete cultures show similar properties even when highly diluted. Up to 30% increases in yields of tomatoes and other crops have been demonstrated after treatment with culture filtrates under conditions where regular amounts of normal fertilisers were applied. This aspect, which may have an important effect on the economics of basidiomycete cultivation, is presently being studied also in the case of *S. pulverulentum*.

CONCLUSIONS

Conversion of starch-rich products to edible mycoprotein affords a method of improving present utilisation of agricultural resources. The high biological efficiency of fungal cultures may be illustrated by comparison with the protein yield when barley is used as pig feed. 1 kg of barley flour supplemented with an inorganic nitrogen source (or possibly a waste containing nitrogen) would give about 500 g (dry weight) of meat-like mycelium containing 150–200 g of high-quality protein. In contrast, the same amount of barley used as pig feed without supplementation would yield only 15–20 g of meat protein. Supplementation would of course increase this figure, but the supplement would have to be high-grade protein.

A further improvement in agricultural efficiency is obtained if fungi are used to convert by-products which are at present wasted or at best utilised at low efficiency. Brans and other cereal, vegetable and fruit residues fall within this category, and we have demonstrated that such material can be upgraded through cultivation of *S. pulverulentum*.

Higher fungi have the advantage of being widely accepted as foodstuff. The production of fungal mycelia by industrial fermentation gives the further advantage of producing a structured material which may be fabricated to give alternative food forms.

International co-operation between industrialised and developing countries is not only desirable but absolutely necessary if we are to combat malnutrition by the development of new food and feed products. The Protein-Calorie Advisory Group of the United Nations plays a most important role in this work, but there is also a great need for establishing an internationally recognised organisation which could carry out independent nutritional testing and practical evaluation programmes.

ACKNOWLEDGEMENT

This work has been supported by grants from the Swedish National Board for Technical Development.

REFERENCES

1. Worgan, J. T. (1968). *Progr. Ind. Microbiol.*, **8**, p. 74.
2. Torev, A. K. (1973). *An Industrial Technology for Production of Higher Fungi Mycelium*, Publ. House of the Bulgarian Acad. Sci., Sofia.
3. von Hofsten, B. and von Hofsten, A. (1974). *Appl. Microbiol.*, **27**, p. 1142.
4. Burdsall, H. H. Jr. and Eslyn, W. E. (1975). *Mycotaxon* (in press).
5. von Hofsten, B. and Rydén, A. L. (1975). *Biotech. Bioeng.* (in press).
6. Worgan, J. T. (1973). In: *The Biological Efficiency of Protein Production*, ed. J. G. W. Jones, Cambridge University Press, p. 339.
7. FAO/WHO Ad Hoc Expert Committee (1973). In: *Energy and Protein Requirements*, WHO Technical Report Series No. 522, Geneva.
8. Eriksson, K. E. and Larsson, K. (1975). *Biotech. Bioeng.*, **17**, p. 327.
9. von Hofsten, B. (1975). In: *Symposium on Enzymatic Hydrolysis of Cellulose*, ed. M. Bailey, T.-M. Enari and M. Linko, SITRA, Helsinki.
10. Spicer, A. (1971). *Trop. Sci.*, **13**, p. 239.
11. Protein Advisory Group (1974). *PAG Bulletin*, **4**(3), United Nations, New York.

DISCUSSION

Zadrazil: In your paper you discussed only one possibility from higher fungi, the production of food, but in Japanese research the other possibility of mycelium production for pharmacological properties has been studied, and this could be one other point for future research.

von Hofsten: I agree. I will admit that we do not hope to find many pharmacologically active compounds in our mycelium.

Wood: Do you think this product is likely to be acceptable? The current UK consumption of mushrooms is only 2–3 lb per capita per year.

von Hofsten: It is higher in other countries. There is a fair amount of consumption in mushroom soups, of course, and such composite foods. We mix our product with ordinary ingredients and we can make mushroom burgers, mushroom sauces or mushroom pizzas. There is a lot more that can be done on this. People from the Rank group have worked many years on this.

Seal: Have you done work on the lignin-utilising ability of the basidiomycete and if so have you determined whether the basidiomycete uses up cellulose first and then goes on to the lignin or does it use it currently with the cellulose?

von Hofsten: Very briefly there is an interesting link between cellulose degradation and lignin degradation in this white-rot fungus, and the presence of lignin in wood enhances the production of cellulases. This is a clear link, but after all, the growth is slow on lignified wood fibres.

Satchell: Can you tell us something about how the cost and productivity of mycelium production compares with that of the existing mushroom industry?

von Hofsten: I wish I could, but not at this stage. I suppose again the Rank people have much more information on this and have done a more careful economic balance sheet. Perhaps Dr Edelman could help us with something.

Edelman: We haven't actually done any significant comparison between a process of this sort and the mushroom industry, because mushrooms are produced for a completely different purpose. As far as we are concerned, we are producing material which we hope will replace meat, or will extend meat, which of course mushrooms do not; mushrooms are sold on the basis of high-quality vegetable delicacy and people consume them in very small amounts. As far as weight is concerned they do of course have a large volume, so the two areas are quite different from each other, and one has nothing to do with the other. The protein content of mushrooms also is quite low. Of the normal mushroom that you buy, in a ¼ lb of mushrooms it is probably less than 20% of the total dry weight, whereas, as we have heard, the protein content of this material is very much higher than that, and becomes significant in the diet.

von Hofsten: I suppose we should be very happy to have a similar market to that of the present mushroom-growing industry.

Edelman: The UK market is 2 lb per head per year consumption.

11

Production of Symba-Yeast from Potato Wastes

H. Skogman

AB Sorigona, Staffanstorp, Sweden

ABSTRACT

This paper describes a method permitting utilisation of waste starch. It is known as the 'Symba process', and has been in full-scale operation for almost two seasons.

The Symba process converts starch and other carbohydrates into Candida *or* Torula *yeast by the symbiotic growth of two yeasts,* Endomycopsis fibuliger *and* Candida utilis, *on these materials.*

Endomycopsis *produces the amylases which are needed to break down the starch to sugars.* Candida utilis, *being unable to feed on starch, quickly 'steals' the sugar as soon as it is formed, thereby growing and producing a yeast product which consists mainly of* Candida utilis. *Thus, although both yeasts grow simultaneously, more than 90% by weight of the Symba yeast is* Candida utilis, *which is favourable with regard to the final composition. By this symbiotic action most of the carbohydrates in the starchy waste streams are utilised in one step, avoiding a costly prestep of hydrolysis by either acid or enzyme.*

The first commercial Symba plant was built in Sweden at a factory producing potato products—mostly potato granules and 'French fries'. Waste streams, as well as solid wastes from the factory, are treated in the plant to produce Symba yeast. At the same time, the waste streams are purified to 90%. The plant will be described. Applications and conditions which must be fulfilled for such waste treatment to be feasible will also be discussed.

INTRODUCTION

In processing potatoes, wheat, tapioca, maize or other raw materials containing starch, considerable amounts of valuable substances are unavoidably lost into the waste streams. Solid wastes, when local conditions are favourable, can be utilised for cattle feed, etc. The liquid waste streams, however, represent a threat to the purity of rivers and lakes, since no such use can be found for them. Ensuing costs of treatment for such waste streams have risen enormously.

H. Skogman

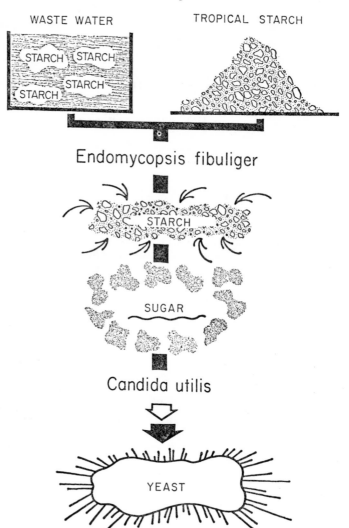

FIG. 1. Symba process.

Processes for concentrating such streams for utilising waste materials have become feasible.

I shall describe a method called the Symba process by which these wastes are converted into high-quality food yeast. The process was developed by the Swedish Sugar Company and Chemap Co. in

Switzerland, and has been in successful full-scale operation in Sweden for two years.

PROCESS DESCRIPTION

Biological processes are commonly used to clean different waste waters. Conventional processes, activated sludge, biofilters, etc., use random mixtures of micro-organisms to consume the organic waste material, which is partly converted into biological sludge. Owing to the undefined nature of this sludge eventual uses of it are limited to low-qualified ones: manure, soil conditioner, etc. For cleaning specific wastes, particularly those containing high concentrations of sugars, *e.g.* whey, spent sulphite liquors, etc., yeasts have been used in more or less pure culture to give feed and food products. The preferred yeasts of species *Candida* and *Saccharomyces* have, however, no ability to produce the enzymes needed to utilise starch. In the Symba process this is made possible by the symbiotic culture of two yeasts, *Endomycopsis fibuliger* and *Candida utilis*, on the starch waste (Fig. 1).

Endomycopsis produces the amylases which are needed to break down the starch to sugars. *Candida utilis*, being a fast-growing organism, 'steals' the sugar as soon as it is formed, thereby growing and producing a product which consists mainly of *Candida utilis*. The extremely high amylase productivity of the *Endomycopsis* strain used limits the need of this yeast to less than 4% by weight in the finished product, which is favourable with regard to the composition of the two yeasts. By this symbiotic culture most of the carbohydrates and many other substances, organic acids, proteins, amino acids. etc., are utilised in one step, avoiding a costly prestep of hydrolysis, BOD of the waste water is thereby reduced by 90%.

PLANT DESCRIPTION

The first commercial Symba plant was built in Sweden two years ago at a factory producing potato products—mostly potato granules and French fries. Waste waters as well as solid wastes are treated in the Symba plant. Figure 2 shows the water system of the potato

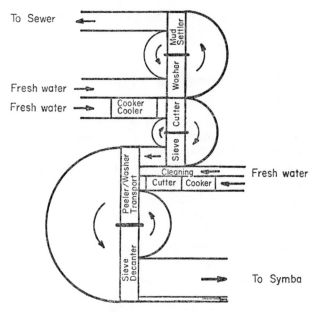

Fig. 2.   Potato factory water system.

factory which has brought water consumption down to 2–3 m³/ton
of potatoes. The Symba plant has a capacity to treat 20 m³/h of
waste water with 3% dry matter (Table 1). From this about 300 kg
of yeast are produced per hour. BOD is reduced by 90% from
15 000 mg/litre to about 1500 mg/litre.

TABLE 1
Symba plant, Eslöv, Sweden

Waste water capacity	20 m³/h
Waste water dry matter content	2–3%
Waste water BOD_5	10 000–20 000 mg/litre
Waste water after Symba BOD_5	1 000–2 000 mg/litre
BOD reduction	4–8 tons/day
Symba yeast production	250 kg/h

Figure 3 shows a flow diagram for the plant. The water and sludge
from the potato factory are collected in buffer tanks to equalise flow
and composition of waste streams. From the buffer tanks a continuous flow of water is taken into the Symba plant.

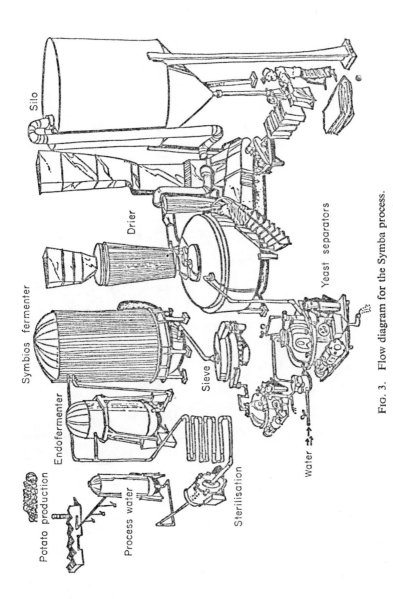

Fig. 3. Flow diagram for the Symba process.

Fig. 4. Heat exchanger and fermenter.

After heat sterilisation the water is pumped into the symbiotic fermenter (Fig. 4), which is aerated with sterile filtered air and cooled. From the fermenter the yeast liquor passes vibro screens, where peels and fibre are eliminated before concentrating the yeast into a slurry by centrifuges. After a wash step the Symba yeast is dried on a ball drier and finally bagged in 25 kg bags. The whole plant is controlled and supervised by 1 man/shift (Fig. 5).

FIG. 5.   Control panel.

PRODUCT DESCRIPTION

The composition of Symba yeast is shown in Table 2. It complies with the norm for food yeasts. Of special note is the low content of nucleic acids and the high vitamin content. Also the amino acid composition is favourable (Table 3), although the content of sulphur-containing amino acids as for all yeasts is somewhat low.

Extensive feeding experiments with Symba yeast have been made by the Swedish University of Agriculture (Table 4). Most important are the experiments where Symba yeast has replaced skim milk, *e.g.* in milk replacers for baby animals and in pet foods. For baby calves up to 40% of the milk protein could be replaced by Symba yeast proteins (Table 5). All the feeding tests have yielded positive results and have not shown any adverse effects at all.

TABLE 2
Composition of Symba yeast: food quality

Protein	48·0%
Fat	3·0%
Carbohydrates	36·5%
Fibre	1·0%
Minerals	5·5%
Water	6·0%
Nucleic acids	4·0%
B-vitamins:	
Thiamine	145 mg/kg
Riboflavine	80 mg/kg
Pyridoxine	35 mg/kg
Niacin	430 mg/kg
Folic acid	20 mg/kg

For food uses the low content of nucleic acids and the bland taste of Symba yeast are special advantages. Uses as in bread and in mashed potato powders look very promising. Combined food products from Symba yeast and different milk products have been developed and will soon be marketed.

TABLE 3
Amino-acids of Symba yeast: food quality
(g/100 g raw protein)

Arginine	4·6
Aspartic acid	10·3
Cystine	1·0
Glutamic acid	13·8
Histidine	2·0
Isoleucine	4·3
Leucine	7·5
Lysine	6·3
Methionine	1·5
Phenylalanine	5·4
Threonine	5·4
Tryptophan	1·3
Tyrosine	4·8
Valine	4·2

TABLE 4
Feeding tests with Symba yeast

	Replacing
Rats	(Compared with casein)
Chickens	Fish and soya meals
Pigs	Fish and soya meals
Baby pigs	Skim-milk powder
Calves	Skim-milk powder/soya meal
Baby calves (1–8 weeks)	Skim-milk powder
Mink	Meat
Pet animals	Meat meal

TABLE 5
Calf experiment 1: Symba yeast in a milk replacer

	Control			Symba yeast		
Ingredients %:						
Dried skim milk		58·4			35·0	
Dried whey		19·0			20·0	
Symba yeast + 0·5 % met.		—			25·0	
Fish meal (Protanimal)		2·0			—	
Animal and vegetable fat		19·5			18·8	
Minerals and vitamins		1·1			1·1	
Chemical composition:						
Crude protein %		25·7			26·5	
Mcal ME/kg, calculated		4·35			4·35	
Ca (g/kg)		11			7	
P (g/kg)		8			7	
Results:			Mean			Mean
No. of animals	6	6	12	7	7	14
Mean birth weight (kg)	41·3	40·3	40·8	42·5	40·4	41·5
Daily weight gain, 0–8 weeks (g)	612	467	539	506	494	500
Daily weight gain, 9–20 weeks (g)	983	853	918	949	878	914
Total milk refusals (kg/animal 0–8 weeks)	2·4	27·2	14·8	2·1	2·5	2·3
Diarrhoea days, total	—	4	4	2	1	3

TABLE 6
*Products giving suitable
wastes for Symba
process*

Potato products:
  French fries
  Granules
  Cubes
  Flakes
  Hashed brown
  Dehydrated
  Chips
Rice products:
  Instant rice
Starch products:
  Wheat starch
  Maize starch
  Glucose, dextrose
  Derivates
Cassava products
Sweet potato products
Vegetable products:
  Carrots
  Red beets
Bakery products:
  Dough
  Bread
  Crackers

FEASIBILITY AND ECONOMICS

Many different wastes and waste waters could be taken care of by the Symba process. Table 6 lists products which give suitable waste streams for Symba yeast production. Some conditions have to be met, however, to make the production feasible. At first, the amount of waste has to be larger than a certain minimum size which varies with the alternative cost for waste disposal but which is normally in the range of 2000–4000 tons/year. This corresponds to a Symba yeast production of 1000–2000 tons/year.

Secondly, the dry matter content of the waste water should be over about 2%. If this is not initially the case, water consumption could normally be reduced by recirculation, which also saves fresh water, or solid wastes could be added to bring dry matter up to this level.

Finally, the production season has to be fairly long. Seasons for production of potato starch and certain vegetables are for instance too short to give sufficient productivity of the Symba plant.

Investments for Symba plants for waste utilisation normally range between £0·7 and £2 million. In many cases raw materials for Symba yeast production could be negatively priced. This gives very favourable operating costs for the process.

Plant sizes are, on the other hand, restricted by the amount of wastes available at reasonable distance from the plant. The total production cost is, however, highly competitive with other SCP processes currently being projected. The Symba process has therefore shown that waste treatment on a full scale could indeed be profitable.

DISCUSSION

Rees: You indicated that the primary use of Symba yeast is in milk for calves. Has there been any change in the dairy industry in Sweden as a result of this? Are you releasing more milk which is available for human consumption either directly or indirectly in the form of dairy-based products?

Skogman: There will naturally be some changes when you start utilising a replacer for the milk protein used. In Sweden as in many other countries there is a surplus of milk being produced. On the other hand, this milk is much too expensive to be used for feeding purposes, and the world market price for dried milk is higher than the value of the milk for feeding purposes, which means that by replacing milk for feeding baby calves, for instance, by Symba yeast, we make a larger part of the milk available for human consumption, and as this is a surplus—for Sweden, at least, this is a surplus product already—this milk will have to be exported at the world market price, but this is higher than the feed price anyhow.

Butcher: Can you tell us the possibilities of utilising the Symba yeast in human food markets, seeing that the yeast for those markets commands a much higher price than animal yeast?

Skogman: As I briefly mentioned we are naturally very much in operation to find the right uses for Symba yeast in food products, but I think the situation is such that you could not claim to sell protein as an addition to foods, just for the purpose of upgrading the protein content. You have to find the right uses of your product in food, and in doing so we try to find those places where either the yeast exerts a certain function in the food product where it is put, or such products where you could replace the more expensive component of the food with the Symba yeast with equal or better function. As a matter of fact I forgot to mention that our aim in making *Candida utilis* from the starch waste is naturally that *Candida utilis* is the best known of all yeasts and has been used in foods and feeds for a long time. The addition of the content of 4% *Endomycopsis* in the product does not make this any more difficult because *Endomycopsis fibuliger* has also been used for a long time. It is used in many composed foods in Thailand where naturally tapioca is a large basis for nutrition and they use the *Endomycopsis* to make the tapioca more tasty, to sweeten the tapioca. It has also been used in Czechoslovakia under the name of 'Fibuli', which was a product which consisted of 100% *Endomycopsis fibuliger*, so we are in the last phase of getting permission from the FDA. Naturally, for this product also there will have to be an official clearance for uses in food, at least in America and Japan, which are the most critical countries in this respect, but we expect to get that permission very soon.

Questioner: Is this for an extracted protein or for the whole cell?

Skogman: This is for the whole cell.

Lalla: Has the process been adapted to use lye peel waste from the potato processing industry?

Skogman: This process was originally developed to utilise powdered waste potatoes, of which in our group of companies we had a lot. Like most waste products, when the amount of waste grew smaller and smaller we turned it over to use lye peel waste waters for the purpose and adapted the process to this type of waste water. Today they use steam peeling and mechanical peeling for the potatoes.

Thomson: Is there any change in the composition of the yeast with different feed material?

Skogman: No. The only change is that the ash content with lye peel water will be a little higher because of the ions from the lye and eventually from the added agent for neutralisation of the lye. Otherwise the product has an ash content of about 6% so we have still 2% to go on the national formula regulations, and it shouldn't be any problem.

Davidson: Our Energy Analysis Unit has been interested in making studies on the frequency of processes such as your own through an energy requirement study. I wonder if you have carried out any energy analysis or any energy study of this process. Studies at Strathclyde University have shown that protein production through milk production is less energy-intensive than via beef production, both of which appear to be much less intensive than SCP production.

Skogman: One should remember that in this case the alternative for getting rid of that waste is to use aerated lagoons or aerated activated sludge plants or anything of that kind to break down the contaminants in the water, so the energy comparison has to include the alternative energy consumption for cleaning the waste.

Russell Eggitt: I may have missed this point in your talk, but what is the concentration of the total solids actually going into the fermenter after it has been sterilised?

Skogman: Between 2% and 3%.

Russell Eggitt: And is there no problem of thickening at this concentration?

Skogman: We would have liked to go up to much more than that from a productivity point of view and that would have been quite possible, but this is one of the problems when working with a waste material. You have to take what you get.

Oguntona: I see you included up to 40% of Symba yeast in the feed for calves. I wonder if you did the same for poultry. I ask this because with some of the yeast materials already on the market, where you go up to several percent you get problems like feed intake, weight gain, diarrhoea, etc.

Skogman: In that case Symba yeast is quite like the others. You have to set a limit as to how much Symba yeast or any type of single-cell protein that you put into poultry rations, because of the lack of some component that has not yet been identified. This lies at about 25% of the feed composition, I think, but up to that limit it gives good results. It should not go higher than that.

Davies: When feeding the Symba yeast–milk mixture to calves, can you feed it immediately or do you have to introduce it gradually?

Skogman: It is directly for the newly born calves—one day old, or so.

Kapsiotis: Do you have any problems with the iron content of the Symba yeast for veal feeding?

Skogman: As our plant is completely stainless steel everywhere, the iron content is not such that it gives any problems.

Kapsiotis: I put the question because BP have experienced this problem because of high iron (Fe) content of their SCP.

Skogman: That must come from some other source, as we do not have a very high iron content.

12

Food from Waste: Leaf Protein

N. W. Pirie

*Rothamsted Experimental Station, Harpenden,
Herts., England*

ABSTRACT

*Potential sources of leaf protein (LP) could sometimes be grown on land that is for
some reason, e.g. shading, unsuitable for other crops. When grown in place of
conventional crops, it is waste of sunlight that will be avoided because leaf crops
can yield more than seed or root crops. Many agricultural by-products are underused
or completely wasted. Thus sugar beet tops and potato haulm in the UK are each
possible sources of 50 000 tons of LP. It is less easy to estimate the potential yield
from vegetable wastes, and some of them would be difficult to collect.*

*The potentialities of tropical by-products such as leaves from sugar cane, cotton
and the fibre plants have been less fully explored. Water weeds, especially in the
tropics, are an immense potential source. Their exploitation would have the added
advantage that it would diminish eutrophication and partly replace the expensive
methods by which control is now attempted.*

*The process of extracting LP yields a partly dewatered fibre containing 1–2% N,
and a 'whey' containing most of the soluble components of the leaf. The former is
cattle fodder even when made from initially unpalatable leaves; because of the
partial dewatering, it can be economically dried. The latter is a substrate on which
micro-organisms can be grown; it could also be used as irrigation water so as to
exploit the NPK in it.*

*Circumventing waste always involves changing traditional habits, and often
involves introducing more elaborate and labour-consuming processes. It has therefore
not hitherto been considered important in some communities except by those with
ethical or ideological motivation. It seems likely that that era is ending and that
more attention will be paid to avoidable waste in future.*

INTRODUCTION

The production of leaf protein (LP) will be more important as a
means for preventing waste than as a means of consuming wastes.
Only water weeds are likely to supply a sufficiently continuous flow
of underexploited leaf, from sources near an extraction unit, to

180

maintain production throughout the season. Gaps in the flow of by-product leaves would be filled by crops grown primarily as sources of LP; in most regions, more protein will probably come from crops than from wastes. Crops that could be regarded as preventers of waste fall into two categories: those grown on land which, though arable, is not at present used for conventional crops, and those grown on land on which forage crops are now suboptimally fertilised.

Crops in the first category obviously keep land from being wasted. Shade-tolerant species can be grown under trees in orchards and plantations where it would be difficult to ripen seed-bearing crops. There are sites where pollutants such as SO_2 restrict the range of species that can be grown; some SO_2-tolerant plants may be useful as LP sources. LP made from plants that manage to grow in spite of pollution by metals such as lead and zinc will probably be itself so contaminated with the toxic metal as to be hazardous.

Crops in the second category keep sunlight from being wasted. In most climates, adequately fertilised leafy crops give larger annual yields of protein and dry matter (DM) than seed or root crops. When green vegetables are grown, this potentiality is fully exploited—but people can eat green vegetables only to a limited extent, though this limit is seldom now reached. Forage crops grown as ruminant fodder are seldom given as much NPK and water as is needed for maximum productivity, *i.e.* for optimal use of sunlight. Parsimonious husbandry is adopted so as to avoid getting forage that is inconveniently lush and that contains more protein than a ruminant needs. A lush protein-rich leaf is ideal for LP extraction. The extra yield resulting from optimal fertilisation would probably justify the cost of the extra fertiliser. More ruminant fodder would be supplied by the protein-depleted residue, and the mechanical removal of water in the course of extracting LP would greatly cheapen drying if that were the method of conservation chosen.[1,2]

THE METHOD OF EXTRACTION

The various methods used in large-scale LP extraction were described in a symposium[3] in 1970. There have been no radical innovations since then and there are no valid patents covering any essential part of the extraction process. The extraction of protein from the cells of a leaf depends more on shearing than on fine subdivision. An extraction unit should therefore rub rather than cut the leaf; intense pressure is unnecessary and may be detrimental. In some extraction systems, *e.g.* sugar cane rolls and screw expellers, the leaf gets rubbed accidentally because of slip and the general inefficiency of these units as presses. From the beginning of sustained work on LP extraction[4] it therefore seemed best to accept pulping and pressing as distinct operations that might have to be performed in separate machines. Large amounts of LP were made, especially in India, in a machine designed to do both jobs,[5] but it was less effective than the pulper and press combination because the extract remained for too long in contact with the fibre.

When it became clear that much of the energy consumed in pulping served only to create wind, and that much of the juice was liberated as a result of leaf rubbing against leaf rather than against parts of the machine, the idea of exploiting the defects of screw expellers, considered simply as presses, became attractive. A screw expeller cannot build up pressure unless the surface of the scroll slides across the fibrous surface of the charge. This wastes energy, even with a smooth scroll, but it does some of the necessary rubbing. In the arrangement shown in Fig. 1, the scroll is broken into a series of paddles so that there is more chewing and less useless friction;

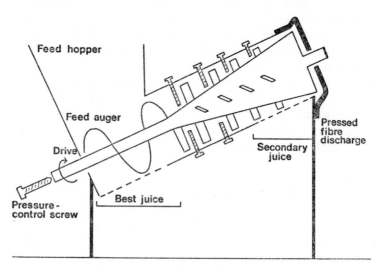

FIG. 1.

pressure would be built up as a result of the repeated rearrangement of the charge. In the conventional screw expeller, juice is forced under pressure through holes or slits in the casing. Consequently, fine particles of fibre come with it and are not easy to remove. In the arrangement illustrated the extract runs under gravity through a gauze from which retained material is continually swept by the incoming crop. The only foreseeable disadvantage of this unit, compared with the pulper and press combination, is that the addition of water to a crop that is rather too dry for normal pulping will not be effective. Added water would be squeezed out before effective rubbing starts and would merely dilute the extract without increasing the percentage extraction of protein. It may be possible to overcome this defect by injecting water at a point near the high-pressure end of the unit.

Various leaf components form complexes with LP in extracts;[6] it is wise therefore to separate coagulum from 'whey' as soon as possible. The only known advantage in delayed separation is that less nucleic acid accompanies the protein into the final product when leaf ribonuclease is allowed to act. Similarly, quick heating to the coagulation temperature is advantageous because it results in a firm and easily handled coagulum. Heating to 70°C is sufficient for complete coagulation, but it is often advisable to heat to 100°C so as to inactivate the enzymes in the extract.[6] The importance of this inactivation depends on the species of plant that is being extracted and on the distribution of enzymes in it.

Thoroughly pressed LP contains 60% water; when made from some species, *e.g.* pea (*Pisum sativum*) and maize (*Zea mays*), it has such a pleasant taste that it can be used immediately. When made from most other species it should be resuspended in water and filtered off again. The suspension should be taken to about pH 4 to facilitate filtration and to ensure the removal of alkaloids. A protein cake made in this way has the keeping qualities of cheese; it can be canned, salted, pickled or dried.

TEMPERATE ZONE SOURCES OF LEAF

Agricultural By-products

In Britain 81% of sugar beet (*Beta vulgaris*) tops are ploughed in, the remainder is ensiled or fed to cattle fresh; a considerable fraction

of what is fed fresh is not in fact eaten. In West Germany only 10 %
is ploughed in, and 63·5 % is dried. Ploughing in is sometimes
justified on the grounds that the N in the tops is a useful fertiliser
for succeeding crops. For various reasons, *e.g.* denitrification and
leaching during the winter, less than a tenth of the N is available to
barley grown after sugar beet.[7] Waste would be diminished if we in
Britain simply followed the established German practice. Sugar beet
leaves contain 1·6–2·8 % N (2·3 % is a common value) on the DM,
and the average yield of DM on the 193 000 ha devoted to sugar beet
in the UK is 5 t ha^{-1}. We are therefore making inadequate use of
about 25 000 t of N. Even if all the tops were fed to cattle, only about
one-seventh would be recovered in edible products. The soft leaves of
sugar beet are extremely easy to pulp, so easy indeed that in large-
scale work it may be advantageous to mix them with leaves from a
more fibrous crop so as to give the pulp enough 'body' to make it
controllable when pressed. If two-thirds of the N in the leaves is
protein N and half of that is readily extractable, we have a potential
source of about 50 000 t of extracted protein and the pressed residue,
containing the unextracted protein, would still be available as cattle
fodder. Our best yield of dry extracted LP at Rothamsted was
820 kg ha^{-1}. Commercial extraction of protein from sugar beet tops
has started in Sweden.

The situation with potato (*Solanum tuberosum*) haulm is similar.
In spite of more than 20 references in a widely used handbook[8] to
the use of haulm hay and silage as cattle fodder, haulm is scarcely
ever used in Britain. Most references to its use[9] come from Germany.
Fear that cattle will be poisoned by solanin and other glycoalkaloids
is widespread, although there is no evidence that the glycoalkaloids
withstand microbial attack in the silo. Even if they are resistant, they
are soluble in slightly acid conditions and would therefore be largely
removed if the silage were pressed on a grid before being used.

Instead of being harvested for use as hay or silage, potato haulm
is wastefully killed mechanically, or with an acid spray, at the
beginning of September so as to facilitate tuber-lifting and as a safe-
guard against blight. The haulm that can be collected from a hectare
at that time can yield 0·3 t of dry extracted protein and 2–3 t DM of
fibre containing 1·5–2 % N.[10] Main crop potatoes occupy 0·23
million ha, but some of the crop is not as well fertilised as the crops
that we have used. It is, however, reasonable to conclude that 50 000 t
of haulm protein could be made. Early potatoes occupy less than

30 000 ha but give about twice the yield of extractable protein. When the extraction of LP from haulm becomes an accepted technique it will be worthwhile considering the advisability of harvesting main crop haulm a little before the customary time in spite of the diminution in tuber yield. The feeding value of the fibre has not yet been measured. When made by heat coagulation in the usual way, the protein curd at Rothamsted and in Poland[10,11] contains less N than curd made from most other leaf species, but its nutritional value for rats is equally good.[12] Protein-rich and -poor fractions can be made by the usual methods of differential coagulation.

By simply destroying the haulm, we are therefore at present wasting the equivalent of a medium crop of beans and a good crop of hay. Soon after potatoes were introduced into Britain, Sir Thomas Overbury is said to have remarked: 'The man who has not anything to boast of but his illustrious ancestors is like a potato, the only good belonging to him is underground.' The sentiment is admirable, but we may have taken the simile too literally.

Horticultural By-products

Some vegetable wastes are used as ruminant feed, but most of them are ploughed in or expensively disposed of in tips. Most of the material is broad-leaved and is therefore well suited for the technique of partial drying and fractionation. The protein-rich laminae dry and become brittle more rapidly than the protein-poor stems and petioles. Classification of partly dried leaf worked well on clovers during the last war[13] and has been used on vegetable wastes.[14,15] Usually, vegetable discards contain so much water that drying is uneconomical; with protein extraction the position is different—the lusher the leaf the better the extraction.

At one time, peas for canning and freezing were harvested on the vine and the whole mass was taken to a factory; the peas were separated and the vines carted back to the farm. Mobile viners now go into the field and drop the vines as they go along. The old arrangement was well adapted to protein extraction. From peas grown on an experimental plot we got 600 kg ha^{-1} of dry extracted protein; this is more protein than is present in the peas. Pea haulm collected from a factory 30 km from Rothamsted did not extract as well as fresh haulm—perhaps because there was an interval of about 3 h before the bruised and battered haulm was pulped. The percentage of haulm N that was recovered as protein N varied from 22% to 47%.[16] If efforts are made to give up vining in the field and revert to the old method of vining in a factory, protein could be extracted from the haulm without delay. However, peas may not ultimately be a useful source of LP; there is little leaf on some new varieties.

When maize is allowed to ripen completely, the leaves are too dry and depleted of protein for satisfactory extraction. From some varieties, harvested at the end of August, only 20% of the protein was extractable.[16] When harvested earlier, *i.e.* at the sweet-corn stage, nearly half the protein was extractable and the yield of extracted protein reached 480 kg ha^{-1}. The area devoted to sweet-corn in Britain is too small for it to be an important source of LP.

Vegetable discards in the USA in 1948 had a wet weight of 4 million t;[14] the weight in 1958 was 21 million t[17] containing an estimated 0·4 million of protein. There have been no similar estimates recently in Britain: in 1951 the wet weight was 0·5 million, the weight sometimes quoted now is 4 million t. The area devoted to open-air vegetables in England and Wales is 0·17 million ha, *i.e.* intermediate between sugar beet and potatoes. The brassicas alone (Brussels sprouts, cabbage, calabrese, cauliflower, sprouting broccoli, etc.) occupy 60 000 ha. The weight of discarded material is not recorded but is probably more than 200 000 t containing more than 3000 t of protein. Material discarded in the field would be fresh and worth extracting; discards at the retail level may possibly not be worth collecting. However, one estimate[18] puts the grand total (wet weight) of all vegetable leafy waste in the field and during marketing at more than 3 million t; much of it is already being collected and some market gardeners pay to have it disposed of.

TROPICAL SOURCES OF LEAF

Agricultural By-products

Anyone who has seen sugar cane (*Saccharum officinarum*) tops being burnt off will agree that they are the most spectacular way in which a potential source of LP is wasted. Burning was introduced because, by removing trash, it made hand-cutting easier, and by removing snakes and scorpions, pleasanter. With mechanised cutting these advantages lose some cogency, and there are technical disadvantages in processing cane that has been fired. Unburnt cane tops are therefore available and there is about 0·5 t of protein in the tops on a hectare. But they are so dry and tough that it is unlikely to be profitable to extract protein from them. They might, however, be useful for giving 'body' to some very lush and non-fibrous leaves, *e.g.* water hyacinth (*Eichhornia crassipes*). When cane is harvested for making sugar, some leaf is inevitably included in the mass and there is a little protein in the cane itself. There is therefore LP in the cane juice and it normally collects in the 'mud'. By a slight change in processing technique, a mixture consisting predominantly of LP and cane wax can be made, and from that, LP with 8% N.[19] In Mauritius alone about 6000 t of protein is discarded in 'mud' annually. The ratio is about 1 t of protein for every 100 t of sugar produced. World production of cane sugar exceeds 60 million t a year; it seems therefore that 0·6 million t of protein, originating largely from leaves, is being discarded.

Unpublished experiments at Coimbatore (India) showed that leaves gathered from cotton (*Gossypium hirsutum*) after the second picking of the bolls yielded 510 kg ha^{-1} of extracted protein. After the third picking the leaves were too dry to extract well. No tests of palatability or nutritional value were made, but elsewhere[20] cotton is being grown as a silage rather than a fibre crop. The methods now used for mechanised cotton picking depend on chemically defoliating the plants; though it may not be easy to combine the collection of leaf with collection of bolls, the area devoted to cotton is so large that the attempt would be worth making. Ramie (*Boehmeria nivea*) is now being grown more extensively than hitherto because of the increased cost of artificial fibres and exceptional resistance of ramie fibre to weathering and water damage. The leaf is scutched off before retting and contains 2·25–4·5% N according to age and level of manuring.[21] Judging from appearance and feel it should extract well, and in (unpublished) experiments at Coimbatore 63% of the protein was extractable; less protein was extracted in other experiments[22] unless alkali was added. Some other fibre plants have similar N contents but a harsher feel; this is in agreement with the observation[23,24] that only 30–40% of the protein in sunn hemp (*Crotalaria juncea*) is extractable and only 20% of that in roselle (*Hibiscus sabdariffa*). The latter has an acid leaf[24] and would therefore probably extract better if neutralised. Kenaf (*H. cannabinus*) was originally grown as a tropical fibre plant; there is now increasing interest in it as a source of paper pulp in New Zealand,[25] Russia and the USA. It has acid leaves and is presumably similar in other ways to roselle.

Some of the jutes (*e.g. Corchorus* sp.) have mucilaginous leaves that give an extract that is difficult to handle; this should be remembered lest it be assumed that every protein-rich leaf could be a source of extracted LP.

In some countries, leaves of jute-type plants are eaten as vegetables. If this direct use could be extended it would be preferable to LP extraction. The use of these leaves as cattle fodder or fertiliser gives a smaller return of human food than would come from protein extraction with use of the fibre residue as fodder.

Although the pulp made when sisal (*Agave sisalana*), and the related fibre plants henequen and furcraea, is scutched can be fermented to yield alcohol, and is sometimes used as fodder,[26] most of it is waste. The pulp is acid. Judging from experience with protein from other leaves, neutralisation after the pulp has been made will not make as much protein soluble as would remain soluble if the leaf were scutched with dilute sodium carbonate so that neutralisation and disintegration are simultaneous. There is no reason to think that this neutralisation would damage the fibre. It may also be possible to recover protein from abaca (*Musa textilis*) leaves, but experience with banana (*M. sapientum*)[23] is not encouraging. New varieties of abaca are being produced as sources of paper pulp; it may be that some of them do not contain so much of the phenolic material that is probably[6] the reason for poor protein extraction. Some of the many species that are being tested, in various parts of the world, as sources of paper pulp will probably yield useful amounts of by-product leaf.

Horticultural By-products

The leaves of many plants cultivated primarily for their below-ground part are eaten on a small scale. Thus cassava (manioc or tapioca, *Manihot esculenta*) leaf is edible after prolonged boiling to drive off HCN. At the usual time of harvest, much sweet potato (*Ipomoea batatas*) leaf is discoloured; some, but by no means all, of the younger leaves are eaten in New Guinea[27] and Sierra Leone; elsewhere they are usually fed to pigs. Some of the leaves of yams in the family Araceae (coco-yam, tannia, eddo, taro, etc.) are eaten. Nevertheless there is much waste. Sweet potato leaves[23] and some of the yams[23,24] extract moderately well; the variety of cassava tested[23] extracted less well but there are many other varieties. The yield of extracted protein from the by-product leaves of various brassicas grown in India was 130–170 kg ha^{-1},[28] and LP was extracted from chicory (*Cichorium intybus*) leaves, also in India.[29] The potentialities of groundnut (*Arachis hypogaea*) leaves depend on the rainfall in the period before the seeds are harvested. In Ghana[23] they extracted reasonably well; in Aurangabad (India) and Nigeria[3] poorly.

WATER WEEDS

Weeds growing on land will rarely be useful sources of LP because the land on which they are allowed to grow is either unfertilised or is for some reason difficult to crop. Species now stigmatised as weeds may, however, be grown deliberately as sources of LP: nettles (*Urtica* sp.) gave 612 kg ha^{-1} from a single harvest;[30] other weeds, *e.g.* fat hen (*Chenopodium album*) and other chenopodiums, extract well. Some Indian weeds[31] also extract reasonably well. A fuller survey of weeds would be valuable because some of them start to grow earlier in the season than conventional crop plants.

Weeds growing in water are an entirely different matter and failure to use them is one of the more scandalous examples of waste. There are no reliable figures for the annual amount spent throughout the world on rather unsuccessful attempts at control—£500 million is sometimes mentioned. About £3 million is spent in Britain alone. In addition to this cost there are the losses caused by restriction of waterways, increased evaporation from irrigation ditches (transpiration by some weeds doubles evaporation) and poisoning of crops irrigated with water to which herbicides have been added to kill weeds. Meanwhile, although the possibilities have been comprehensively reviewed,[32] very little is spent on finding uses for water weeds. The subject has comic aspects. While India spends large sums on herbicides, and increasingly elaborate machines are devised in the USA to batter weeds to death, farmers in the Yangtse delta deliberately cultivate water hyacinth as a pig food.[33] It is also used as pig food, but not deliberately cultivated, in the Democratic Republic of Vietnam, and it is beginning to be used as cattle fodder in India and Indonesia. When animals are used to consume weeds, land animals are preferable to fish or manatees, in spite of the labour involved in getting the weed out of the water, because the nutrients in the weed are then removed from the water, where they cause eutrophication, and reappear as dung for use as fertiliser on arable land. Where eutrophication is not a problem, extraction equipment would be mounted on a barge, the extract would be coagulated on it, the protein allowed to settle, and the 'whey' discarded into the waterway. Only the pressed fibre and concentrated curd would be brought to shore. Where eutrophication is a problem, as much of the crop as possible should be removed from the water.[34] It would be easier to move pressed fibre and coagulated juice to shore from time to time, instead of collecting and landing the weed itself. The final processing could be done on land. Furthermore, by this arrangement, waste heat from the propulsion and harvesting equipment would be available for coagulating the juice and drying the fibre.

Hyacinth is the most troublesome and abundant of the weeds. The DM in the standing crop may weigh 80 t ha^{-1}. The DM of the leaves contains up to 5% N; the whole floating plant, including roots and floats, contains 2·5%. It would be whole floating plant that would in practice be used. There is general agreement[22,35–37] that at leaf pH (6·6) only 10–20% of the protein is extracted and that up to 60% can be extracted if alkali is added. If the 'whey' is ultimately to be used as irrigation water, it would be reasonable to use K_2CO_3 or NH_3 as the alkali, and H_3PO_4 as the acid that would have to be added before coagulation. The position is somewhat similar with Nile cabbage (*Pistia stratiotes*); it is abundant, it is the principal food for pigs in some places,[38] and less than 20% of the protein is extracted at about pH 6.[23,24,37] Extraction with added alkali does not seem to have been tried. The floating fern, *Salvinia auriculata*, is a widespread pest. Only one attempt (Rothamsted, unpublished) seems to have been made to extract protein from it; 34% of the total N was extracted, two-thirds of it was protein N, but the curd was only 24% protein.

The main advantage of using these three water weeds as sources of LP is that weeds and eutrophication have to be controlled and it would be reasonable to get at least a small return from the process of control. Some rooted weeds on the margins of lakes and slow-moving rivers are such good sources of LP that they may be worth cultivating in these otherwise underused places. From mixed weeds collected in Hertfordshire,[30] 47% of the protein was extracted, and from water lily (*Nymphaea lotus*) in Ghana, 40%.[23] From an early harvest of lily in Alabama[39] the extracted protein accounted for 61% of the leaf N; the yields from *Justicia americana* and *Alternanthera philoxeroides* were a little smaller. Unfortunately, *Typha* and

Phragmites, which produce very heavy growths in suitable climates,[40] do not extract well, while duckweed (*Lemna minor*), which extracts well, is seldom troublesome.

BY-PRODUCTS FROM LEAF PROTEIN EXTRACTION

It can be argued that just as it is a mistake to attach the label 'weed' to plants for which we have not yet found a use, so it is a mistake to attach the label 'by-product' to some fractions resulting from a separation. The labels tend arbitrarily to assign relative importance, and they justify an outlook based on disposal rather than use. When protein is extracted from leafy material, the fibre residue contains more than half the original DM. Fibres from 13 crops harvested at different ages and after different manurial treatments contained 0·9–3·3% N;[16] the larger values were given by crops that initially contained the most N, but there is no strict proportionality. A greater fraction of the total protein is extracted from those leaves that contain most protein and, as has often been pointed out, species vary in extractability. Most fibres contain 1·5–2% N; they are more digestible by ruminants than hay containing the same amount of N because they are made from younger and less lignified leaves. In the extraction process most of the water is removed from the fibre; a crop that initially contained 10–20% DM yields a fibre containing 30–35%. Consequently only 2 t of water has to be evaporated from the fibre to make 1 t of DM, whereas 5–10 t has to be evaporated from the original crop. With increasing fuel costs this saving may be nearly as important as the extracted protein.[2,41] Crops grown as ruminant feed are often dried purely for convenience—ensiling would often be as effective a method of conservation. When very lush leaves (*e.g.* haulm from peas, potatoes and sugar beet, or water weeds) are ensiled, there is serious loss of effluent and local pollution by it. There is no loss when the pressed fibre is ensiled.

No generalisation can be made about the composition of the 'whey' that remains when coagulated protein is removed from a leaf extract.[42] It always contains carbohydrates, non-protein N and most of the P and K that was present in the crop. It is therefore a good medium for the cultivation of micro-organisms; this will probably be its ultimate use. At first, however, it will be simplest to use it as irrigation water.

EPILOGUE

Clearly there is much unheeded, and some deliberate, waste of material from which LP can, or probably could, be made. It is at first sight surprising that this should be so: the people concerned with food production in industrialised countries are popularly supposed to be equally concerned with making money. But the 'affluent society' depends on waste,[43] and waste is one aspect of 'conspicuous consumption'.[44] Waste is also convenient. Ploughing in pea haulm saves trouble, and flushing out a byre obviates heavy labour that is, to most people, disagreeable. At certain ratios of food and labour costs, the value of what is conserved is less than the costs of conservation: in these circumstances, the prevention of waste is more an ethical than an economic matter. Much nonsense has been written in the guise of ecology, but a persistent, even fanatical, concern for the prevention of waste leads people constantly to reassess the possibilities of using material now thrown away. Economy is a feature of the more successful systems of primitive agriculture: little is wasted of the plants grown or gathered. These systems are also labour-intensive and so help to prevent drift to the towns. China seems to be setting a good example, perhaps because politicians there have more personal experience of farming than politicians elsewhere. Mao Tse-tung wrote in 1955: 'Diligent and frugal operation ought to be the policy of all our agricultural co-operatives—of all our enterprises in fact.' The title of an article in a book organised in honour of Lord Boyd-Orr on the occasion of his 70th birthday was 'The circumvention of waste'.[45] That book argued that with adequate exploitation of existing agricultural knowledge, the world's increasing population could be adequately fed. This still seems to be true[46,47] and it is a welcome sign of returning sanity that the importance of circumventing waste is now gaining recognition. Much attention is now being given to recycling waste: provided it can be done economically, it is more important to avoid producing waste in the first place. That is the point of this paper.

REFERENCES

1. Pirie, N. W. (1942). *Chem. & Ind.*, **61**, p. 45.
2. Pirie, N. W. (1966). *Fertil. Feed. Stuffs J.*, **63**, p. 119.
3. Pirie, N. W. (1971). *Leaf Protein: Its Agronomy, Preparation, Quality and Use*, International Biological Program, Handbook 20.

4. Pirie, N. W. (1953). *Rothamsted Exp. Sta., Ann. Rep. for 1952*, p. 173.
5. Davys, M. N. G. and Pirie, N. W. (1963). *J. Agric. Engng. Res.*, **8**, p. 70.
6. Pirie, N. W. (1975). In: *Protein Nutritional Quality*, ed. M. Friedman, Marcel Dekker, New York.
7. Widdowson, F. V. W. (1974). *J. Agric. Sci., Camb.*, **83**, p. 415.
8. Watson, S. J. and Nash, M. J. (1960). *The Conservation of Grass and Forage Crops*, Oliver & Boyd, Edinburgh.
9. Bugdol, G., Graupe, B., Lattermann, W. and Reimold, A. (1967–8). *Jahrb. Tiernährung Fütterung*, **6**, p. 72.
10. Carruthers, I. B. and Pirie, N. W. (in press).
11. Hanczakowski, P. (1970). *Przem. ferment. rol.*, **14**(10), p. 25.
12. Henry, K. M. and Ford, J. E. (1965). *J. Sci. Fd. Agric.*, **16**, p. 425.
13. Hannah Dairy Res. Inst., *Rep. for 1947*, p. 14.
14. Willaman, J. J. and Eskew, R. K. (1948). *USDA Tech. Bull. 958*.
15. Livingston, A. L., Knowles, R. E., Page, J., Kuzmicky, D. D. and Kohler, G. O. (1972). *J. Agr. Food Chem.*, **20**, p. 277.
16. Byers, M. and Sturrock, J. W. (1965). *J. Sci. Fd. Agric.*, **16**, p. 341.
17. Oelshlegel, F. J. Jr., Schroeder, J. R. and Stahmann, M. A. (1969). *J. Agr. Food Chem.*, **17**, p. 791.
18. Bowbrick, P. (1975). Personal communication.
19. Parish, D. H. (1960). *Nature*, **188**, p. 601.
20. Smith, L. S. and Hale, W. H. (1972). *Cotton Growing Rev.*, **49**, p. 61.
21. Squibb, R. L., Mendes, J., Guzman, M. A. and Scrimshaw, N. S. (1954). *J. Brit. Grassland Soc.*, **9**, p. 313.
22. Ghosh, J. J. (1967). *Trans. Bose Res. Inst.*, **30**, p. 215.
23. Byers, M. (1961). *J. Sci. Fd. Agric.*, **12**, p. 20.
24. Matai, S., Bagchi, D. K. and Raychaudhuri, S. (1971). *Science and Engineering*, **24**, p. 102.
25. Withers, N. J. (1973). *N.Z. J. Exp. Agric.*, **1**, p. 253.
26. Frank, P. J. (1957). *E. African Agric. J.*, **22**, p. 165.
27. Kimber, A. J. (1972). *Papua New Guinea Agric. J.*, **3/4**, p. 80.
28. Deshmukh, M. G., Gore, S. B., Mungikar, A. M. and Joshi, R. N. (1974). *J. Sci. Fd. Agric.*, **25**, p. 717.
29. Mahadeviah, S. and Singh, N. (1968). *Indian J. Exp. Biol.*, **6**, p. 193.
30. Pirie, N. W. (1959). *Rothamsted Exp. Sta., Ann. Rep. for 1968*, p. 94.
31. Gore, S. B. and Joshi, R. N. (1972). In: *Symposium Tropical Ecology*, ed. P. M. Golley and F. B. Golley, Athens, Georgia, p. 137.
32. Little, E. C. S. (1968). *Handbook of Utilisation of Aquatic Plants*, FAO, Rome.
33. Anon. (1974). *China Reconstructs*, **23**(9), p. 36.
34. Boyd, C. E. (1970). *Econ. Bot.*, **24**, p. 95.
35. Datta, R. K., Chadrabarty, P. R., Guha, B. C. and Ghosh, J. J. (1966). *Science and Culture*, **32**, p. 247.
36. Taylor, K. G., Bates, R. P. and Robbins, R. C. (1971). *Hyacinth Control J.*, **9**, p. 20.

37. Matai, S. (1973). Abstracts of seminar 'Noxious aquatic vegetation in tropics and sub-tropics', Ind. Nat. Sci. Acad. and UNESCO, New Delhi, p. 58.
38. Epstein, H. (1969). *Domestic Animals of China*, Tech. Comm. 18 of CAB Animal Breeding and Genetics.
39. Boyd, C. E. (1968). *Econ. Bot.*, **22**, p. 359.
40. Dykyjova, D. (1971). *Photosynthetica*, **5**, p. 329.
41. Pirie, N. W. (1975). *Nature*, **253**, p. 239.
42. Festenstein, G. N. (1972). *J. Sci. Fd. Agric.*, **23**, p. 1409.
43. Hodgson, J. L. (1933). *Great God Waste*, published by the author, Eggington, Beds., England.
44. Veblen, T. (1899). *The Theory of the Leisure Class*, Macmillan, London.
45. Pirie, N. W. (1951). In: *Four Thousand Million Mouths*, ed. F. LeGros Clark and N. W. Pirie, Oxford University Press.
46. Pirie, N. W. (1974). In: *Human Rights in Health*, ed. K. Elliott and J. Knight, Elsevier, Amsterdam, p. 99.
47. Pawley, W. H. (1974). In: *Human Rights in Health*, ed. K. Elliott and J. Knight, Elsevier, Amsterdam, p. 119.

DISCUSSION

Tannenbaum: I have two questions. (i) I have heard that over 50% of the protein in most leaves is one enzyme—ribulose diphosphate. I was wondering if that is true? (ii) Could you comment on the problem of chlorophyllase inactivation?

Pirie: Whether it is one enzyme or whether it is a group of enzymes, with varying similar properties, I regard as a little open, but it is certainly a powerful enzyme. You get one action out of the leaf that has fairly uniform properties. It is true there is a dominant type of protein called fraction A protein. Now the chlorophyllase action is no trouble if you make protein in the proper way. For various reasons which I have explained, you reheat the juice suddenly. It is technique to a large extent because you get a good hard curd out with a sudden heat. By sudden heat I mean within a second, taking it from room temperature up to curdling point. It also has the advantage of killing or inactivating enzymes. Nobody has ever run into trouble with chlorophyllase except when they heat in a lethargic way.

Bu'lock: What happens to the alkaloid content if you are using potato haulm in this process?

Pirie: All the alkaloids known to me are removed and for convenience one always washes the protein at about pH 4. Convenience because if you don't do the washing at pH 4 you get your filters bunged up. So to get the subject-matter to filter easily, you use pH 4. They come into the whey and if one was processing potato crops on a large scale, you would get a useful source of glycoalkaloids on the 100 tons sort of scale and someone would eventually find a good use for it. All you have got to do then is add an alkali and it falls out. Somebody will find a use for it.

Hay: Does the leaf protein possess any undesirable flavour characteristics?

Pirie: Well, undesirable is a matter of point of view, or point of taste. When it is fresh it has very little flavour from most of the species we use, but there are some species which do carry a flavour through. I think some would be completely impossible from that point of view, but most species give a product which, when it is fresh, has very little flavour. As it gets older and oxidises it builds up the flavour of oxidised lipids. Now these are what you pay extra for in kippers and China tea, and this is the selling point of China tea, it is this flavour.

Thomson: As a somewhat reluctant gardener it strikes me that weeds grow rather well, they don't seem to need much cultivation, they don't need much attention. Has anyone really looked at the possibilities of particular types of weeds in terms of total production?

Pirie: Yes. Nettles give an excellent source. You can get from a single cut of nettles about 600 kg/ha of extracted protein and it will grow again in three months or so. And fat hen is an excellent one, but fat hen you can eat straight. It is perfectly good and edible in its own right. Nettles aren't bad but you have to take them very young. The trouble with weeds as a crop is getting correct germination. The whole art of using weeds is not to germinate at once because you might germinate at the wrong period. You plant fat hen seeds and you'll find them coming up any time from now to five years hence, so that is inconvenient if you are farming, but there is an enormous range of new plants waiting to be explored. Our yields are all obtained on perfectly ordinary crops chosen for some other purpose, and in the end when this gets better accepted we will breed plants especially.

The group of plants that I attach particular importance to are the chenopodiums, fat hen, and Good King Henry, and there is a nice one from Bolivia—quinoa. It grows up to about 6 ft and gives marvellous leaves, and it has the great advantage that you can go on extracting protein even when the leaf has got mature. All these plants, as soon as the flower head begins to form, are similar in that the protein won't extract so well.

Thomson: What is the fertiliser input required for these sort of plants?

Pirie: To get 2 tons/ha the amount of fertiliser needed is probably uneconomically large.

13

Protein from Potato Starch Mill Effluent

B. J. OOSTEN

Koninklijke Scholten-Honig Research NV,
Foxhol (GR), The Netherlands

ABSTRACT

The high nutritional value of potato protein has been known for quite some time. However, the recovery of this material from the effluent of a potato starch mill could be accomplished only a few years ago.

To do this it is necessary either to change the starch recovery process fundamentally or to install additional, high-quality equipment. These changes result in a more concentrated effluent, which improves the economics of the protein recovery process. Owing to the higher prices for proteins and, in particular, the ever increasing charges on water pollution, the production of this highly valued protein will be increased in the very near future.

The increasing prices of energy press for the development of new protein recovery processes, which is an area of main interest for KSH.

The composition of potato protein was first studied over 70 years ago by Sjollema[1] in The Netherlands. During the Second World War more reliable studies, due to applying better analytical procedures, were carried out by Groot and Kentie.[2] From these amino acid analyses it could be concluded that potato protein, being a vegetable protein, should be considered a remarkably nutritive protein. Table 1 gives the amino acid analysis of potato protein. It can be seen that all the essential amino acids are present. The high biological value of the protein is also evident from a comparative rat feeding test carried out by Pol and Den Hartog.[4]

It may be wondered why potato protein was isolated on a commercial scale only about 15 years ago, while the production of potato starch was taking place as far back as 1840. Among the reasons are the following:

1. The protein becomes available at a very low concentration, that is, a large volume of water has to be treated per unit weight of protein.
2. Evaporation of the protein-containing stream is not possible due to severe fouling of the equipment.
3. Separation of the coagulated protein is very difficult due to very low sedimentation rates and poor filterability.
4. Low market prices for protein.

Notwithstanding these characteristics, Sjollema carried out experiments on a technical scale back in 1905.[1] At the end of World War I an installation for protein recovery was built but it never went on stream, since the end of the war intervened. In the 1930s technical experience was gained in Germany, but a commercial production level was not reached. In short, many experiments did not result in a commercial plant.

TABLE 1
Amino acid analysis of some proteins[3]

Product	Potato protein	Skim milk powder	Soya flour
Crude protein content (N × 6·25)	80%	36%	45%
amino acids/16 g N:			
Lysine[a]	8·2	7·8	6·2
Arginine[a]	5·5	3·6	7·2
Methionine[a]	2·2	2·6	1·4
Cystine	1·9	0·9	1·5
Isoleucine[a]	6·2	5·6	4·9
Leucine[a]	10·5	9·8	7·6
Phenylalanine[a]	6·9	4·8	4·9
Tyrosine	6·3	5·0	3·5
Tryptophan[a]	1·3	1·3	1·3
Threonine[a]	6·1	4·6	4·2
Histidine[a]	2·3	2·8	2·5
Valine[a]	7·4	6·9	5·0
Alanine	5·1	3·4	4·3
Asparagine acid	13·4	8·0	12·0
Glutamic acid	11·4	22·0	18·8
Glycine	5·5	2·0	4·2
Proline	5·4	10·0	5·5
Serine	6·0	6·1	5·6

[a] Essential amino acids.

During the last decade there have been some changes: firstly the pollution problem, the water pollution caused by a potato starch mill being tremendous; secondly, protein prices are fluctuating at a higher level; thirdly, improved technology, that is, better equipment and better processes. I shall try to show how this works out for a potato starch mill.

The starch of a potato is contained in the cells of which the potato is composed. To recover the starch, one has to tear the cells and this sets free not only the starch but also the cell fluid, usually called fruitwater. This fruitwater contains about 5% dissolved material, about 1·5% high molecular proteins, which can all be coagulated upon heating, about 1·5% amino acids and some peptides. The remainder is a mixture of sugars, organic acids and minerals, mainly potassium and phosphorus compounds (*see* Table 2).

TABLE 2
Composition of fruitwater

Crude protein	2–3%
Coagulable	35–60%
Minerals	
Organic acids	
Saccharides	
Vitamins	
Enzymes	
Total: about 5% dissolved material	

The figures given in this table are approximate values only. The composition of this fruitwater is quite variable, due to potato variety, manuring, time elapsed between harvesting and processing, temperature of potatoes during transportation and storage, etc.

Since this fruitwater is set free to make possible the recovery of starch, it is clear that one cannot possibly recover starch from potatoes without creating a severe pollution problem. What can be tried is to reduce the dilution of this fruitwater as far as possible. To achieve this, two cases will be shown.

In our potato starch plant in Germany a decanter was installed immediately after the rasps. With this system about two-thirds of the fruitwater is set free and can be used for protein recovery. The remaining one-third of the total amount of fruitwater becomes available at the end of the process, diluted with the water used for washing the starch free from fruitwater. This diluted stream is used as a fertiliser in the neighbourhood of the plant. This is old practice and the farmers like it for their land.

In our potato starch plants in The Netherlands this method cannot be applied, since there is no irrigation possible as in Germany. Here the fruitwater is set free diluted with the process water, that is, at a concentration of about 1·1 % total solids. A fundamentally new starch recovery process has been developed by KSH. The new process is based on the separating function of the hydrocyclone. The most important characteristic of this new process is the very low water consumption for recovering the starch, yielding a waste stream with about 3·1 % solids. The significance of this low water requirement for the energy required to solve the water pollution problem deserves at least some attention.

There are nowadays still plants in operation which require 6 m³ or more per ton of potatoes, yielding a waste stream with about 0·55% dissolved solids. The relation between required volume of wash water and the solids concentration in the total effluent is shown in Fig. 1. For a given tonnage of potatoes the pollution is a given quantity, but with higher concentrations in the effluent, less energy is required for solving the pollution problem, since a smaller volume of water has to be handled. This is illustrated in Fig. 2.

Another important characteristic of this KSH process is that all the pollution is found in only one stream, as opposed to all other known processes. This implies that the protein contained in the potato is all in one stream. If this stream can be treated, the maximum yield of potato protein is possible.

To isolate the protein from the pure, undiluted fruitwater, use is made of a process which KSH bought from a rival company. Owing to the agreement with this company, it can only be said that this process involves the coagulation of the protein by heating the fruitwater by steam injection. The end-product contains about 8% humidity and 75–80% protein on dry substance.

This process can work satisfactorily, but we think it has as a drawback a high energy requirement. Therefore, we in KSH have been looking for other processes which would require less energy. Much time and effort have been devoted to applying ultrafiltration to potato fruitwater. Many severe problems were met. Most of these problems were due to particular characteristics of potato fruitwater; for instance, it has an outstanding tendency to foam, it contains small fibres (the remainders of the potato cells), it contains small

B. J. Oosten

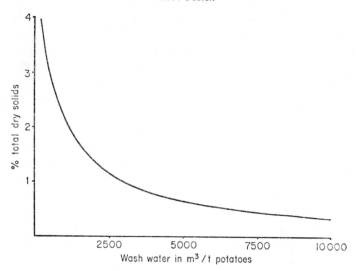

Fig. 1. Wash water versus percentage of total dry solids.

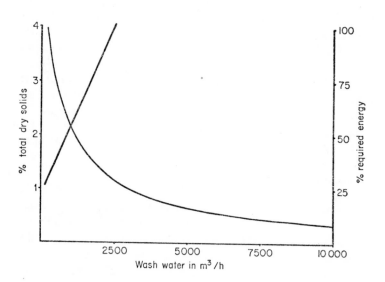

Fig. 2. Total dry solids and energy versus wash water.

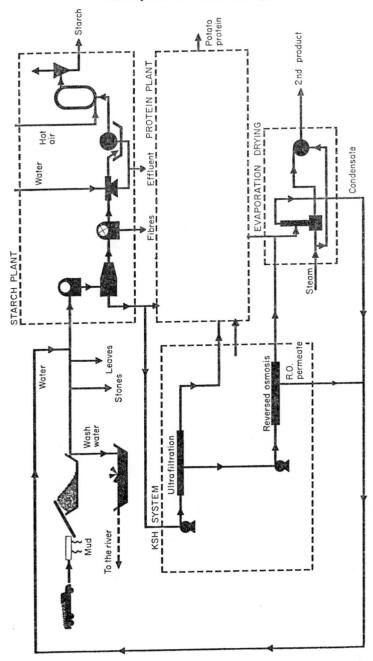

Fig. 3. Potato starch mill.

mud particles, many sorts of bacteria in abundance and some coagulated protein. It took quite some effort to get the development into the commercial phase. During the last campaign an ultra-filtration unit has been in operation which could handle several m³/h of undiluted fruitwater, and this volume could be reduced several times. The system is illustrated in Fig. 3.

The concentrate of the ultrafiltration contains all the coagulable protein and this protein can be isolated comparatively easily. The energy requirement of this new process, that is, ultrafiltration, and recovery of the protein as a product with 8 % humidity is, as compared with the first-mentioned process, about 40 % lower.

The permeate of the ultrafiltration contains the low molecular weight material, that is, sugars, organic acids, amino acids, and potassium and phosphorus compounds. During the last campaign this liquid was evaporated to a fluid with a 60 % solids concentration. The Kjeldahl nitrogen of this liquid is about 6 % (on dry substance); in other words, about 37 % of the dry solids are amino acids and peptides. At the moment we are trying very hard to find a market for this product.

TABLE 3
Composition of second product

Moisture	2%
Ash	25%
Amino acids	35%
Polysaccharides	8%

Somewhere in the process one component can be isolated: asparagine, a non-essential amino acid. The asparagine, a very high purity product, is for sale.

This evaporation process again has the same drawback as the first-mentioned protein recovery process: it requires much energy. For this reason we are experimenting on a technical scale with reverse osmosis units of different suppliers. We feel that a part of the evaporation process can profitably be replaced by reverse osmosis. To what extent this can be done is dependent on the economics, that is, on prices for energy and on investments. More long-term testing is needed before a decision can be made as to how far evaporation can be replaced by reverse osmosis. To find this out is one of our objectives for the near future.

REFERENCES

1. Sjollema (1907). *Chemisch Weekblad*, **4**, p. 637.
2. Kentie, A. (1946). *Voeding*, **6**, p. 214.
3. De Noord, K. G. (1974). *Chemisch Weekblad*, **70**, p. 10.
4. Pol, G. and Den Hartog, C. (1966). *Br. J. Nutrition*, **20**, p. 649.

DISCUSSION

van der Wal: I listened with great interest to your paper, and I observe that when comparing both processes you have given figures for the decrease in energy requirement. Will you please comment also on the other major cost component—is there a difference in investment as well, either in one or the other direction?

Oosten: We think there is a difference in investment. We made an estimate and the investments for both processes are about the same, apart from slight differences in running costs. Actually it is going into commercial production this coming spring in one of our plants in The Netherlands.

Bookey: When you have a seasonal product like this, and you mentioned that the protein and the fibre were going into cattle feed, is there any difficulty in disposing of this on a seasonal basis, in the sense that it isn't a regular supply for the manufacturers?

Oosten: Yes, indeed. The high molecular protein does not give a problem that cannot be solved, but the problem we are facing now is that 60% of solids are slurry. We have to find an outlet for them. Instead of evaporating this to 60% solids you might consider using this liquid as a liquid fertiliser, as is done in Germany. We have a project in co-operation with the Institute for Soil Fertility in The Netherlands and at a university, and this project investigates the possibility of using this liquid as a liquid fertiliser, but you face many problems. You are producing this liquid in the autumn when the farmers already have a problem with rainfall, and the problem then is not one of getting the product on to your land but of how to avoid your water problem. There is an advantage in that the concentration is quite high, about 4% solids. This implies that you could use this liquid as a fertiliser on meadows and so on. An additional problem is that the structure of the soil is such that you cannot go there with heavy equipment, so it has to be very light equipment. It looks as if there is quite some manpower required to get this liquid fertiliser on to the land, so that is one reason why we decided to evaporate the liquid in Germany and try to find an outlet for the concentrated slurry of 60% solids, but indeed it is a problem. For one thing, you can only produce this material for four months of the year.

Zadrazil: Can you tell me how much potato waste—dry waste—is produced per year in The Netherlands?

Oosten: We are producing about 2000 tons of potato protein and roughly 10 000 tons of slurry of 60% solids. I think it has to be multiplied by ten

to get the total production of these materials in The Netherlands, *i.e.*
20 000–25 000 tons of potato protein and 100 000 tons of 60% slurry. These
are very rough estimates.

Brown: In quoting those figures for the material, which looks like Marmite
but isn't, it occurred to me that it might be a competitor to corn steep
liquor, and the people who might be interested in that are the industries
that make antibiotics, and the enzyme fermentation industry where corn
steep liquor is an essential commodity nowadays for fermentation processes. As anyone who operates in this industry knows, we do have a
certain amount of problems with bulk control.

Oosten: You may know that we do have an interest here as well, so we are
familiar with the outlet of corn steep liquor for these opportunities. I
think one of the problems with corn steep liquor is its variation in composition.

Chubb: What is the price relationship between the potato protein and
vegetable oil cakes for animal feeds, soya, rapeseed and groundnut
meal? Is it cheaper than these?

Oosten: $400 per ton. One point I also forgot to mention is that the
overall reduction in pollution in this process is 99% or better.

14

Protein Recovery from Meat, Poultry and Fish Processing Plants

R. A. GRANT

Ecotech Systems (UK) Ltd,
Creekmoor, Poole, Dorset, England

ABSTRACT

Each year in the UK alone, tens of thousands of tons of protein and fat are lost in effluents from abattoirs and poultry and fish processing plants. Such effluents are highly polluting and can impose heavy loads on public sewage treatment works.

A process has been developed which allows the separate recovery of fat and protein from effluents accompanied by a large reduction in the BOD level. The protein recovery system involves two stages, the first stage being a flocculation pretreatment whereby a proportion of the soluble protein is rendered insoluble and is recovered by air flotation or sedimentation followed by dewatering and drying. Residual soluble protein is extracted from the effluent by passage through a bed of newly developed ion-exchange resin. Should the effluent contain a large amount of fat, this is recovered prior to protein recovery by air flotation. By such treatment it is possible to produce a colourless effluent with a relatively low BOD value ($> 90\%$ reduction). Protein may also be recovered from the regenerant solution from the ion-exchange bed by heat coagulation, dewatering and drying.

Protein recovered from effluents has been evaluated nutritionally by amino acid analysis and by feeding trials in pigs and poultry. Good growth rates were obtained with no evidence of toxic effects.

In terms of plant size, the new system is more compact than conventional sewage-type or biological treatment plants and compares favourably with respect to capital cost. Running costs may be offset by by-product recovery in the form of animal feed protein and tallow.

INTRODUCTION

Waste effluents from meat, poultry and fish processing plants contain large amounts of protein and fat and usually have much higher BOD levels than town sewage.

It has been estimated that between 2% and 5% of the total carcass protein is lost in the effluent from abattoirs and poultry plants. In

205

the UK alone this amounts to tens of thousands of tons per annum
with a potential value in the region of £100/t; for the world as a
whole this loss will be increased by a factor of about 100. At a time
when world population is increasing rapidly and outstripping food
production in many areas, such a wastage is hard to justify if the
means of preventing it are available.

Conventional biological effluent treatment plants suffer from the
inherent disadvantage that potentially valuable materials are degraded
to useless sludge which in itself presents a disposal problem. On the
other hand, in the case of physico-chemical treatment plants capable
of recovering useful by-products the revenue from sale or reuse of
recovered material can defray at least in part the capital and running
costs of the plant.

In the past, various processes have been introduced using chemical
precipitants to remove proteins from solution. Mostly, these have
involved the use of toxic compounds such as iron salts which results
in the precipitated protein being useless for nutritional purposes.

The work described below, much of which was carried out in New
Zealand, had as its principal objective the development of a system
capable of achieving a high standard of purification of effluents from
meat and poultry plants while at the same time recovering non-toxic
by-products suitable as animal feeds.

ION EXCHANGE

The new ion-exchange resins (registered name 'Protion') consist of
cross-linked regenerated cellulose modified by the introduction of
anion or cation exchange groups. These resins are available in a
granular form in a wide range of grain sizes and have markedly
superior hydraulic properties and physical stability compared with
the fibrous cellulose ion exchangers usually employed for protein
adsorption in the laboratory. Conventional ion-exchange resins
based on synthetic organic materials such as polystyrene have
negligible capacities for protein molecules. The granular regenerated
cellulose ion exchangers, however, have protein capacities comparable
with fibrous or micro-crystalline cellulose ion exchangers of the order
of 0·5 g protein/g resin. The new resins have been evaluated over a
considerable period of time in applications ranging from laboratory-
scale enzyme production to effluent and water treatment. Because

of their excellent hydraulic properties, Protion resins are suitable for use in conventional types of ion-exchange plant as well as in continuous and fluidised bed systems. By varying the grain size and degree of cross-linking, it is possible to 'tailor' the resin for specific applications in water and effluent treatment and biochemical processing.

The new resins are available in four main types—weakly basic (DEAE), strongly basic (QAE), weakly acidic (CM) and strongly acidic (SP)—corresponding to the main types of conventional resins used for water treatment and covering a working pH range of 2–12. In general, adsorbed protein is readily desorbed by washing the resin bed with salt or buffer solutions; alkaline brine has been found particularly suitable as a regenerant solution where the resins are used for effluent treatment.

EFFLUENT TREATMENT PROCESS

It is generally undesirable to pass raw effluent containing fat and suspended solids directly into the ion-exchange resin beds and a good deal of work has been devoted to the development of a suitable pretreatment which could be integrated with the ion-exchange process to give a complete effluent treatment system. Where the effluent contains a large amount of fat and/or suspended solids, the bulk of this material can be removed by air flotation. This is preferably carried out at a pH of between 3 and 5. This technique has been employed for a number of years in the meat industry for fat recovery.

A considerable proportion of the protein present in the effluent may often be readily flocculated by neutralising the acidified effluent with lime and adding a suitable flocculant. Recovery of the flocculated protein by flotation or sedimentation allows the quantity of resin required to be considerably reduced while at the same time making it possible to achieve a higher degree of purification in the treated effluent from the ion-exchange stage.

In order to recover protein as a dry product from the spent regenerant solution from the ion-exchange resin bed, this is neutralised to an optimum pH determined by experiment and the protein coagulated by heating. After heat coagulation the insoluble protein is readily dewatered by mechanical means prior to drying. The sedimented protein sludge from the flocculation process is similarly treated to yield a dry product.

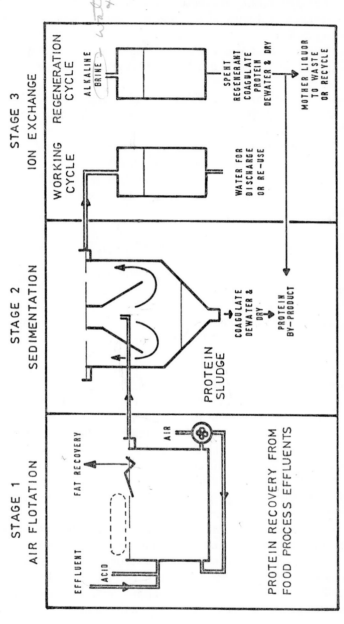

Fig. 1. Process flow diagram.

In terms of plant size, the new system is considerably more compact than conventional sewage-type or biological treatment plants and compares favourably in terms of capital and running costs. In certain cases it is possible to treat effluent up to a very high standard and BOD values of less than 10 mg/litre have been achieved. The overall process is shown diagramatically in Fig. 1. The resins and processes described in this article are covered by British and foreign patents.

BY-PRODUCT COMPOSITION

Samples of dried effluent protein recovered from the flocculation and ion-exchange stages were analysed for protein nitrogen, fat, ash and amino acids. Table 1 shows the composition of dry material recovered from the ion-exchange regenerant solution; the true protein content averaged 68% with an ash content of only 3·7%. The same samples

TABLE 1
Composition of dry product

Sample	N	g/100 g P	Ash	Protein
A2	9·80 ±0·2	0·70 ±0·02	5·1	61·3 ±1·0
B2	11·81 ±0·08	0·02 ±0·05	2·3	73·9 ±0·5

were analysed for amino acids by ion-exchange chromatography and the results (Table 2) compared with various reference proteins. The amino acid pattern is evenly distributed with no significant deficiencies. The essential amino acid contents of the two samples (with the exception of tryptophan) are compared with the FAO recommendations for human nutrition (Table 3); in both samples the content of essential amino acids appeared adequate. A similar analysis for amino acids was carried out on a sample of protein recovered from the effluent from a poultry processing plant (Table 4). In certain instances, as in the case of effluents from processing operations such as cooking or rendering, the effluent may contain considerable amounts of fat firmly complexed with protein and present in a colloidal state. This results in the dried floc protein by-product containing appreciable quantities of fat; this does not impair its value as an animal feed.

TABLE 2
Amino acid composition of recovered solids from Gear Meat Co. works effluent (g amino acid/16 g nitrogen)

Amino acid	Recovered solids		Reference proteins			
	Fraction		Fibrin	Haemo-globins	Serum proteins	Casein
	A	B				
Lysine	8·8	8·5	9·1	9·1	10·0	8·5
Histidine	3·9	5·9	2·9	8·0	3·3	3·2
Arginine	4·4	4·7	7·8	3·9	5·8	4·2
Aspartic acid	14·3	9·4	11·9	9·8	10·3	7·0
Threonine	7·9	4·5	7·3	5–6	12·6	4·5
Serine	7·7	5·7	12·5	5·5	18·2	6·8
Glutamic acid	19·3	10·0	15·0	8·1	14·2	23·0
Proline	6·6	3·2	5·3	4·7	5·5	13·1
Glycine	5·5	3·5	5·4	5·3	2·0	2·1
Alanine	8·8	6·8	4·0	9·8	—	3·3
Half-cystine	trace	trace	3·8	1·0–2·2	7·0	0·8
Valine	11·0	8·2	5·6	9·0	7·5	7·7
Methionine	2·8	3·2	2·6	1–3	4·0	3·5
Isoleucine	5·5	4·1	5·6	0–2	3·4	7·5
Leucine	17·1	15·0	7·1	14·4	10·1	10·0
Tyrosine	5·5	3·2	6·0	2·9	5·5	6·4
Phenylalanine	9·9	7·9	4·5	7–8	5·2	6·3
Ammonia	—	1·1	—	—	—	—

TABLE 3
Essential amino acids
(g amino acid/16 g nitrogen)

Amino acid	FAO[a]	Egg	Fraction		Casein
			A	B	
Isoleucine	4·2	6·8	5·5	4·1	7·5
Leucine	4·8	9·0	17·1	15·0	10·0
Lysine	4·2	6·3	8·8	8·5	8·5
Phenylalanine	2·8	6·0	9·9	7·9	6·3
Tyrosine	2·8	4·4	5·5	3·2	6·4
Threonine	2·8	5·0	7·9	4·5	4·5
Tryptophan	1·4	1·7	—	—	—
Valine	4·2	7·4	11·0	8·2	7·7
Sulphur containing:					
Total	4·2	5·4	2·8	3·2	4·3
Methionine	2·2	3·1	2·8	3·2	3·5

[a] Food and Agricultural Organisation, '*Provisional Pattern*' *of Essential Amino Acids for Human Nutrition*, Rome, 1957.

TABLE 4

Amino acid analysis of protein recovered from poultry processing plant effluent (μmol/100 μmol)

Aspartic acid	10·8	**Threonine**	5·1
Serine	7·7	Glutamic acid	11·5
Proline	4·5	Glycine	6·9
Alanine	8·9	Cystine (half)	1·2
Valine	7·4	**Methionine**	1·5
Isoleucine	5·3	**Leucine**	9·1
Tyrosine	2·3	**Phenylalanine**	3·8
Lysine	6·6	**Histidine**	2·3
Arginine	4·9		

Essential amino acids in bold. Tryptophan not estimated.

FEEDING TRIALS

A standard feeding trial on chicks was carried out on recovered effluent protein from the Gear Meat Co., Wellington, New Zealand. The composition of the experimental rations is shown in Table 5 and the relative growth rates, food consumption and feed efficiencies are shown in Table 6. The basal ration consisted of wheatmeal, maize meal, barley meal, lucerne and salt, and contained 13% protein. Therefore at the 50% level it contributed 6·5% protein. To this was added casein, meat meal or effluent protein to contribute a further 6·5% protein.

The ten treatments were arranged in a randomised block with two replicates. The 280 chicks used were crossbred WL/AO cockerels randomised in groups of 14. The reference ration was fed to all chicks for the first week, the chicks were then weighed and the experimental rations fed for three weeks and the chicks weighed again. Feed consumption was recorded weekly. The ratio feed consumption (g)/weight gain shown in Table 6 is a measure of the efficiency of the feed. The dried effluent protein was approximately equal to the meat meals and casein in nutritional value, slightly inferior to fishmeal and superior to the meat and bone meals and protein extracted from grass which were tested at the same time. It is apparent that this effluent protein can be used as a concentrate for poultry production. There was no evidence of toxic side-effects in either the chicks or young rats which could be attributed to the

TABLE 5
Composition of experimental rations

	A	B	C	D	E	F	G	H	I	J
Basal	50·0	50·0	50·0	50·0	50·0	50·0	50·0	50·0	50·0	50·0
Premix	2·0	2·0	2·0	2·0	2·0	2·0	2·0	2·0	2·0	2·0
Bonemeal	5·5	4·0	2·0	1·25	—	4·25	—	0·75	2·75	4·5
Sugar	35·2	34·4	33·9	35·05	32·95	36·0	34·35	34·95	36·35	30·5
Casein	7·3									
Mm 41		9·6								
Mb 43			12·1							
Mb 44				11·7						
Mm 45					10·8					
Mb 46						12·0				
Mm 47							9·9			
Grass protein								12·3		
Fishmeal 6									8·9	
Effluent protein										13·0

TABLE 6
*Chick growth, food consumption and feed efficiency of
experimental rations*

	Body weight gain/chick 1–4 weeks	Food consumption/ chick 1–4 weeks	Feed consumption(g)/ weight gain
A Reference ration (casein)	137	359	2·62
B Mm 41	147	400	2·74
C Mb 43	103	347	3·38
D Mb 44	100	302	3·02
E Mm 45	166	413	2·49
F Mb 46	83	282	3·42
G Mm 47	141	386	2·73
H Grass protein	104	338	3·16
I Fishmeal 6	169	418	2·48
J Effluent protein	125	345	2·75
MSD 5%	25	91	0·54

TABLE 7
Pig trial rations and results

	Ecotech effluent by-product %	Control %	Whey %
Barley	42·0	43·0	31·2
Maize	41·75	43·0	31·2
Meat meal (60%)	11·0	13·75	10·0
Whey mix (12·4%)	—	—	26·75
Trace nutrients	0·25	0·25	0·25
Steamed bone flour	—	—	0·6
Effluent by-product	5·0	—	—
	100·0	100·0	100·0
Estimated total protein (%)	17·0	17·0	16·9
Results:			
Original liveweight (kg)	14·0	14·3	14·4
68 trial days liveweight (kg)	39·5	41·6	33·4
68 day gain (kg)	25·5	27·3	19·0
Average daily gain (kg)	0·38	0·40	0·28

recovery process. Samples tested bacteriologically had low total counts and were negative for coliform organisms.

A feeding trial was also carried out on pigs using dried floc protein from the save-all effluent from a New Zealand meat works. The composition of the experimental rations and the results obtained are shown in Table 7. A satisfactory growth rate was obtained over 68 days when the diet included effluent by-product at the 5% level.

INDUSTRIAL APPLICATIONS

Typical results for meat works effluents with respect to BOD, COD and protein levels are shown in Tables 8, 9 and 10. Generally speaking, the best results were obtained using the combined flocculation plus ion-exchange process. However, there is a great variability in the composition and strength of effluent from different abattoirs and poultry plants and also in the consent conditions imposed by local authorities for discharging to sewers so that, depending on the circumstances, either or both of the process stages may be required. In some cases a separate fat recovery stage will also be necessary to meet the requirements. Table 11 shows approximate values for protein and fat in different effluent streams of a meat works. Although the concentrations are relatively low, in terms of total output the quantities involved are quite large; 1000 ppm of protein or fat represents about 1 t/10^6 litre (4·5 t/10^6 gal) of effluent which would be an average daily output for a New Zealand works producing frozen lamb.

In the case of an effluent from a herring processing plant, the COD level was reduced by 90% using the flocculation process only; the dry product yield was 2 g/litre.

TABLE 8
Residual BOD (%) in treated slaughterboard effluent

Treatment	Sample					
	1	2	3	4	5	Means
Flocculation	38	41	31	23	27	32
Ion exchange	10	13	23	19	18	17
Flocculation + ion exchange	0[a]	5	12	7	0[a]	5

[a] Value too low for measurement by standard method.

TABLE 9
Residual COD (%) in slaughterboard effluent after treatment

Treatment	Sample							
	1	2	3	4	5	6	7	Means
Flocculation	19	40	31	37	35	31	31	32
Ion exchange only	18	31	31	28	25	27	15	25
Flocculation + ion exchange	0[a]	14	9	22	0[a]	11	0[a]	11
Initial level (ppm)	305	110	708	554	274	703	858	645

[a] Value too low for measurement by standard method.

TABLE 10
Residual protein (%) after treatment in slaughterboard effluent

Treatment	Sample					
	1	2	3	4	5	Means
Flocculation	29	40	32	29	47	35
Ion exchange	36	21	18	23	45	28
Flocculation + ion exchange	5	5	6	8	5	6
Initial level (mg/ml)	0·63	0·70	0·39	0·18	0·43	0·47

TABLE 11
Approximate concentration in ppm in different wastes

	Slaughter-board (ppm)	Save-all (ppm)	Skinwash (ppm)
Protein	500	500	800
Fat	100	300	1 000
Ash	250	1 000	2 000
Chloride	75	100	80
Total solids	1 000	2 000	4 000

For a poultry plant carrying out cooking as well as slaughtering and dressing, the effluent had an average COD value of 4000 after the bulk of the fat had been removed by air flotation. In this case, the combined flocculation plus ion-exchange treatment reduced the COD level to 160 (96% reduction).

Industrial-scale fat recovery, protein sedimentation and ion-exchange plant are shown in Figs. 2 and 3.

Fig. 2. Full-scale (100 000 gal/day) poultry effluent plant. Fat recovery and protein sedimentation stages.

ECONOMICS

The costs of biological treatment of industrial waste have been evaluated by Chipperfield.[1] He concludes that the evidence casts considerable doubt upon the validity of the traditional view that bio-degradable industrial wastes are most effectively and cheaply treated

Fig. 3. A 4 ft diameter ion-exchange unit.

at local sewage works. The evidence suggests that industry should consider wholly or partly treating liquid wastes at source. The possibility of reuse of water should also be considered carefully in view of rapidly increasing water costs.

The question of the disposal of industrial effluents with domestic sewage and the related costs has also been reviewed by Calvert.[2] The cost range is given as approximately 10–25p/1000 gal, but this will have considerably increased since the date of the review and may now be as high as 75p/1000 gal in some cases. The same author also states that biological treatment on site is not always desirable and the fact that it may appear economical may be a fallacy of the Mogden formula.

In view of the foregoing it appears that a strong case can be made for physico-chemical effluent treatment on site with by-product recovery to offset capital and running costs. This appears to apply particularly in the case of meat and poultry works and may also apply to other food processing effluents.

ACKNOWLEDGEMENT

The author wishes to express his warm appreciation of the co-operation of many colleagues and, in particular, that of the Director and staff of the DSIR Physics and Engineering Laboratory, Lower Hutt, New Zealand, and the management and staff of the Gear Meat Co., Wellington, New Zealand.

REFERENCES

1. Chipperfield, P. N. J. (1970). *Chem. & Ind.*, p. 735.
2. Calvert, J. T. (1970). *Chem. & Ind.*, p. 733.

DISCUSSION

Cerletti: I have two questions to ask:
    (i) To what extent are proteins denatured in the air flotation stage?
    (ii) You mentioned the use of flocculants to improve protein flocculation. What kind of flocculants did you use?
Grant: Denaturisation does take place but does not always lead to insolubilisation. Secondly, it is not always necessary to add specific flocculant aids. In order to promote the size of the floc and the ease with which it can be settled or floated, one can add one to two parts of polyacriline, for instance, which would promote the growth of the floc.
Russell Eggitt: This question may be a little difficult to answer but I do realise that the answer depends on the problem of effluent disposal. If one could take an average situation, what do you think would be the size of a poultry processing establishment, possibly in terms of daily throughput of broilers, at which it becomes economically viable to establish one of these protein recovery plants?

A second minor question is, what sort of life do you get with the resin?
Grant: I would say the economics would be favourable in the case of a poultry unit processing 20 000 birds a day producing 100 000 gal of effluent. I would say that would be a viable operation.

Secondly, with regard to resin life we carried out life-testing trials with an accelerated life-testing rig and it has been estimated that the life of the resin would be in excess of 1000 working cycles. In point of fact we have never had resin which has become so badly contaminated that it couldn't be revitalised by treatment with warm caustic soda solution. It is possible that the most reasonable estimate for resin life would be approximately 1000 working cycles.

Clift: How specific is the ion-exchange resin to blood proteins? Can it be modified to handle other food proteins, *e.g.* milk proteins?

Grant: The resin can be made selective, and if one likes to go to the trouble of collecting blood separately you could produce γ-globulin. Other high-quality proteins could also be produced. The resin can be used for isolating expensive proteins.

Clift: I was really considering whether this could be a more economical process than ultra-filtration for use, for example with skimmed milk?

Grant: It would depend on the strength of the solution, I would think. It is more efficient for recovering protein from very diluted solutions.

Mann: One of the main constitutents of the effluents of a slaughterhouse is blood, particularly with regard to BOD. If much work is going on just now to recover blood from slaughterhouses and improve its utilisation, then one of the major protein constituents is lost. Will your process still be economical if blood is recovered in another way?

Grant: In the case of large works in New Zealand they do save as much blood as they can and produce dried blood as a by-product. A lot of protein comes from the washing operation. In a small slaughterhouse, blood is the main constituent, but in large units where secondary processing is going on you will find there is much less blood. The same applies in some of the poultry works where the effluent contains much less blood.

Lalla: When you said it is economical and feasible to operate a plant at 100 000 gal/day, did you think of negative costing of the effluent disposal or is it economical from the sale of by-products?

Grant: Taking an average situation and comparing it with the costs of disposal to a sewer or the installation of a biological treatment plant. For instance, in a plant of 100 000 gal/day capacity, one might recover half a ton a day of tallow which can be sold. In fact we have a plant where the tallow is being sold and firms producing poultry could recycle the recovered protein back to the poultry farm. Compare this with a biological treatment plant where there is no possibility of by-product recovery. You have the capital costs and running costs of the treatment plant itself, together with the costs of disposal, which is rapidly increasing at the moment because of transport.

Evans: Could you tell us how the protein is released from the ion-exchange resin and the concentration at which it is released?

Grant: We use a regenerated treatment which consists of alkaline brine, and this normally removes protein readily from the resin. It is possible to reach a protein concentration of 10% in the regenerated solution from which the protein can be recovered by coagulation. If necessary the mother liquid can be made alkaline and recycled.

Emery: Could you say a few words about the control problems in such a process, particularly in terms of the measurement of saturation and breakthrough in the ion-exchange problems and so on, and the degree of technical skill that would be required in order to operate such a process.

Grant: With regard to the running of the plant, the first part of the plant is subject to automatic control. The operations requiring operators would be say centrifuging the protein sludge or rendering the fats down into tallow. We have a plant where the operator is a labourer who has been upgraded to a technician. He is not really a skilled engineer but he manages to operate the plant quite successfully, provided he has access to skilled people if he requires them.

15

Recovery of Dairy Waste

S. G. Coton

Milk Marketing Board, Thames Ditton, Surrey, England

ABSTRACT

The sources and extent of general wastage in the dairy industry are described; about 1–4% of milk input to dairies and creameries is wasted. The economics and nutritional value of this wastage is calculated. Attempts to recover the wastage have been made in some instances but it is doubtful if recovery processes are economically justifiable.

A major part of the paper is concerned with whey, which constitutes a special problem, the extent of which is described and the nutritional value of the whey wastage calculated. Methods of treatment are discussed. 'Conventional' treatments, including drying, direct animal feeding and lactose extraction, are briefly described together with newer 'unconventional' treatments at greater length. These 'unconventional' processes—gel filtration, ion exchange and ultrafiltration—generally aim at extracting the 0·7% of true protein from whey in undenatured form. Ultrafiltration is now reaching a commercial scale. All three processes produce a lactose-rich by-product which, for economic success, must be utilised. Possible lactose utilisation includes fermentation either to a protein-rich biomass or other product, e.g. alcohol, or by enzymic conversion to galactose/glucose syrup which may have a relatively ready acceptability in foodstuffs or for subsequent fermentation. Neither process is yet established on a commercial scale.

INTRODUCTION

The dairy industry wastes very little. With the exception of whey utilisation, which is a special case and is the subject of a major part of this paper, waste from modern dairy plants constitutes only 1–4% of milk input. This 1–4% is, however, of itself a very significant quantity. For example, milk production in the United Kingdom, which is sufficient for only 60% of UK demand for dairy products, was, in 1973, 2997×10^6 gal. 1–4% of this is 30×10^6–120×10^6 gal, valued at 1973 farmers' prices at £6·9–£27·6 million.

The BMA Committee on Nutrition recommend that a man on

221

'medium work' requires a minimum of 3000 kcal and 87 g protein per day. Using these recommendations, the food value of 1% wastage is sufficient for the calorie needs of 83 000 men and the protein needs of 146 000.

GENERAL DAIRY WASTAGE

Milk has a high BOD (100 000–120 000 ppm) and, even when diluted, as it is in effluent, conventional effluent treatment is expensive. Costs of treatment are variously quoted, but range usually between 1·0p and 2·0p/lb BOD. The problem is illustrated by the capital expended on effluent treatment plants; a large modern creamery with a through-put of 100 000 gal/day and costing, say, £5 million will probably include an effluent plant costing roughly £0·4 million.

The wastage arises largely from drainage and washing of tankers and equipment plus spillages. An immediate aim is therefore to reduce these direct wastages by fairly obvious means of good house-keeping and management. Attempts have been made to segregate first plant rinses from other waste streams and to recover the material from this directly back into product. One dairy in Sweden has been extensively equipped with this in mind. These attempts often, how-ever, involve a concentration step, and the expense of this together with the cost of separating first rinses from general effluent may well make the process economically unattractive.

Dairy effluent is usually treated conventionally, by aerobic diges-tion processes, simply because there is no proven effective alternative which might result in the recovery of useful material. Dairy effluent is sufficiently concentrated to be a disposal problem but too dilute for any but very inexpensive processes for material recovery to be economically justifiable. Fermentation processes to produce useful biomass, which figure prominently in this symposium, are very unlikely to be applicable to general dairy effluent.

WHEY CONSIDERED AS A SEMI-WASTE MATERIAL

The situation is, however, somewhat different with whey. Whey is the fluid separated from milk or skimmed milk in the process of making cheese or casein. Its composition varies slightly with origin, but an average composition of whey from Cheddar and similar cheese is given in Table 1. World cheese production is increasing fairly

TABLE 1
Composition of liquid whey
(amount per 100 g)

Item	Liquid whey
Water	93·1%
Crude protein (N × 6·25)	0·9%
True protein (N × 6·25)	0·7%
Fat	0·3%
Lactose	5·1%
Ash	0·6%
Calcium	51 mg
Phosphorus	53 mg
Iron	0·1 mg
Sodium	—
Potassium	—
Vitamin A	10 IU
Thiamin	0·03 mg
Riboflavin	0·14 mg
Niacin	0·1 mg
Ascorbic acid	—
Food energy	26 kcal

Source: *Composition of Foods*, Agricultural Handbook No 8, USDA, 1963.

rapidly with a corresponding increase in whey production, as shown in Table 2.

Using once more the recommendations of the BMA Committee on Nutrition (1950), the world whey production of 70·7 million tons (1973) could provide protein for the yearly needs of $20·36 \times 10^6$ men and calories for $17·02 \times 10^6$ men. The UK produced only 58% of its 1973 cheese requirements, but this involved the production of 1·5 million tons of whey which could provide protein for the yearly needs of 432 000 men and calories for 361 000 men.

'CONVENTIONAL' WHEY PROCESSING

It follows from these figures that a major aim of the dairy industry in producing food from waste must be the utilisation of whey. This is already achieved to a considerable extent by what might be termed conventional technology, including drying to whey powder, lactose extraction and direct feeding to animals.

TABLE 2
Estimated world whey production
(estimated at 8 kg and 5 kg whey per kg of cheese and cottage
cheese respectively)

	1966	1971	1972	1973
		('000 tons)		(preliminary)
USA	8 618	10 883	11 804	11 836
Canada	774	998	1 019	935
Belgium–Luxembourg	282	290	282	230
Denmark	1 000	960	1 048	1 024
France	4 878	5 603	5 960	6 136
Germany, Federal Republic	2 512	3 285	3 482	3 568
Ireland	136	264	364	328
Italy	3 918	3 840	3 880	3 960
Netherlands	1 864	2 424	2 504	2 616
United Kingdom	872	1 296	1 469	1 447
Total Western Europe	20 105	23 045	24 189	24 541
Australasia	1 352	1 440	1 502	1 512
Other developed countries	496	768	800	832
Total developed countries	31 345	37 134	39 314	39 656
USSR	3 456	3 624	3 808	4 016
Eastern Europe	4 968	6 088	6 090	6 300
Total developing countries	17 344	19 344	19 736	20 723
Total world	57 113	66 190	68 948	70 695

Of these, whey powder production is the most important single factor. Whey powder production in 13 countries is shown in Table 3. Most of this whey powder has been used in animal feed except in the USA, where the use of dried whey for human food accounted in 1973 for 53 % of total US whey powder production; uses included baked goods, ice cream, processed meat and processed cheese. During 1973 and the early part of 1974, world prices for whey powder increased rapidly at a time when prices for animal feeds were also rapidly increasing. More recently there has been a sharp fall in price which will discourage expansion of powder manufacture.

The simplest means of utilising whey is to feed it directly to pigs. Large quantities are used in this way (for example, in the UK approximately 40 % of production is used in this way), but higher transport costs, considerable seasonality of supply and poor storage properties make it comparatively unattractive to the pig farmer and therefore comparatively unprofitable to the whey supplier. Lactose extraction is another well-established use for whey, with the mother liquor from the extraction being dried and used in animal feed. Uses for lactose, which include pharmaceuticals, are, however, fairly limited and little market expansion is likely.

Whey-based beverages have achieved modest popularity in a few countries but are unlikely to be users of major quantities of whey.

TABLE 3
Whey powder production

	1966	1970	1971 ('000 tons)	1972	1973	Whey drying as % of total whey supply 1973
USA, total	214	282	308	346	338	40
of which for food	110	133	145	171	178	—
Canada	19	20	24	25	24	36
EEC	93	210	274	325	389	30
of which France	26	80	115	148	170	39
Netherlands	28	51	65	71	99	53
Germany, FR	15	43	48	56	66	26
United Kingdom	11	13	14	15	15	15
Belgium	6	7	10	9	9	55
Others	7	16	22	26	30	6
Austria	1	7	8	9	11	35
Finland	6	12	14	17	17	65
Total 13 countries	333	531	628	722	779	34

'UNCONVENTIONAL' WHEY PROCESSING

There has been a recent upsurge of activity in 'unconventional' whey treatment, but bridging the gap between 'conventional' and 'unconventional' treatment is deionisation generally by electrodialysis or, less commonly, ion exchange. Deionised whey powder is now fairly well established and finds its major outlet in the baby food industry for the production of so-called humanised baby foods. It is normal practice to reduce inorganic constituents by about 90%.

The 'unconventional' processes of gel filtration, ion exchange and ultrafiltration aim at extracting the protein from whey in undenatured form. True protein amounts to about 0·6–0·7% in whey. It has an

excellent amino acid spectrum, as shown in Table 4. In the undenatured form proteins also possess functional properties of high
solubility, aeration, heat gelation and stability in acid solution. These
functional properties indicate use in the flour and sugar confectionery
industries, in the soft drinks industry and, in respect of the excellent
nutritional value, in, for example, baby foods.

TABLE 4
*Amino acid composition of whey
protein obtained by ultrafiltration*

Amino acid	mg/g N
Lysine	176
Histidine	52
Arginine	50
Aspartic acid	219
Threonine	129
Serine	92
Glutamic acid	364
Proline	118
Glycine	38
Alanine	100
Cystine	60
Valine	117
Methionine	44
Isoleucine	114
Leucine	221
Tyrosine	62
Phenylalanine	65
Tryptophan	36

Gel Filtration

Gel filtration has now reached the stage of a large pilot plant for
recovery of whey protein. The process uses a cross-linked dextran
gel in a column through which the whey is passed. The smaller
molecules, minerals and lactose are entrained in the dextran gel more
readily than the protein molecules, and on elution of the column with
water the protein fraction elutes first, followed by lactose and then
minerals. There is no concentration during the process.

Ion Exchange

A description of ion exchange used for protein recovery is the
subject of a separate paper in this symposium and therefore I intend

only to draw attention to its possibilities as a process for treatment of whey with the potential advantage over ultrafiltration, with which I shall deal more fully, of producing a better separation of protein from other constituents, but the disadvantage of achieving a lesser concentration of protein.

Ultrafiltration

Ultrafiltration is at present the most promising of the methods for extraction of protein from whey. Ultrafiltration and the closely related technique of reverse osmosis are membrane processes in which a fluid, in this case whey, is applied under pressure to a selective membrane; in the case of reverse osmosis, water, and in the case of ultrafiltration, water and some smaller molecular weight solutes pass through the membrane. Thus, in the case of reverse osmosis, all solutes, and in the case of ultrafiltration, solutes not passing through the membrane are concentrated. A practical problem in these membrane techniques is membrane polarisation, the build-up at the membrane surface of solute concentration as the result of passage of solvent through the membrane. This reduces flux through the membrane and means are provided in all ultrafiltration and reverse osmosis equipment to avoid stagnation of fluid at the membrane surface either by using highly turbulent flow conditions across the membrane or by laminar flow in short passes with frequent shear of the fluid.

Ultrafiltration plants for use in the food industry have membranes cast internally in tubes or in flat plate form, roughly analogous to a plate heat exchanger.

A second practical problem is that of ensuring good microbiological quality. A merit of ultrafiltration is that concentration and separation occur at near-ambient temperatures, and therefore denaturation of protein with consequent impairment of functional properties is avoided, but by the same token the hazards of microbiological spoilage are increased. The hazards are mitigated by avoiding operation in the temperature range of most rapid growth (in general, the range for mesophilic organisms), by reducing residence time in the plant to a minimum, and by hygienic plant design. In practice, plants operate at about 10°C or about 50°C, the latter having the advantage that flux rates, being temperature-dependent, will be significantly higher at 50°C than at 10°C.

There are three possible modes of operation of ultrafiltration plants: as a batch process, as a straight-through plant and as a series of recirculation loops with a bleed from one loop to the next with increasing concentration in the successive loops until the final one which operates at the desired final concentration and from which the product is bled (Fig. 1). Batch plants involve undesirably long

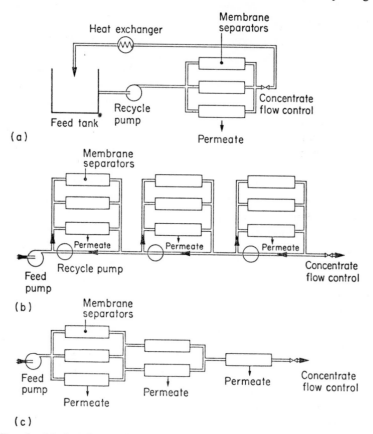

FIG. 1. Modes of operation of ultrafiltration plants: (a) single stage batch recycle; (b) continuous flow multi-stage recycle ultrafiltration; (c) continuous single pass operation.

residence times. Straight-through plants are not yet feasible because of the difficulty of avoiding membrane polarisation with this configuration, and consequently most plants are built with internal recirculation loops. A tubular plant of 10 000 gal/day capacity with two recirculation loops has been installed by the Milk Marketing Board.

The degree of concentration which can fairly readily be achieved by whey ultrafiltration is between 25% and 30% solids, of which about two-thirds is protein; this represents a concentration of the original protein of between 24 and 29 times. The proportion of protein to other solids can be increased to a level approaching 100% by adding water to the concentrate followed by further concentration in an ultrafiltration plant. Concentrate is normally spray dried.

LACTOSE UTILISATION

The extraction of protein for human consumption from whey represents a valuable upgrading of a low value or no value by-product, but if whey is regarded as an effluent problem, then the extraction of 0·7% protein scarcely reduces the problem relative to the 5% lactose which remains in the permeate from the ultrafiltration process. Commercial utilisation of the lactose-rich permeate is not immediately obvious, and this is the probable reason for the comparatively slow development of commercial ultrafiltration of whey.

It is, of course, quite easy to extract lactose from permeate, but the market for lactose is strictly limited and therefore alternative means of lactose utilisation are desirable. The two alternatives being pursued most vigorously are fermentation and enzymic hydrolysis to galactose/glucose.

Fermentation of lactose by yeast, in particular *S. fragilis*, has been quite extensively investigated with the aim of producing cell mass and, therefore, by aerobic fermentation, but alcohol production is an obvious alternative. Fermentation by many other micro-organisms has also been investigated, though less extensively than yeast fermentation, again generally with the aim of producing protein-rich biomass. The commercial application of this work is inhibited by comparatively unattractive economics. The least expensive product is likely to result from a fermentation plant receiving its whey permeate by direct pipeline from an adjacent cheese creamery. Large cheese creameries now have capacities in excess of 100 000 gal/day of milk, 90% of which, in volume terms, will appear as whey. However, because of the seasonal production of milk, the average throughput of a cheese creamery is not likely to be much in excess of 60% of maximum. This implies a fermentation plant to handle a maximum of say 100 000 gal/day and an average throughput of 60 000 gal/day, unless it is envisaged that whey is transported from other creameries. The cost of transporting a material of 95% water content or evaporation before transport must be quite high and reduces the prime advantage of lactose as being a cheap fermentation substrate.

Fermentation plants tend to be scale-dependent for their economics and the throughput of even a large cheese creamery is well below the optimum size for a fermentation plant. Table 5 represents a model

TABLE 5

Model costing for fermentation of whey permeate, **100 000** *gal/day (454 000 litres/day) maximum capacity*

Assumptions:
1. Permeate at nil value
2. Lactose 5%; biomass yield 43% of lactose
3. Average throughput 60% of maximum capacity

Costing:

Item	£/year × 1 000	£/ton of product
Depreciation (10% of capital)	175·0	81·9
Energy costs	157·0	73·4
Chemicals	62·9	29·4
Water	2·9	1·4
Packing	14·3	6·7
Labour	22·4	10·5
Repairs and maintenance	28·1	13·1
Total	462·6	216·4

Exclusions: Interest on capital, administration and selling costs, effluent treatment.

costing of a biomass produced from whey permeate at 100 000 gal/day maximum, 60 000 gal/day average. With the assumptions made, and most importantly that the substrate is included at nil value (a condition quite unattractive to the dairy industry), the ex-factory price of the biomass would be in excess of £216/ton. This level of price is acceptable for human nutrition but quite unacceptable in present market circumstances as an animal feed.

METHANE PRODUCTION

It is perhaps a little outside the scope indicated by the title of this symposium, 'Food from Waste', but my paper, dealing as it does largely with whey utilisation, would be incomplete without mention of the possibility of anaerobic fermentation of lactose permeate to produce methane which can be used in the steam-raising plant of a cheese creamery. The permeate, as it leaves an ultrafiltration plant, is likely to be at about 50°C and therefore no energy needs to be added in order to operate the anaerobic process at about 30°C, at which temperature the residence time and therefore the capital involved in the fermentation plant is minimal.

A model costing based upon pilot-plant work indicates that this process may have economic attractions.

DISCUSSION

Emery: Could you tell me what the molecular weight distribution of the whey protein is?

Coton: I'm sorry, I cannot.

Butcher: Do the quoted costs in Table 5 on the fermentation plant include drying costs, and what percentage saving do you think there would be if the yeast was processed without drying?

Coton: Yes, it did include drying as part of the cost.

Butcher: How much do you think would be the saving if the drying costs were excluded and the material was further processed?

Coton: My off-the-cuff answer there would be about 20% of that cost.

Evans: It might help the first questioner to know that the proteins are α-lactalbumen and β-lactoglobulin.

16

The World Food Problem

G. D. KAPSIOTIS

*Food and Nutrition Development Strategy Service,
FAO, Rome, Italy*

ABSTRACT

*The bold and simple definition of the world food situation is that there is not enough
food produced or available to meet the needs of most developing countries. The
problem is as old as humanity, but its true and frightening dimensions are underlined
by the present world food crisis. The main cause of the crisis is attributed to disastrous
climatological conditions in 1972. Other factors, such as increased economic
activities in affluent countries resulting in high demand for commodities and the
worldwide inflation and monetary instability since 1972, had their cumulative effect
in creating a critical food situation. The steep increase of grain prices has also
driven the prices of other foodstuffs to levels beyond the economic reach of the
poorer people. This leads to the reduction in effective demand which does not
encourage increased production. The energy crisis, the shortage and high cost of
fertilisers and of all agricultural inputs since 1973 brought the world food situation
to its most desperate point. The World Food Conference, convened by the United
Nations in Rome during November 1974, tried to get to grips with the world food
problem and propose measures to redress this situation and prevent impending
disaster. Some of the resolutions made during this conference are reviewed in the
paper. It is hoped that the World Food Conference will prove a breakthrough in the
world food situation, but the practical results will be the measure of its achievements.
The resolutions were in fact only an expression of political will, but results cannot
be obtained if this expression is not put into active political will at both international
and national level. For a multitude of developing countries, but also for the developed
countries, poverty is closely tied with the world food problem, and eradication of
poverty has to be the moving element in the political will to solve the world food
problem.*

It is a disturbing and, I would say, morally unacceptable fact that
certain quarters voice the philosophy of natural selection for the
human race. There are people supporting the 'lifeboat' theory or, if
you like, the theory of 'triage'. Brought within the context of
survival of mankind, these so-called theories imply that food and

economic aid should be extended only to selected countries—this with the apparent hope that they board the lifeboat in order to assist in the survival of those on it. Other countries—on whose decision?—should be left to starve quietly by themselves. Perhaps some of you have read an article published in February 1975 in *Newsweek* under the title of 'Triage: Deciding Who Shall Live' by V. Tarzic Vittachi. He very aptly points to the false analogy that 'we do not fight our way aboard the boat called earth: we were all born aboard'. He envisages earth as a badly managed ocean liner and suggests that 'only if we put our new-found technological knowledge and our humane sense of mutual considerateness to work redesigning the ship by stripping it of its wasteful class divisions and eliminating its dispensable luxuries the liner-earth could carry us all—and perhaps even our children—to our destination'. The implication is quite clear: in the era of humanitarianism it appears that the rich and powerful are losing, if they have ever developed it, the sense of reason and humane behaviour. For years developed countries pledged their intention to devote 1 % of their national income to assist the economic and social development of the poor developing countries of the world. Practically none—one or two exceptions might exist by now—reached even a small portion of that pledge. In preparing, encouraging and conducting wars, much higher percentages have been used. It is commonplace now to talk of the cost of the conquest of space. Funds, energy and creativeness have been used abundantly—but not for the direct or indirect benefit and development of mankind.

Let me return to the theme of this presentation: the 'world food problem' is as old as humanity but its true and frightening dimensions came to the forefront because of the present food crisis. What, however, triggered the worldwide awareness were not the implications which the food crisis might have—and actually has—for the nutrition and health of large masses of population, mainly in the developing countries, but the sudden depletion of reserves of cereals. What alarmed political leaders of the world was the 'cereal crisis'. The chronic or continuing world food crisis with its inseparable problems of poverty, inequitable distribution, under- and malnutrition has over decades been receiving only grudging attention. The World Food Conference (WFC) held in Rome in November 1974 brought together the countries of the world to deal essentially with the world cereal crisis. The chronic food crisis that has been afflicting much of the population of the poorest and most overpopulated

countries was not the impulse behind the Conference. However, as
I shall refer to it later, the World Food Conference gave consideration to the problems related to nutrition and health during its
deliberations.

The present world food crisis—more precisely the cereal crisis—
originated from a combination of longer-term problems and
temporary setbacks, and emerged suddenly in a pronounced form in
1972. The disastrous weather conditions in that year resulted in poor
harvests. An unusual coincidence of a number of developments, such
as increased economic activities in affluent countries resulting in a
high demand for commodities and the worldwide inflation and
monetary instability since 1972, had their effects in exacerbating an
already difficult food situation. The concurrent appearance in the
cereal market of two large consumers, *i.e.* the USSR and China, led
to a further dwindling of the depleted reserves. The steep rise of
grain prices has driven the prices of other foodstuffs to levels beyond
the economic reach of poorer people. The energy crisis, the shortage
and high cost of fertilisers, pesticides and other agricultural inputs
since 1973 have contributed to bringing the world food situation to
its most desperate point. Particular hardship has been inflicted on the
poorer people in the developing countries, who spend the major part
of their income on staple foods and essentially cereals. With dwindling international food reserves and limited funds, the food aid programmes were cut and the food-deficit developing countries have
been facing difficult problems in financing much higher food import
bills.

It would be expected that higher world cereal prices would stimulate the attempts to increase local production, both to contribute to
self-sufficiency in view of the drying-up of international food
assistance and/or to increase exports, taking advantage of the
international demand and higher prices. However, the prospects are
poor for most countries, because of the inability of their producers to
respond in time to benefit by strong demand and predictable high
prices, and because of the simultaneous increased cost of transport,
storage, fertilisers, pesticides, seeds, energy, etc.

As mentioned earlier, the problems of food production are
closely related to the equally vital issues of nutritional adequacy of
available food supplies within countries and to the extent of under-
and malnutrition. Cold statistics do not reveal the quantitative food
availability, as it is extremely difficult to assess the tremendous

quantities used for non-food purposes, that is, for seed, animal feed, for sustaining rodents and insect pests, from lack of or faulty storage. Statistics have been able to reveal even less about damage inflicted on the nutritional value of grains by insects and moulds during harvest, storage and transport. Combined losses of quantity and quality in most developing countries might account for over 30% of the staples produced. The mere creation of necessary infrastructure for adequate storage and transport facilities could solve the staple food problem in many countries.

The 'assessment of the world food situation', constituting the base document at the WFC, shows that out of 97 developing countries, 57 had a deficit in food energy supplies in 1970—and certainly the situation is not better now. In the Far East and Africa, 25% and 30% respectively of the population is estimated to suffer from significant undernutrition. Altogether in the developing world malnutrition affects some 460 million people, with its consequences on health and physical growth, capacity of children to learn and adults to work, and high rate of infant and child mortality. The average rate of growth of food production in developing countries, which was 2·7% in the recent past, has to rise to 3·7% per year just to match the growth in demand. The performance has to be even higher if malnutrition levels are to be reduced substantially and broader economic and social objectives are to be achieved.

In the fact of the alarming food situation the General Assembly of the United Nations arranged for the World Food Conference. The Conference was 'entrusted with developing ways and means whereby the international community, as a whole, could take specific action to resolve the world food problem within the broader context of development and international economic co-operation'. The over-riding importance of that Conference lies in the fact that for the first time the nations of the world attempted to make a direct political approach to the world food problem. As the very first expression of intent the Conference made the Declaration on the Eradication of Hunger and Malnutrition and solemnly declared that:

'Every man, woman and child has the inalienable right to be free from hunger and malnutrition in order to develop fully and maintain their physical and mental faculties. Society today already possesses sufficient resources, organisational ability and technology and hence the competence to achieve this objective. Accordingly the eradication of hunger is a common objective of all the countries of the international community, especially of the developed countries and others in a position to help.'

The Declaration went further with a series of recommendations to states and stressed that 'it is a fundamental responsibility of Governments to work together for higher food production and a more equitable and efficient distribution of food between countries and within countries'.

The Conference adopted some twenty resolutions emanating from the basic conclusion that the solution of the world food problem required co-ordinated action on three important points:

1. To increase food production, especially in developing countries.
2. To improve consumption and distribution of food.
3. To build a system of food security.

To achieve the objective of increased food production the WFC decided to call for the immediate establishment of an International Fund for Agricultural Development. The Conference considered this a notable achievement. The implementation of many of the specific action programmes and policies to transform the agriculture of developing countries will definitely require large investment by the developing countries and a greatly increased flow of financial resources for agricultural development from outside. The preparatory documentation for the Conference estimated the required increase of external resources from the present level of US$1500 million a year to about US $5000 million a year by 1980. The Conference did not arrive at proposing any level of funding but expected that funds would be forthcoming from voluntary contributions from traditional donors and from new potential donors, in particular the oil-exporting countries. Concurrently, in order to increase, co-ordinate and improve the efficiency of financial and technical assistance to agricultural production in developing countries, the Conference requested the United Nations Development Programme, the World Bank and FAO to organise a Consultative Group on Food Production and Investment in Developing Countries. Whereas not a penny has so far been pledged for the proposed Fund, the three agencies already have agreed to establish the Consultative Group.

An important action of the WFC was to give its strong support to the early implementation of the concept of world food security by ordering an International Undertaking on World Food Security.

The central feature of this Undertaking, proposed by the Director-General of FAO, is that countries should undertake to adopt national stockholding policies in order to arrive at and maintain at least a minimum safe level of basic food stocks, principally cereals, for the world as a whole. As a necessary adjustment to this the Conference established a Global Information and Early Warning System on Food and Agriculture to be operated by FAO with the participation of all governments.

The Conference finally, in order to provide political strength for follow-up action, called for the formation of a World Food Council at ministerial–political level. It will be an organ of the United Nations General Assembly serviced within the framework of FAO, with headquarters in Rome. The Council is now being organised in consultation between the United Nations and FAO. Mr John A. Hannah, formerly of US-AID, has been appointed by the Secretary-General of the UN as Acting Executive Secretary of the World Food Council, which will hold its first session during 23–27 June 1975.

I have tried to give in a nutshell the happenings and the outcome of the World Food Conference. You probably are impressed by the vast range of measures and programmes proposed and adopted by a Conference—wholly political. For FAO it has given considerable satisfaction in seeing much of what it has been advocating for many years accepted at the political level. It appears that finally the political leaders have decided to come seriously to grips with the world problems of food, of nutrition and health and of poverty within the context of economic and social development.

It is hoped that the World Food Conference will prove to have been a decisive breakthrough in the world food situation. The measure of success will be assessed by the magnitude and importance of practical, concrete and long-lasting results. Spectacular achievements are of course not to be expected for they are in any event deceiving and have a very short life.

What will decide whether there is hope of solving the world food problem, at least of alleviating malnutrition, preventing or foreseeing famines, and eradicating poverty, is the political will. It is this political will within a nation which will decide whether investments, efforts, ingenuity will be devoted to food and agricultural production, to the improvement of the nutritional health of its people or to meet the needs of other sectors of the economy or to satisfy the requirements of national prestige or pride. It does require a strong and decisive political will to promulgate measures needed to create economic and social justice in rural areas through agrarian reforms, increased employment and equitable distribution of income.

At the inter-nation level, the expressions of political will voiced during the Conference should be translated into action if there is a real intent to bring about the hoped-for change. I mentioned earlier that developed countries pledged to devote, over a period of years, 1 % of their national income to assist in the economic and social development of the poor countries of the world. This still has not been achieved. Should now the Declaration on the Eradication of Hunger and Malnutrition be a sincere one, the political will has to be put into action and the flow of financial resources and technical assistance to developing countries has to be raised to meaningful levels, and at the same time contributions to food aid programmes, whether for emergencies or development purposes, have to be increased in order to make the concept of world food security a reality.

The world—in particular that part which suffers from all kinds of deprivation—is now waiting in anxiety to see whether the political leaders of powerful and traditionally or newly-rich countries have derived inspiration from the World Food Conference to take charge in changing the predicament and never to consider the 'lifeboat' or 'triage' theories.

DISCUSSION

Hearne: We have heard much during the course of this symposium about growing protein, and of course we have this tendency in the FAO to regard the more important problem as the food energy gap rather than the protein gap except in special circumstances. Would Dr Kapsiotis express an opinion on how he sees the development of SCP in the world market?

Kapsiotis: I would say there is a place because the need for food exists. Let us take the soya beans which are imported to Europe. France and most of the European countries have the same problems in agriculture, and soya beans produced at a competitive price certainly can meet the demand for animal feeding and release foods which are used in other ways for animal feeding, *i.e.* release them for human feeding. This is one thing which is very important, and then of course trying to prevent waste is something which may release foods in parts of the world which can certainly be good for the great number. I am told there are 500–600 million people who are starving, and what can be saved can be easily made available for them at prices which can be kept low if we do not create artificial shortages.

Seal: What importance does Dr Kapsiotis attach to the problems of post-harvest spoilage in foods produced in the developing countries, and does he feel that this could help in alleviating the world food problem? We saw in the Tate & Lyle film that there is something like 70% wastage in pine-apples, and it seems to me that one could try and help the problem by perhaps including storage facilities to prevent these problems arising.

Kapsiotis: I do think storage and transportation facilities in developing countries are two elements which are most needed. I gave a general figure of 30% waste of agricultural products due to lack of storage and trans-portation. The experience of relief in a recent famine showed us in a very dramatic way that food had arrived at the port but could not be moved where it was needed and could not be stored whilst waiting for distribution. Take India for example. The biggest problem is the storage of their cereals and this is the real test in the whole production system in developing countries. One of the worst problems is the lack of adequate storage, whether at farm level or village level or in the big silos. I think this may be the crucial point in agricultural production.

Selby: Just to take this point a stage further, I think this problem has been aggravated really by the fact that we, certainly in the UK, have been living much more hand to mouth in terms of cereals over the last few years than perhaps we did say five, six or seven years ago; and in fact it strikes me that this is perhaps the area which really needs to be concentrated upon. If you are talking in terms of 30% post-harvest deterioration, which I was aware of already, if you are talking about a national stockholding policy for cereals, we are really talking about the same sort of problem, are we not? In fact we are going in the future to have to think in terms of the use and storage of cereals which are not, as are traditional for ours in the UK now, and in Europe, very short-term between harvest and use. I think it is a completely different view we have to have on how we use our cereals.

Kapsiotis: I think you are right. Actually the International Undertaking of the World Food Security System provides for immediate stockpiling of 10 million tons of cereals with the next crop, and this of course necessitates the creation of storage facilities. This can be in the existing cereal-exporting countries, say England and Canada, but the problem really lies in channel-ling the aid as quickly and as efficiently as possible, or just keeping stable prices in the international trade for cereals.

Selby: It seems to me, if I may just comment, that this is perhaps an area where there is going to be a need for work. Perhaps we don't understand all the problems which are going to arise if we adopt this totally different approach to the way in which we harvest and use our material.

Evans: I wonder if Dr Kapsiotis could comment on how he sees the future ability of developing countries to be self-supporting. To what extent is this a temporary problem that can be overcome with development, and to what extent is it a problem that has no solution that we can foresee?

Kapsiotis: I think this is a terribly difficult question to answer. The aim is to make the countries self-sufficient in the area in which they exist. How-ever, with the present situation and the shortage of fertilisers, high cost of energy, high prices of everything, it has to go through a conditional period with massive assistance from outside, until the countries can stand on their feet and start producing in the normal way for their own needs or for export. But at this stage it is a long-term project to help the countries to become self-sufficient. I gave the figure of $5000 million a year in aid which is needed to keep pace with the same rate of production growth. It is not an easy problem.

Bookey: I wonder if you could come down from the strategic to the tactical level and give us some idea of the work you are envisaging in certain areas, such as storage, water management or the provision of nitrogenous fertilisers, and say what you see, optimistically, happening in the next few years on areas such as these.

Kapsiotis: Actually, much is happening, and there are projects which are financed by the United Nations, by FAO and by the countries themselves. There is enough work being done, but again we are always up against the priorities that the countries themselves establish. It is not always the increased food production; there are other priorities—the highways or the army, or whatever. This is the stumbling block, but a lot is happening now, irrigation, land reclamation and many such projects.

Mrs Parry: How does Dr Kapsiotis suggest that we might implement the recommendations of the World Food Conference? Individual members of developed countries feel immensely sympathetic as each new famine crisis occurs, but it must be admitted we are overwhelmed by the size of them and how we can translate our sympathy into practical terms—not only the question of supplies, but how we can perhaps change nutritional habits in developing countries and offer to train personnel from these countries who could then go back and give assistance with better understanding.

Kapsiotis: There are two approaches—a political approach, and the creation of a local council. Individual countries may hope to channel their aid through the World Food Council. Training is a matter of what resources the governments themselves or the international organisation can put at the disposal of this type of development. I said in my paper that there are some countries who reach close to the 1% of the national income which is considered as a target for aid to the developing countries, but again it is how far the country itself pays the Treasury and how far the person who is trained abroad goes back to the work for which he has been trained. If 10% of the people who are trained abroad go back to their country to do the work for which they have been trained, it is a very optimistic figure.

Further discussion at the conclusion of Session IV:

Chairman (Professor Aylward): Let me say how much I would like to thank Dr Kapsiotis on behalf of everyone here, for he rightly pointed out the fact that recent FAO figures showed there was a great deal of protein around the world. Secondly, he pointed out that it has been shown that in many developing countries there is a real energy gap, and that this may be extremely important in relation to disease. Now Dr Kapsiotis did not say, as far as I know, that everyone had sufficient protein, and that there was no protein problem, and even at the risk of abusing this position at the moment here I may say that I myself am extremely disconcerted by the new bandwagon that is running, to some extent in this country, but also abroad, which simply says there is no protein problem. We have a situation where to say that in Britain seems to me the height of absurdity. There is a protein problem in Britain, and one can get it simply by the examination of our import figures. What is it, £3000 million a year for food and feed imports, and in that figure there is a great deal of roundabout protein for food or feed. Now when someone says 'What's the use of these new technologies—how can the Africans, by implication, afford them?' I think this is the wrong way of looking at it. The Africans in many places have plenty of protein, mainly in groundnuts and other things that they send over to us. We are the people, I am afraid, some of us, who are likely to be short in the future because we may not be able to afford to import food. Now this is a gloomy doctrine on my part, but I do believe that one has to return to some principles of arithmetic. I think this country, and indeed all the industrialised countries with large populations, have got to set their own house in order, not because we want to change food habits, but because we have got to live more efficiently if we want to maintain current standards of living. Now I hope I have not too much misinterpreted Dr Kapsiotis' figure, and I will give him a moment to reply to me.

Kapsiotis: Mr Chairman, what happened is that the nutritionists got together with the statisticians and made a slight mess! There is a need for protein and there is a need for biomass production.

Chairman: I knew what Dr Kapsiotis' views on this were and it was in view of what was said later in the afternoon by some other speaker that I raised this point about a protein problem.

17

A Versatile Continuous Ion-Exchange Process
for Protein Recovery

D. T. JONES

*Development Division, Viscose Group Ltd,
South Dock, Swansea, Wales*

ABSTRACT

*Ion-exchange celluloses have been used for laboratory protein separations for about
25 years but have not been suitable for large-scale industrial applications due to
poor hydrodynamic properties. A new type of regenerated cellulose ion exchanger
has been developed which is capable of being produced in a wide variety of forms.
These are capable of being used in the recovery of protein from industrial process and
effluent streams. The first generation of media has been produced in a granular form
and a continuous ion-exchange system has been developed whereby the medium is
taken successively through an adsorption, desorption and wash stage, then returned
to the first stage. The continuous stirred tank reactor concept is used for the reaction
at each stage, but various separation means may be employed depending on the
particular application. A 10 000 gal/day pilot plant has been run successfully for
three months recovering protein from an abattoir effluent. The system has also been
applied to the recovery of protein from milk whey, soya concentrate plant effluent,
gelatine plant effluent, and meat and vegetable processing streams. The process
produces a concentrated stream of protein unchanged in form from that present in
the original liquors. The isolation of the protein from this concentrate can be carried
out in a variety of ways depending on the end-use requirements for the particular
protein.*

We have heard constantly of the utilisation of wastes for the production of microbial or fungal proteins and the recovery of protein from
various waste streams in the food industry. All the authors have
stressed the importance of protein as a food source and the system
I am going to describe is capable of isolating and recovering protein
from practically any protein-containing stream.

The basic process is one of the application of a special form of
cellulosic ion exchanger in a continuous dynamic system. Ion-
exchange celluloses have been used for laboratory protein separations

for about 25 years but have not been suitable for large-scale industrial applications due to poor hydrodynamic properties.

Although the cellulose ion exchanger shown in Fig. 1 is a highly modified material, microcrystalline and cross-linked, it still retains its fibrous form which dictates its hydrodynamic properties.

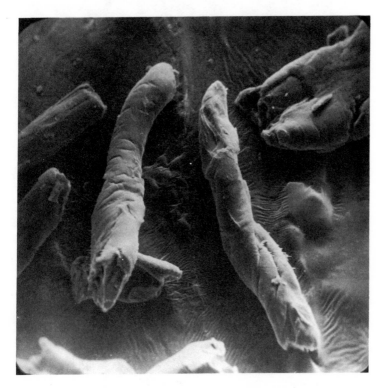

FIG. 1.   Fibrous cellulose ion exchanger.

Figure 2 illustrates a new form of cellulosic ion exchanger produced from regenerated cellulose through the Viscose process. This first-generation material is produced by grinding a film of regenerated cellulose. The particulate shape ensures much improved hydrodynamic properties.

Figure 3 illustrates the advantages of the Vistec laboratory-grade material compared with competitive laboratory materials.

Vistec medium, which is the name that has been given to the new

FIG. 2.   Vistec medium.

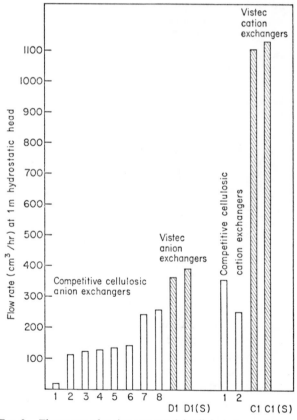

FIG. 3.   Flow rates of major commercial cellulosic ion exchangers.

ion-exchange material shown in Fig. 4, is produced by the Viscose process. In the Viscose process, cellulose is reacted with caustic soda and carbon bisulphide to produce cellulose xanthate which is dissolved in dilute caustic soda solution to give a solution known as Viscose. The cellulose may be regenerated from Viscose in a variety

Xanthation:
$$R_{cell}ONa + CS_2 \rightarrow R_{cell}OCSSNa$$

Regeneration:
$$2R_{cell}OCSSNa + H_2SO_4 \rightarrow$$
$$2R_{cell}OH + Na_2SO_4 + 2CS_2$$

FIG. 4. Viscose process.

of forms and microstructure depending on Viscose composition and regeneration conditions.

In the Vistec patented process (Fig. 5) the ion-exchange cellulose derivative is first formed, then the derivative is taken through the Viscose process and regenerated as Vistec ion-exchange cellulose

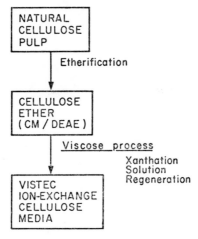

FIG. 5. Vistec media process.

medium. The versatility of the process is shown in Table 1 where Vistec medium is compared with another fibrous cellulose exchanger and the variation of structure is illustrated by the fact that the protein uptake can be varied widely at approximately the same ion-exchange capacity. Another illustration of the versatility of the

TABLE 1
Illustration of variability protein uptakes

Ion-exchange cellulose material type	Ion-exchange capacity (mg/g)	Protein uptake (albumin capacity) (mg/g)
Natural fibrous cellulose derivative	1·14	288
Commercial microcrystalline cross-linked derivative Whatman DE-52	1·00	313
Vistec Medium E-2	1·13	928
Vistec Medium E-3	1·09	798
Vistec Medium E-4	0·99	480
Vistec Medium E-7	1·11	366

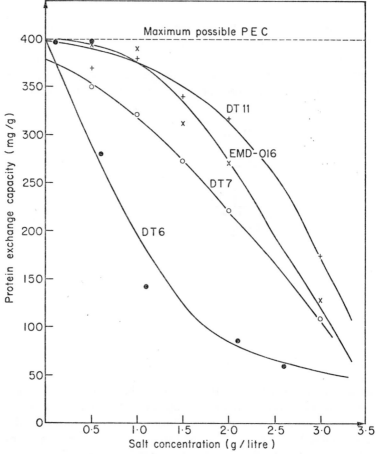

FIG. 6. Variation of protein exchange capacity with salt concentration of solution for various media. pH of solution = 9·0.

material is shown by Fig. 6, illustrating different tolerances to salt concentration. This is required as many protein streams in the food industry are contaminated with salt.

The new material has been applied in a continuous ion-exchange system (Fig. 7) composed of a stirred tank where the ion-exchange medium is intimately contacted with the protein stream followed by a separation device for separating the medium from the now treated substantially protein-free stream. In this particular flow diagram this is shown as a settling cone, but it may well be a centrifuge or rotary vacuum filter or other suitable device. In Stage 1, the protein adsorption stage, protein is removed from the feed liquor by adsorption on to the medium. The medium is then taken to the protein desorption stage where a concentrate of the isolated protein is produced by desorbing either with competing ions such as those from sodium chloride or preferably by change of pH. If necessary, a third stage is used where the medium can be washed and conditioned ready for recirculation back to Stage 1 to adsorb further protein. The process is subject to the normal parameters controlling ion-exchange processes so that the normal adsorption isotherms, rate isotherms and pH dependence all apply.

The consequence of all these controlling parameters is shown in Fig. 8 where a protein stream has been treated with different rates of media throughput in the stirred container. It will be seen that as the media rate is increased, the efficiency of protein removal increases quite rapidly to a maximum approaching 100%, while the efficiency in use of media decreases. In this particular case it will be seen that the optimum media throughput is about 20 g/min, giving a protein exchange efficiency of around 200 mg/g. All the parameters and results were combined in mass balance equations which were used for design of a versatile pilot plant based on the simple concept shown in Fig. 7.

The pilot plant shown in Fig. 9, nominally 10 000 gal/day, was built at ICD/Clarke Chapman, Derby, to substantiate the correctness of the small-scale experiments and to investigate any scale-up problems. It was also used to confirm the practicability under industrial conditions of the continuous ion-exchange process described. This pilot plant ran for three months at a British Beef Abattoir in Watford, recovering protein from the total abattoir effluent. The results confirmed that there were no scale-up problems and that the process concept could be utilised on an industrial scale.

D. T. Jones

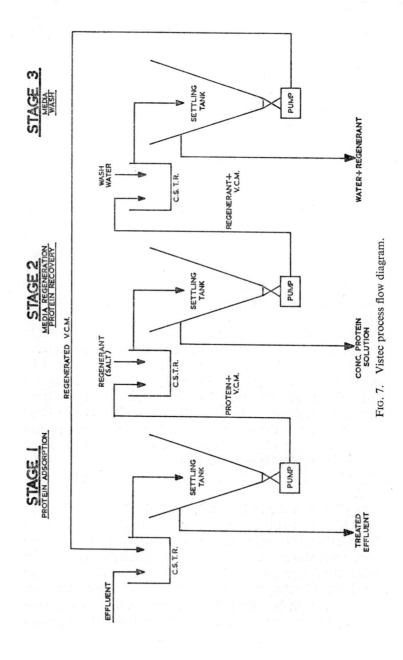

Fig. 7. Vistec process flow diagram.

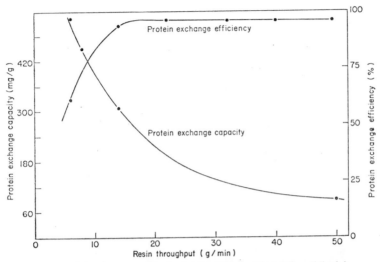

FIG. 8. Stirred reactor experimental results (residence time 7·7 min).

FIG. 9. Pilot plant, ICD/Clarke Chapman, Derby.

TABLE 2
Abattoir effluent: Pontardawe results

Source	Before treatment		After treatment		% Efficiency		
	Protein (mg/litre)	BOD (mg/litre)	Protein (mg/litre)	BOD (mg/litre)	Protein removal	BOD removal	Protein recovery
Killing floor effluent	7 550	4 409	850	94	87·8	98·1	86·0
Total abattoir effluent	1 700	3 470					
1000 h			185	50	89·1	98·5	
1400 h			240	118	85·8	96·5	82·5
1700 h			245	113	85·5	96·7	

TABLE 3
Abattoir effluent: Thames Water Authority results

Source	pH	Suspended solids (mg/litre)	4 h N/80 PV (mg/litre)	4 h N/8 PV (mg/litre)	Total N (mg/litre)	5 day BOD (mg/litre)
Effluent pit outflow	7·6	468	200·0	528	406	3 400
Pilot plant Stage 1 effluent	8·6	400	70·4	131	70·4	710
% reduction		14·6	64·8	75·1	82·6	79·1

The results listed in Table 2 illustrate the efficiency of protein removal and protein recovery from a 10 litre/min plant built at Pontardawe, near Swansea. As can be seen, it was successful in continuously recovering over 80% of the protein over a period of 7 h.

Even though the pilot plant at Watford was following a planned programme and no attempt was made to optimise maximum removal of protein, analyses carried out by the Thames Water Authority (Table 3) show a reduction of over 80% in the total nitrogen.

Table 4 illustrates a run in the programme at Watford when conditions approaching optimum appertain. There was a removal of 90% of the protein with a concentration step of about 6:1. The simple system, as illustrated in the flow diagram which was shown above and built into the pilot plant, is only capable of giving a limited concentration step due to the carryover of absorbed solution in the ion exchanger.

The application of a counter-current system and pH desorption is

TABLE 4
Abattoir effluent: Watford results
(a) 0900 h, 24 Oct. 1974

Sample	Total N (g/litre)	Non-protein N (g/litre)	Protein N (g/litre)	Protein concn. (g/litre)
Raw effluent	0·42	0·114	0·306	1·91
Treated effluent	0·113	0·093	0·020	0·13
Concentrates	1·28	0·083	1·20	7·50
Wash water	0·043	0·042	0·001	0·006

Protein removed = 93·2%.

(b) 1300 h, 24 Oct. 1974

Sample	Total N (g/litre)	Non-protein N (g/litre)	Protein N (g/litre)	Protein concn. (g/litre)
Raw effluent	0·295	0·097	0·198	1·24
Treated effluent	0·096	0·076	0·020	0·13
Concentrates	1·30	0·075	1·225	7·65
Wash water	0·041	0·035	0·006	0·037

Protein removed = 89·5%.

shown in Fig. 10, which illustrates the treatment of milk whey where the process has been reduced to two steps—a two-stage adsorption and a three-stage desorption unit. Adsorption at a low pH allows practically full utilisation of the capacity of the media, and desorption at a high pH through a three-stage desorption unit allows a

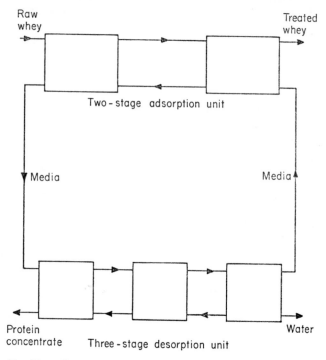

Fig. 10. Flow diagram showing counter-current adsorption and desorption units.

considerably improved concentration step and eliminates the need for a wash section. Table 5 describes an alternative process utilising milk whey.

The system as described has been used on a laboratory and pilot scale for the isolation and recovery of protein from milk whey, soya concentrate plant effluent, gelatine plant process and effluent streams, fish and vegetable processing streams. The process produces a concentrated stream of protein unchanged in form from that present in the original liquors.

The isolation of the protein from this concentrate can be carried out in a variety of ways depending on the end-use requirements for the particular protein. In the case of simple blood effluents, such as those from an abattoir where the end-product could be used as animal feed, straightforward coagulation with acid and heat followed by filtration and drying can be used. In the case of milk whey and soya whey proteins where the structural properties are important, spray or freeze drying may be used.

TABLE 5
Alternative processes for milk whey treatment
(whey flow rate = 100 000 gal/day (315 litre/min))

Process	Media circulation rate (kg/min)	Protein concentrate (g/litre)	Vol. rate of conc. (litre/min)
A	22	20	71
B	9	25	57
C	9	42	34
D	9	48	30
E	8	60	24

A. *Single* CSTR's in both adsorption and desorption units with settling cones used for dewatering.
B. A *three*-stage counter-current adsorption unit with a *single*-stage desorption unit with settling cones as dewaterers.
C. As B, but with a *two*-stage counter-current desorption unit.
D. As C, but with a *three*-stage desorption unit.
E. As D, but with centrifuges/filters used for dewatering prior to and within the desorption unit.

Table 6 gives the results of freeze-dried protein recovered from milk whey uncontaminated with either fat or lactose. This is 100% soluble. The amino acid analyses shown compare favourably with published analyses.

This sample illustrates the advantages of the Vistec process in that it is not only capable of recovering protein from various waste food streams, or indeed any stream containing soluble protein, but it is also capable of isolating the protein and producing it in a much purer form than has hitherto been possible. Fractionation of proteins can also be achieved. The versatility of the material and the process ensures that it can be adapted and optimised to cope with most streams.

TABLE 6
*Amino acid analysis of recovered
milk whey protein*

Amino acid	g/16 g N
Lysine	6·50
Histidine	1·73
Ammonia	1·30
Arginine	1·00
Aspartic acid	8·66
Threonine	6·43
Serine	4·73
Glutamic acid	23·46
Proline	8·82
Glycine	1·80
Alanine	5·19
Valine	6·512
Methionine	0·179
Isoleucine	7·043
Leucine	12·4
Tyrosine	1·198
Phenylalanine	3·35

DISCUSSION

Selby: Could you make a comment about the biostability of the material? Is the degree of substitution sufficiently high to keep it biostable?

Jones: Not completely, no. As you will probably gather, in order to stop breakdown we are limited in the substitution we can use, and though we can overcome this to a certain extent by cross-linking, this leads to loss of some activity. At the degree of substitution one is supposed to use, there are various problems and we are currently taking the material through various pH and other tests.

Tannenbaum: I have two questions. First of all, are these systems apparently better than the dextran ion exchangers which also have a much higher capacity than the cellulose types? Secondly, what about economics of process, particularly the cost of the resin?

Jones: With regard to the dextran material, the cells in ion exchangers—the ones we produce—are much more stable, especially with regard to changes in volume, change of pH and also concentration. They do not suffer the same shrinkage as dextran materials. They are much more stable in an industrial system. One can pump them and, in fact, we pumped the material around 5000 cycles, which you would probably never do with the dextran material.

The answer to your other question is more difficult, of course, and I would like to explain that specific cases call for specific solutions and specific costs. We have looked at the cost of recovering blood protein from a simple situation like an abattoir, and the capital costs involved were about £60 000 for the plant including the running charge, which is a fair proportion of it. The running costs, including capital write-off, etc., were about £29 000 but there was a payback from saving of waste disposal charges, and this gave a cost of protein of about £100 per ton; so if you could sell your protein for more than £100 per ton you could make a profit or run your treatment plant for nothing. In a factory situation the picture is much more complex than I have described, and there you may be talking of a much more expensive plant, but again, one can hopefully recover the protein in convenient form depending on whether you want it pure or if you want it completely isolated from any other product.

Cerletti: In the treatment of industrial effluents contaminated by other material, *e.g.* fats, do you foresee a pretreatment before ion exchange? Would fats flowing through the resin clog it?

Jones: I think in practice one would have to use pretreatment if one was after an effluent treatment plant, because the ion-exchange plant *per se* does not remove fat or suspended solids. I think if you took note of the Thames Water Authority analysis it showed there there was a certain change in suspended solids. Fat is not absorbed, it goes through the process. This is one of the strengths of the system, really, in that it is capable of accepting the protein without being contaminated by the other materials.

With regard to fats flowing through the resin and clogging we have not experienced this and we have not found any contamination of the resin by fat as such in the dynamic system. The fat does not affect the medium.

Thompson: I have been working with some novel materials and can to some extent cover the point Dr Selby raised; being composed of titanium dioxide these materials are much more resistant to chemical than bacterial attack. They are very highly resistant indeed. The capacities are somewhat less than these viscose resins. We visualise being able to use them in quite substantial size columns and we have in fact operated columns of the order of 35 m—that is, something like 45 column volumes per hour with whey and other industrial effluents—so I think the particular contamination problems in some instances may not be very great and one can operate in a way that minimises this in a column mould. The system is not as far advanced as the one described but it has other characteristics which may be of interest.

Rawlings: Talking about the specificity of these columns, do you know if they happen to separate nucleic acids from proteins?

Phillips: On a mass scale we have carried out separation of protein from nucleic acid in single-cell protein, so the possibility exists of separating nucleic acids using Vistec media.

18

Nutritional and Toxicological Evaluation of Novel Feed

P. VAN DER WAL

Institute for Animal Nutrition Research (ILOB),
Wageningen, The Netherlands

ABSTRACT

Nutrients from waste are, either directly or after some processing, usually upgraded to human food via farm animals. The nutritional (and toxicological) evaluation of wastes as an animal feed is therefore the most relevant one. Such an evaluation can, if properly designed, serve to a large extent as preclinical testing for human food as well.

A more intensive testing of novel feed than in the past is required. Because products tend to find a faster and wider application, the degree of novelty due to production and processing is more marked and the consumer's attitude is more critical. New techniques allow a more accurate evaluation.

An international standardisation of testing based on the principles of Guideline 15 of the Protein Advisory Group (PAG) of the United Nations is essential. International scientific communication and trade will thus be promoted.

For identification and to create a base for adequate testing, a detailed description of the chemical composition and the production process is required for a novel feed.

Biological testing of nutritional and toxicological characteristics is concerned with nutritional value for the animals, safety for the animals, and safety of the animal products for the human consumers.

Digestion and resorption of feed ingredients, the requirements for nutrients and the susceptibility to toxins are specific for an animal species and may vary with their physiological stage. The biological evaluation has therefore to include, apart from the classical rat tests, also experiments with the main target species during various stages of the life-cycle. The fowl and the pig are mostly used. Animal products destined for human consumption are thus obtained for further investigation.

The extent to which an evaluation scheme has to be applied depends on the degree of novelty judged from analytical data and the production system. The scale of production and the impact of a new product can sometimes partly be taken into consideration.

INTRODUCTION

Toxicology in these days is the work of a group of highly trained specialists, and my position is that I have been leading such a group more or less successfully over the last decade.

When going through the papers presented in the last few days, and taking especially the one by Professor Tannenbaum, it struck me that I am completely in agreement with one of his general remarks—wastes are usually in the first place either directly, or after upgrading, suitable for animal feeds and not as human food. Reasons may differ but are usually found in some characteristics like poor organoleptic qualities, chemical and bacteriological safety aspects, inconsistent qualities and quantities, and too limited quantities to pay for sophisticated upgrading required to create palatable and acceptable human food. A few more shortcomings are sometimes found, such as low protein content, low nutrient content, poor digestibility of nutrients, so far overcome by microbial upgrading by fermentation.

The reasons I have mentioned, and the fact that wastes are primarily, in my opinion, suitable for animal feed, led me to agree with the Chairman of the Organising Committee that the title of my paper should be 'Nutritional and Toxicological Evaluation of Novel Feed'. Categories of waste products offer specific problems with regard to nutritional and toxicological evaluation. It is too much to mention them all, except for a few examples. Most farms produce relatively small wastes, unlike the huge farms in Arizona where you see mountains of manure. So I think we may state that waste exists in limited amounts, and that is an important fact if you want to upgrade it. Agricultural wastes, like manure, also have the specific problem of recycling of pathogenic micro-organisms, a highly interesting and important point. Industrial, and mainly agricultural industrial products, have other characteristic points which run into difficulties, and I mention the specific point of seasonal variations, again a hard point to be overcome if you want to apply a lot of sophisticated upgrading. Other wastes, not even mentioned here, both solid and sewage, have problems which I personally am inclined to consider as prohibitive unless we are rather shrewd—the amount and nature of toxic residues that you can think of, and aspects like that, are beyond imagination.

There are also different principles with regard to evaluation of the particular problem concerned. I shall stick to principles in the short

time we have available. I do not like it, preferring to stick to facts
rather than to principles, but I think in this case, covering such a
wide area, we cannot avoid this question of principles. You are going
to be aware of some interesting interactions that may occur from
now on; I have been watching these from different places from three
groups involved in work that we have been dealing with in the last
few days: the group taking care of the development, the one evaluating the product, and the potential consuming group. Now the usual
sequence is that the symposium starts off with enthusiastic and con-
structive talks by people who have been doing a very good job in
creating new products, and then comes the toxicologist and he sends
up endless lists of tests and requirements, and a murderous glint
comes into the eyes of the developers, and I can understand that,
because the consumers feel increasingly uneasy realising what might
occur if all the odds end up against them. In observing these interactions I am inclined to ask for a *carte blanche* along the lines 'Don't
shoot the pianist, he's doing his best'! More seriously, let us be aware
that as evaluators of safety and quality we are not only safeguarding
the interests of the consumer but at least, to the same extent, the
interests of the producer. It is by no means a pleasure to be faced with
catastrophes after having spent an enormous amount of money on
development. Let us now see whether we can combine caution with
commonsense.

First of all, is there any need for evaluation of novel food with
regard to nutritional value and safety? In the physical sense I think
the answer to that would be 'yes'—and more so than in the past,
because there is a faster and a wider application than in the past of
novel products themselves. In the past we took a fruit from a tree,
threw it into the trough of a pig and watched to see whether he did
well. If he did, the farmer did the same thing the next day, and it
spread to the next village, the next country, and it took centuries
before it spread all over the world, and in the meantime we got to
know that the product was useful and safe within certain limits.
Now novel product development is expanding so rapidly that we
need more detailed testing. The great degree of novelty in products
seems to be due to more modern production techniques, more
severe processing solvents, higher temperature, and last but not least
a more clinical attitude. We can illustrate this best by the situation
in Japan, after SCP was tested and introduced on the market.
Suddenly lots of papers and action groups became aware of the

situation and asked 'Who is saying that this product is safe and useful?' Well, the answers which were given were not satisfactory, and the struggle is still going on, and that situation occurs everywhere in the world.

It is not difficult to mention at least six guidelines for testing either in the course of development or already being applied. Today in Germany, France, the EEC, UNICEL—some of the names may not even be familiar to you—there is the Protein Advisory Group of the United Nations who publish Guideline No. 6 for the testing of food for humans, followed by Guideline No. 15 and accompanied by Guidelines of the Union of Pure and Applied Chemistry. These are more or less well combined, the standard tests being internationally accepted as far as the basic principles are concerned. I think that is a great thing, and we owe a great deal to the United Nations for having taken these initiatives, and especially the Protein Advisory Group, because if producers are faced with different guidelines for testing all over the world, country by country, then that is the end of many projects. It is out of the question that work falling into very different lines can be carried out. It is simply too expensive and there is no need for it. Secondly, if we are going to continue to have separate guidelines for separate countries, what about international trade? What about scientific communication on matters of this kind? So I make a strong plea for standardisation of novel product testing.

CHEMICAL CHARACTERISATION

What do we need for evaluating a product? First, a general characterisation. Why do we need that? First of all for identification. It struck me listening to the previous papers of this symposium that not everybody seems to be aware that it is not enough simply to state that a product is satisfactory with regard to value and safety. If these data have to be applicable to later stages of that same product, then we have to deal with a well-identified process, and therefore any applicability of the results depends upon the proper identification of the process conditions. Even small alterations, in our experience, may have catastrophic effects. We need characterisation also to provide a technical basis for biological tests. We match the design, and the test rations, adequately. We want to determine the degree of novelty and judge what risks are involved in a new product, and finally, if one wants to introduce a new feed, then this is done on hard facts, on amino acid content, or available amino acid content, figures introduced in computers, and all these figures have to be provided by the producers, thus providing a basis for biological tests and determining the degree of novelty of the products concerned. You need a good chemical analysis, a description of physical properties, and finally the bacteriological status; for example, bacteria, moulds, the presence of salmonellae, and so on. Not only must this be done for characterisation of a product, but it must be ensured that no major alterations of these characteristics occur later on when the process and the product are applied. Otherwise any research is without any value.

There are striking dissimilarities among different types of SCP in regard to their chemical composition. These are manifested as quite different concentrations of protein, nucleic acid, fat and fibre.

BIOLOGICAL EVALUATION

What I do not like when talking about biological evaluation is the word 'toxicology'—I would like it done away with. The reason is that in our experience the use of the word itself is often sufficient to lower a curtain on the other side of which logical thinking is considered to be the privilege of a specialised class. This is not the ideal of all toxicologists. The risk that such an attitude can easily lead to abuse of the system is too well recognised. I invite you to dwell around in the field of toxicology with all curtains raised.

Let us go through some questions with regard to biological testing in general. Is there a need for biological testing, since we know such a lot already from the general characterisation? The answer is 'yes', because we do not yet know enough about the physiological ability of the nutrients—that can only be surmised. And we do not even know, we cannot even completely identify, the possible toxins. A very important question is, what do we want to learn from biological testing? Well, if my assumption is correct and we are dealing primarily with animal feed, then three questions are of primary importance:

1. What is the nutritional value for animals for which the products are designed? If there is no value, then stop your work.
2. What is the safety for the animals?
3. What is the safety of the products from the animals for the human consumer?

We have mentioned the word 'animal' three times. Now, whilst testing we get answers which vary with the animal species to which we put these questions. The answers vary furthermore with the physiological age of the animals. Why? Because animal species at different ages are different with regard to digestion of the feed, and with regard to transport of the nutrients through the gastrointestinal wall. They have specific requirements for the nutrients and they have specific susceptibilities for toxins. That brings us to one conclusion and that is that we have to include as species for the biological tests the animals on which the product is produced—the target species. That is also the only way to get further exploration of the animal product destined for human consumption. And here we are at the crucial point.

The problem is also that it is difficult to transfer, with certainty, experimental results from one species to another, but finally, ultimately, an evaluation of a feed with farm animals has to be done in more than one species. The rat is included because it is a generally accepted standard laboratory animal with a short life-span, so generation tests over a long period of time, over a total life-span, are easily done. If we are aiming for the human market, then, as also said in PAG Guideline No. 15, we may think of the sheep as an extra animal, but in general for clarity I am prepared to defend the point that one could restrict oneself to rats, fowls and pigs. Wider application later on may demand further studies.

CONCLUSION

It is obvious that an elaborate scheme of testing need not necessarily be applied for every new product. For example, a man frying his potatoes in a different way from his grandmother is producing a novel product, but there are other circumstances when impact of a product can and must be one of the barometers upon which it is judged, and what degree of investigation is necessary. This sounds opportunistic but there is no way out. A local farm production asks for a different approach. Of course we have to prohibit processes that have detrimental effects, that is clear, but on the other hand a weigh-in of the impact of the new process seems relevant to me if one judges the amount of tests required. The criterion is sound judgement, from the product and process characteristics, of the degree of novelty and the risks that are deducible from that with regard to toxicity, pathogenic micro-organisms and nutritional value. So the story is not as bad as you might think.

In conclusion, I did not want to discourage anybody but repeat what I said earlier. I would like to try to combine caution with commonsense and I am aware that nutritional and toxicological evaluation has to be done on behalf of the consumer as well as on behalf of the producer.

DISCUSSION

Evans: What is the cost of carrying out a test on a new product by the rat/fowl/pig procedure that you described?

van der Wal: Well, currencies being what they are, it gets more expensive every day. It is easily one million guilders and more.

Questioner: What is that in honest money?

van der Wal: I would say it is considered the most honest money in the world! It is about five guilders to the pound by now.

Stanton: I am worried about your conventional choice of organisms. Does this mean that in the preliminary screening of new natural products the little *Tetrahymena* has no value in the scheme of biology screening?

van der Wal: I didn't condemn any test, I was just advocating a group of tests that might lead in most cases to the useful answers that may lead to a clearance, so I am not in a position and I am not intending to condemn other tests, but I would like to emphasise again that I am still inclined to make a strong plea for unification. That is not changed by the fact that in some circumstances some tests might have a certain preference. The unification of testing is of such overwhelming importance that I would maintain a plea for that, and I'm saying 'All right, this is a basic testing scheme, but in some cases additional tests can be of great value'. Does this satisfy you?

Wimpenny: Suppose you had an organism that was well known, how much could you short-circuit these tests if you grew it on a different substrate from the one that it had been aseptically grown on? I was thinking of *Candida utilis*, for example, the food yeast, which we might grow on say hydrolysed sewage sludge, or something like that. Would this in fact cut the amount of testing needed, or would it have to be exactly the same?

van der Wal: I think the answer to your question was more or less included in my remarks. The degree of novelty for production processes and production characteristics in my view determines the degree of testing. This is an indirect answer but I do not intend to give direct ones, it would not be wise, but in general terms the better the organism is known and the more experience there is with it, then the less likelihood there is of it presenting trouble.

Wimpenny: So would you say it would be better in that sense to aim to choose an organism that is well known to start off with and make it fit the new substrate rather than to go looking for another organism that would be better suited to that substrate?

van der Wal: I said in the beginning I hate to talk about personal philosophies and here we are reaching such a point, so I refer you back to my previous answer.

19

The Socio-Economic Implications of Producing Food from Wastes

L. G. PLASKETT

Biotechnical Processes Ltd, High Wycombe, Bucks., England

ABSTRACT

Massive production of food and feed from wastes is probably inevitable in a few decades. This is deduced because:

(i) Exponential growth of future agricultural output is not credible.
(ii) Synthetic food makes too high a demand upon resources.
(iii) Public pressure against pollution is justified.
(iv) A population dependent upon food from fossil carbon would be courting disaster.
(v) Largely unused organic wastes are a major renewable reservoir of carbon compounds.

It is socially and economically urgent for us to recognise now that the pressures to recycle carbon will become irresistible.

Implications from fairly quickly operating rational organic waste recycling would be enormous. The wealth of national economies may well come to depend largely upon their ability to produce and reprocess organic matter. The demand for investment and ingenuity would be unprecedented in the food and agriculture industries. All sources of organic matter would be treated on their merits according to composition, whether or not they are repulsive.

Ultimately, by using wastes very efficiently for food production, one eliminates waste. From thoroughly scavenging present industrial wastes, a natural development is to reprogramme agriculture to provide feedstocks for bioengineering plants. The wild lands would be harvested too for their crop of miscellaneous organic matter.

This is probably not a preferred way of life for mankind, but it is the direction in which population growth drives us.

In the intermediate stages numerous small-scale, low-energy processing plants will be needed, to save transport costs. Waste recycle economics are marginal, creating a challenge to technologists to develop processes with low-cost inputs and equipment.

Private enterprise is poorly attuned to waste utilisation, so government incentives and controls can be expected. New large differences may appear in national incomes, related to the level of success achieved in this field.

The foods produced from wastes are expected to be as similar as possible to those now consumed.

THE FUTURE IMPORTANCE OF FOOD FROM WASTES

The primary thesis upon which this paper is based is that foods and feed must be produced from wastes on quite a massive scale within a few decades. This change is likely to make great technological demands and will call for a high degree of flexibility of outlook in industrial management and government. Appreciation of the inevitability of this change is crucial because without it the necessary measures cannot become the subject of firm budgets and plans. Indeed, the situation gives rise to certain dangers: human societies generally have not mastered techniques of so-called long-range planning for the period 5–10 years hence, let alone the 20–30 year span needed to cover major changes in resource procurement. The main danger, therefore, is that of drifting in an unseeing fashion into serious, ever-worsening shortages of conventional resources so that we become very late in adapting our technologies and management. When such changes are introduced only from desperation there is usually insufficient research and development time and they are accompanied by economic stresses which could have been avoided.

I turn to examine the primary thesis.

The main reason for using wastes for food production would be that organic matter is, or is going to be, in short supply.

THE LIMITATIONS OF AGRICULTURAL OUTPUT

The principal sources of renewable organic matter are agriculture and forestry, with forestry being unimportant in food production up to the present time. There is a voluminous literature which attempts to plot the future course of world agricultural output; it is a tremendous subject and obviously it is not possible here to deal with all the arguments about the chances of agriculture meeting the future demands to be made upon it. It is only possible to summarise the author's own conclusions from what has been written.

Firstly, there does appear to be something of a consensus of opinion that rise in agricultural output cannot follow an exponential pattern that would keep pace with world population; output improvement is more likely to follow a linear pattern and hence, if nothing else changes, the gap between food production and food needs will widen.

Secondly, although it is not exactly a consensus, there is rather widespread doubt as to for what period even the linear increase in agricultural output can be maintained. Improvements in fertiliser application, introduction of high-yielding varieties, improvements in management practice are to a large extent exploiting once-off opportunities and, once such practices have been widely adopted, no other similar sources of improvement will be available. This point cannot be affirmed with certainty but few serious writers now contend that over the next two to three decades the battle to make conventional agriculture meet the needs of the population can be other than a losing game.

Increase of conventional agricultural output is concentrated upon staple crops, such as wheat and rice, but the opportunities for further increases in yields of these preferred commodities are not good. It is true that a 6 t/ha yield of cereal grain in the UK, for example, represents only a 2·0% conversion of incident radiation during the growing period[1] whereas there is a theoretical maximum conversion of 18%.[2] Whilst, superficially, this indicates a great potential for improvement, significant gains in photosynthetic efficiency have in practice been hard to achieve, most improved yielding varieties achieving results by better harvest index, *i.e.* better ratio of usable to non-usable portions of the plant. This type of change can produce quite a dramatic effect over a few decades but does not lend itself to a sustained yield improvement.

Whilst there is obviously scope for some argument over the future course of staple crop yields, it is clear that other factors are coming into play which may be more influential in determining future food supplies than is the difference between optimistic and pessimistic forecasts for yields per hectare. These are:

(i) The pressure to produce fuel and other non-foods from agricultural sources. The route by which to achieve eventual independence from fossil fuel supplies is quite unknown, but serious proposals have already been made for 'energy forests' or 'fuel plantations' which would produce organic matter for the purpose of fuelling electricity generating stations.[3] Clearly, any such extra burden placed upon agriculture, although it is a reasonable first response to fuel shortage, would compete with food production.

(ii) The growth of mechanical ploughing is likely to be affected by escalated fuel costs; furthermore, an end to growth in world oil consumption, which seems inevitable quite soon,[4] will add a further constraint.

(iii) Cutbacks in fertiliser application have already been seen as a response to high prices. Presumably this marks the end of a time in which energy inputs into farming have been allowed to exceed greatly the energy content of the outputs. Yet many of the recent increases in agricultural yields per hectare have been based upon extravagant energy inputs.

(iv) In many countries techniques adopted for increase of agricultural output have set in motion long-term changes which will affect productivity adversely, for example soil erosion, depletion of soil water resources, depletion of soil minerals and the salting-up of irrigated land.[5]

'SYNTHETIC' FOOD TOO DEMANDING UPON RESOURCES

As agriculture is essentially a means for converting atmospheric CO_2 into desirable organics, it is not surprising that alternative means of effecting the same conversion have been widely discussed in the literature. There is fairly widespread agreement that complete chemical synthesis of nutrients from CO_2, without intervention of biological processes, is inconceivable for production of bulk foods on account of huge demands for energy and capital. The same is true of sophisticated systems for culturing micro-organisms from inorganic starting materials, such as those algal systems which would have depended upon artificial illumination and rapid pumping of the algal suspension.[6]

Algal systems which utilise sunlight as an energy source are in a stronger position, but practical application on a large scale will remain very dependent upon reducing the technology required to very simple terms and reducing the capital requirements to levels appropriate to developing country economics.

THE FOLLY OF FEEDING AN EXPANDING POPULATION FROM FOSSIL CARBON RESOURCES

Impressive systems now under development for producing protein-rich biomass from hydrocarbons or hydrocarbon-derived methanol have received much publicity and are well known.[7] This ingenious technology seems certain to make its impact, at least on animal feed markets. In terms of social effect and long-term economics, animal feed from this source will presumably be beneficial so long as it is only used to help maintain the high levels of animal protein intake which are customary in developed countries. However, any trend towards making expanding populations dependent upon food from fossil carbon sources could have extremely serious political, social and economic consequences as oil supplies become more expensive and more difficult to procure. This example, more than any other, highlights the very great need for long-term planning in provision of food supplies. Food from hydrocarbons would be an entirely acceptable source if used in conjunction with a scheme that would replace it when hydrocarbon supplies become scarce. Without that provision the unfettered growth of this source of food supply might merely prepare the way to an unprecedented disaster in world nutrition.

PUBLIC PRESSURE AGAINST POLLUTION

Undoubtedly public pressure to abate pollution is justified. Although not all the environmental damage we see from pollution comes from organic wastes, a substantial part of it does.

However, waste disposal technology, so frequently applied to organic wastes and effluents, is normally entirely different from waste utilisation. The whole technical discipline of waste treatment,[8] in so far as it affects organic wastes, will require radical reappraisal if the primary thesis of this paper—the future shortage of total organic matter—were to become widely accepted. Currently one can discern some intellectual confusion between waste disposal on the one hand and waste utilisation on the other. In practice only rarely will the optimum method for low-cost disposal coincide with an optimum use of the material concerned. Disposal produces no economic benefit apart from avoidance of environmental damage and is always a cost upon the producer of the waste. Utilisation normally demands more investment but produces economic benefits related to the present and future value of the recovered material. Avoidance of the disposal costs is always a factor in calculating the benefits of a utilisation process.

Public pressure against pollution is hence a real and justified factor in promoting utilisation of organic wastes. Its effect is indirect, however, since by creating a disposal cost it merely makes waste utilisation more attractive than it would otherwise be.

The main direct incentive to waste utilisation will still be the future shortages of organic material.

ORGANIC WASTES A MAJOR RENEWABLE RESERVOIR OF CARBON COMPOUNDS

The total amount of organic waste material which arises in the course of satisfying present economic needs is immense: there is no country as yet where the potential value of this material has been recognised and a route prepared for its exploitation. Consequently, it is commonplace to:

(i) grow a crop for one part of the plant only and discard the remainder (*i.e.* partial harvest);
(ii) discard processing wastes arising post-harvest;
(iii) discard forestry wastes;
(iv) burn or dump waste timber, waste paper, plastics and other non-food organics after a single use.

Annual world productions of various agricultural and processing wastes have been estimated:[9] the total for wheat straw, wheat bran, maize stover and cobs, barley straw and sugar cane bagasse amounts to some 637 million tons. The amount of waste paper arising in the UK alone is over 7 million tons annually—a figure in excess of the UK wheat crop—yet only a small percentage of it is recycled. UK farm waste has been estimated to be worth £100 million—even with present technology—and its volume is obviously very great.[10]

The production of primary agricultural and forestry products is itself an extremely wasteful process. The inputs of energy for water transport, soil preparation, fertiliser, crop-care procedures and harvesting are usually many times greater than the energy content of the output; consequently the output itself—the whole of the output—needs to be treated as a scarce resource. Moreover, the amount of available wastes is certainly significant in relation to world food requirements.

FEEDSTOCK FOR BIOENGINEERING PLANTS

Concern to obtain maximum amounts of recognised staple products such as rice and wheat has enforced a concentration upon upgrading the yields of the marketable portions of these particular crops. Yet if adequate and viable technology can be developed to utilise cellulose (for example, by hydrolysis) or to upgrade the protein content of mainly carbohydrate materials (for example, by micro-biological processing), this offers scope, depending upon climate, for partial switching to crops with the highest dry matter yields, such as sugar cane, sugar beet, potatoes and crops grown for leaf protein, followed by fractionation and conversion of the dry matter into the desired composition. This would amount to a reprogramming of agricultural production to provide the desired feedstocks for bio-engineering plants producing bulk human food ingredients and animal feeds. Inevitably, the changes involved must be gradual and linked to consumer acceptance of the products; but if they are to happen at all the necessary technologies and policies need to be developed now. Fortunately, the necessary bioengineering technologies are at a stage to repay priority investment.

The processes involved would best be designed *ab initio* so that wastes do not arise.

THE IMPLICATIONS OF RATIONAL WASTE RECYCLING

It is commonplace today to overlook the extent to which wealth and economic well-being depend upon organic produce coming from the soil. Three factors have caused this, especially in developed Western countries:

(i) Power from oil (coming from past photosynthesis) has temporarily relieved agriculture of the need to provide its own energy requirements; it also supplied energy to support much other economic activity.

(ii) Large exportable surpluses of food and feed arose in lightly populated countries.

(iii) Exportable quantities of food and feed arose in certain other countries; these were not surpluses but were attracted by prices in developed markets.

These factors have largely released the UK livestock industry, for example, from the limitations otherwise imposed by the productivity of the local soil.

This order of things is already changing, as exemplified by the price of oil, the increasing competition for exportable food surpluses and the tendency for many exporters to consume more of their own produce. This seems likely to force each country progressively to make more efficient use of the produce of its own soil for food and non-food use alike. The disappearance of factors (i) to (iii) above will presumably be a slow and irregular process and countries with major reserves of fossil fuels, especially oil, will continue to be in a privileged position. However, it is not unreasonable to foresee a future pattern of development in which there would be a closer connection between national wealth and the national capability to produce or control the production of organic matter. The latter is a function of geography and climate and also of the industriousness and management ability of people. Over and above these factors one would expect to see superimposed a marked effect upon national wealth derived from an ability to utilise the national production of organic matter with greatest efficiency. The effect would be a marked one because the economic benefit to be derived from a given area of land may differ, conceivably by several hundred percent, between good conventional agricultural practice on the one hand and systematised bioengineering on the other.

UNPRECEDENTED NEED FOR INGENUITY AND INVESTMENT

To achieve the situation described above, an explosive growth would be needed in the practical technologies connected with processing biological materials, especially bioengineering. To bring this about calls for a new understanding by governments of the potential importance of this field and an equal understanding in industrial management. Government policy to develop this area of technology would have to be linked with industrial exploitation projects in order to gain the benefits that are available. However, these far-seeing policies seem completely essential to avoid future shortages of organic raw materials.

The need for fresh ingenuity, and hence for training and research, would probably be unprecedented within the food and agriculture industries. The investment needs would also tend to be greater than those which have been common in these industries hitherto. As the investment will be hard to find and processing energy expensive, the pressure will probably fall upon technologists to generate low-investment, low-energy bioengineering plants. These may also have to be of modest size, since transportation of wastes to large central processing plants is inclined to be uneconomical.

This type of challenge to the technologist is actually itself an important socio-economic implication of a food-from-waste policy. Today's technologists are principally attuned to designing sophisticated plants, highly capitalised, involving energy-consumptive stages of heating, stirring, comminuting, etc. Indeed, the technological and scientific communities have come to admire sophisticated, energy-consumptive equipment. A new situation, tending to reverse that trend, will affect technologists and scientists directly.

SEGREGATION OF WASTES

Recycling of wastes of all kinds is made easier if the different types of waste can be kept segregated. For example, separation of the different types of municipal waste after collection is expensive and is one of the disincentives to full utilisation of the organic material it contains. It can be expected that some pressure will be brought to bear upon households and industry to separate waste types; however, the resulting benefit to individuals or companies may not be large enough for this approach to be successful.

HARVESTING OF WILD LANDS

The total higher plant biomass greatly exceeds the total biomass attributable to food crops.[5] Wherever there is natural vegetation the 'wastes' arise simply by the death of plants, individual leaves, etc., and fall upon the ground to rot, and such wastes are obviously replaced continuously by new photosynthesis.

Some harvesting of this source of 'waste' material can be expected in future, though it is now commonly restricted to firewood gathering and grazing. More systematic efforts could no doubt be devised to glean this material, which must be large in volume, geared so as to avoid damaging the replacement capability of the vegetation.

ORGANIC MATTER TREATED ON ITS MERITS
ACCORDING TO COMPOSITION

It is obvious that many organic wastes are most unattractive materials—even offensive. Decaying vegetation, food processing wastes, mouldy materials, animal excreta, even human excreta are among the organic resources we cannot continue to ignore. It is certain that, if total organic matter is going to be scarce, it will not be possible to indulge prejudices against using some organic materials which are disgusting to us. Certainly animal excreta may contain fibre and protein of considerable value, and all excreta contain significant nitrogenous compounds. Subject to hygienic conditions being fully met, there is presumably going to be an economic pressure to utilise all forms of usable organic matter. No doubt these substances can be utilised in the community without being drawn sharply to our notice, and this would be the best solution. Most of us, untrained in chemistry and biology, are unable to view disgusting substances dispassionately on the basis of chemical composition.

The ultimate waste product of all human activity is the human cadaver, but it seems safe to predict that prejudice will preclude its utilisation even for some centuries to come.

NOT THE PREFERRED WAY OF LIFE FOR MANKIND

Intuitively one feels that the efficient scavenging and utilisation of wastes does not constitute a preferred way of life. To do these things will add the constraints of 'good housekeeping' to departments of our lives which are more free and easy at present. The careful segregation and recovery of wastes will not be attractive or provide any satisfaction. However, it is contended here that the population explosion now in progress will make changes of this kind inevitable because our present and potential sources of unused organic material are a richer resource than the as yet unrealised increases in agricultural output. If only it were a political and practical possibility to control population at a modest level and live on 'the fat of the land' it would doubtless be immensely preferable. But it seems inevitable that largely unrestrained population growth will have the effects described above.

NEW FOODS AS SIMILAR AS POSSIBLE TO EXISTING FOODS

There is a strong tendency to conservatism in food habits. This has been seen both in developing countries, where there has been consumer resistance to new foods introduced to improve nutrition, and also in developed countries, where the consumer has clung to familiar foods in spite of advertising designed to change his habits.

It is therefore reasonable to suppose that, as far as practicable, food from wastes will be used for production of familiar food items, and passage through animals for meat and milk production will no doubt be a common application in developed countries. Where vegetable or fungal foods are used directly as sources of protein for human consumption, they will probably continue to be processed into forms which resemble as closely as possible their animal protein counterparts.

GOVERNMENT ACTION

Without government guidance it seems unlikely that private industry can be expected to harness waste materials efficiently and optimally. Most private industry acts in pursuit of quite short-term profit and also, rather than plan the overall utilisation of a resource, will often select the most profitable portions, leaving the residue unexploitable. Some governmental control, guidance and incentive will therefore be necessary to secure the efficient scavenging of wastes in a private enterprise system. Given such action in good time it can be anticipated that industry would respond, but this again highlights the crucial need for forward planning in this area.

REFERENCES

1. Wareing, P. F. and Cooper, J. P. (1971). *Potential Crop Production*, Heinemann Educational Books, London.
2. Monteith, J. L. (1966). *Exptl. Agric.*, **2**, p. 1.
3. Szego, G. C. and Kemp, C. C. (1973). *Chem. Tech.*, May, p. 275.
4. Schumacher, E. F. (1973). *Small is Beautiful*, Blond & Briggs, London.

5. Borgstrom, G. (1969). *Too Many: A Study of Earth's Biological Limitations*, Macmillan, London.
6. Desrosier, N. W. (1961). *Attack on Starvation*, Avi Publ. Co. Inc., Westport, Conn., USA.
7. Gounelle de Pontanel (1972). *Proteins from Hydrocarbons*, Proceedings of a 1972 Symposium at Aix-en-Provence, Academic Press, London.
8. Koziorowski, B. and Kucharski, J. (1972). *Industrial Waste Disposal*, Pergamon Press and Wydawnietwa Naukowo-Techniczne, Warsaw.
9. Worgan, J. T. (1972). *Utilisation of Agricultural and Food Industry Wastes by Microbiological Processes*, British Food Manufacturing Industries Research Association Symposium.
10. National Agricultural Centre (1975). 'Muck '75' (announcement of a national farm waste management demonstration).

DISCUSSION

Thomson: How do you get your figure of 18% for the efficiency of photosynthesis?

Plaskett: I am not personally an expert in this particular area, but I took the figure from a publication by J. L. Monteith, 'The photosynthesis and transpiration of crops', *Experimental Agriculture*, 2 (1966), p. 1. It is an attempt to deduce more or less the first principles in biochemical reactions. I think it is probably one of the higher estimates.

Questioner: Most quotes are in the area of 8–10%.

Plaskett: I didn't want to do my own case too much justice.

van der Wal: I may have missed the point, but I wonder what you mean by 'synthetic food'. To my knowledge there is only one really important synthetic food and that is the group of amino acids. They give a tremendous return of energy investment, so I have a question mark at the sentence. If on the other hand you included SCP I think I might understand your statement. Did you?

Plaskett: No.

van der Wal: Then I stick to my first remark: what do you consider as synthetic food?

Plaskett: I was meaning by synthetic food the production of organic compounds by chemical synthesis with the energy being provided by whatever fuel or energy source is most prevalent industrially at that time. I was excluding in that definition a biological production. I was speaking of chemical synthesis which is a fantastic idea, even though you say it is not. Well, we have, of course, the greatest diversity of opinion in the literature concerning the future opportunities for different methods of supplying bulk nutrients. I wouldn't think that chemical synthesis was so fantastic if I could see a really abundant supply of cheap energy employed, but I do not see it.

van der Wal: I still stick to my point, which is based on the practical importance of the synthetic amino acids, and the argument for that is they have tremendous return for energy investment. So it is by no means fantastic, it is today's practice.

Plaskett: It makes no difference to my case to concede your point. I am speaking here of bulk nutrients rather than those specialised things which have a catalytic effect on the utilisation of other materials in food as well.

Worgan: Can I just comment on that point. I think there is a difference between true synthesis, that is, from carbon dioxide, water and nitrogen, and conversion of the fossil fuels. If you use a fossil fuel for conversion then the energy required is much less even when the fossil fuel used as raw material is included. In the future if the fossil fuels become scarce then it will be very much more expensive to synthesise amino acids.

van der Wal: I should perhaps just explain that since I am talking about long-term possibilities I have rejected high oil consumption processes from the future pattern. I think inevitably if enormous quantities of oil are required by a process in relation to the nutrients produced, unless it is some very specialised nutrient of high value because of the special effect, it is not going to be economically viable for many years to come.

Bookey: I wonder if we could look at the marginal case here which Dr Plaskett is talking about. At one end we have what Dr van der Wal described as taxi-loads of nutritionists and bus-loads of biochemists and, believe you me, armies of engineers! A lot of resources go into this and in spite of what you were saying about the need to develop simpler and cheaper processes I think they can be relatively expensive. At the other end, this food is going into areas of the world which at the moment are underfed, where there is a marginal need for extra food—an area of the world which on the whole will find it difficult to pay for what would be expensive extra supplies of food. How do you see this inbalance within the world being corrected? It is the old, old problem, but I think looking at it marginally really does show it up. There has got to be a complete change of attitude, perhaps with governments, and where do you see this coming from? Where do you see the sensitive pressure points at which to effect this change?

Plaskett: I quite agree that research and development will be expensive and the initial technology transfer, if I can use that expression, will be expensive. My own opinion is that we have to try and do this in a way that makes the processes themselves expensive in labour rather than expensive in cash.

Tannenbaum: I very much agree with Dr van der Wal's point of view. I think the essential point is that from an energy point of view, let us say, for example, that you take a protein which is deficient in lysine. The addition of a very small amount of lysine becomes equivalent to the addition of a large amount of protein, that is, poor proteins require much higher levels of protein in the diet to give an equivalent nutritional depth. Small amounts of lysine can be equivalent to that larger amount of protein and what that means is that at the higher protein level you are basically taking in an expensive and possibly energy-intensive material such as protein and using it really in a way you would use a cheap energy source, which would require much less energy to produce only to get that additional lysine.

Plaskett: Yes, I already agreed with this, but I think it makes little difference to the overall case on account of the fact that we seem to be facing such serious future deficiencies of bulk nutrients both in terms of protein and perhaps even more important in terms of calorie supply. The synthesis of lysine is a special case—it obviously does improve the utilisation of protein, and I think it should go on.

Tannenbaum: There are other synthetic sources of energy, such things as butane diols, for example, which have been suggested as synthetic energy sources, and I don't see why it has to come strictly from fossil fuel. You can pyrolyse cellulose and then use the products to convert to suitable energy sources. Ultimately, at some point in the future, if we had relatively inexpensive energy (even solar energy) one could take cellulose and regenerate the equivalent of fossil fuel energy.

Plaskett: I think if we have cheap and abundant sources of energy the whole problem becomes several times easier, but at the moment I don't see that source.

20

The Bioplex Concept

C. F. FORSTER and J. C. JONES

Wessex Water Authority, Redcliffe Way, Bristol, England

ABSTRACT

Considering the Earth as a single ecological system, cyclic processes are extremely commonplace, both for the inorganic and organic components of the world's structure. Indeed this type of cyclic operation is essential to the biology which sustains life. Whilst recycling has been operated successfully by nature for many millions of years, man has, particularly since the Industrial Revolution, largely discarded the concept of recycling waste materials and has preferred the concept of 'disposal by destruction'. In recent years the attention of a wide spectrum of people throughout the world has been sharply focused on the wasteful use of natural resources, particularly by the developed nations. It does not need complex computer models, which are available, to suggest that these cavalier attitudes must be changed if our present standard of life is to survive.

'Disposal by reclamation' has been examined so widely that it is difficult to understand why it is not an accepted technique. Considering only organic wastes (i.e. those derived from solar energy), recycling schemes based on hydrolysis, on pyrolysis and on fermentation have been shown to be technically feasible and in some cases economically attractive. However, these processes have one common feature: as well as being waste-consuming they are waste-generating. The underlying philosophy behind the Bioplex approach is that organic wastes would be treated by a stream of processes so that the waste from one would become the raw material for another. To do this would require not only chemical and microbiological units but also the harnessing of macrobiological productivity. The result would be units which would be flexible in their production capability. Furthermore, the technologies available for use in this type of complex mean that the processes could be tailored to blend with the environment in which the complex was situated.

INTRODUCTION

The natural recycling of matter, such as carbon, sulphur and nitrogen, is an essential part of living systems. The exception to this general rule is post-Industrial Revolution man, who voraciously consumes natural products and prefers 'disposal by destruction' to any form of recycling. Despite this, natural decomposition processes do return some of the waste organics to the various natural cycles. However, the conversion routes through solar energy and the primary producers are too slow for the demands of the developed countries.

The very finite nature of the world's elemental matter together with increasing consumer demands and slow natural conversion rates means that if we are to avoid the disasters predicted by the 'global modellers', the natural cycles must be short-circuited and a Recycling Revolution must begin. In terms of carbon—and it is intended to concentrate on this element—this means that it must be kept in a reduced form for as long as possible. There are several possibilities for the 'philosopher's stone' which can effect this transmutation of waste. Microbes, with their ability to break down and grow on a wide range of organic compounds and at the same time yield useful by-products (Table 1), are one obvious choice.

TABLE 1

Range of chemicals available from fermentation

Gases	Methane, hydrogen sulphide
Alcohols, ketones	Ethanol, butanol, acetone
Organic acids	Malic, citric, fumaric, itaconic, lactic, propionic, tartaric
Amino acids	Glutaric, ketoglutaric, aspartic, lysine, threonine
Polyols	Glycerol, mannitol
Polysaccharides	Xanthan gum
Vitamins	Riboflavin, B_{12}
Sugars	Fructose, sorbose

Similarly, other practically omnivorous biological producers, rats, ducks, rabbits, fish or pigs, considered in mixed-species-farming situations, would achieve a valuable conversion of waste into protein.

There have already been a considerable number of proposals for recycling routes. Porteus has outlined a process, which would convert the ever-increasing amount of paper in domestic refuse to ethanol,[1,2] based on acid hydrolysis of the cellulose followed by fermentation. Finnecy[3] also based his recycling proposals on refuse but preferred the technologies of pyrolysis and incineration. Liquid wastes have also been examined as the raw material for recycling processes.[4] Probably the best documented of these is spent sulphite liquor which has been used to produce both a range of organic chemicals and microbial protein.[5-7] Sewage sludge, an embarrassing by-product from the treatment of domestic effluents, has also been scrutinised by recycling scientists. A review of this work shows that sludge has a considerable potential for 'disposal by reclamation'.[8] This list could be extended to cover agricultural wastes,[9,10] food industry effluents,[11,12] and the unwanted debris from a miscellany of manufacturing industries,[13,14] but in nearly all these schemes the proposed recycling process is not only waste-consuming but is also waste-generating. In Bioplex the biological conversion of wastes consists of exploiting the chemical activities of living creatures in such a way that the waste from one creature becomes the food for another. In this way the productivity of any one site can be brought to a maximum whilst the waste is minimised. A further benefit is that transport costs from one process to another are minimised and any changes due to biodeterioration during transit are prevented.

A BIOPLEX MODEL

The validity of the Bioplex philosophy can be checked by examining two simple models: one in which the waste from a unit process is recycled directly to the feed line, and one in which several unit processes are used in series. In both cases the weight of product obtained follows a geometric progression as the number of stages or the number of recycles is increased. Thus the use of three stages, assuming a similar productivity (*i.e.* 10% conversion) and wastage rate (*i.e.* 60%) in each stage, will increase the amount of product by 96% (Fig. 1). A similar model for a multi-stage process with recycle could also be developed to show the potential for even higher yields (Fig. 2). Although this shows the benefits of recycling in relation to a single-pass straight-through system, it also shows that as the number of stages is increased, so the benefits of a recycle phase are reduced. It may well be, therefore, that in a Bioplex system with more than three conversion stages a recycle pathway may not be economical. Thus each combination of production units will have to be examined as a unique case. In addition, productivity and wastage rates could be varied as far as possible to optimise the overall yield from any one group of wastes.

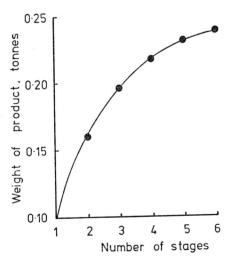

FIG. 1. The effect on overall productivity of increasing the number of production stages. Weight of product = $PF(1+W+W^2+ \cdots +W^{n-2} + W^{n-1})$ where P = productivity = 10%; W = waste = 60%; F = feed rate = 1 t/day; n = number of stages.

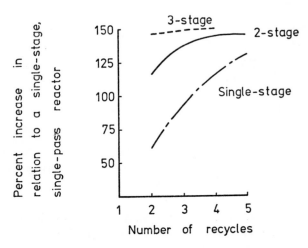

FIG. 2. The effect of recycling on the overall productivity.

However, although information on the conversion rates of food to body weight for several animals is available (Table 2), this is usually derived from experimental work involving specially prepared food. In addition there is little or no information relating to the conversion of food to energy or to waste.

TABLE 2
Animal feed conversion data

Species	% of feed converted to body weight	Faecal waste (dry basis) % feed
Rabbit	25	—
Steers (dairy)	5·9	39
Steers (beef)	6·3	38
Swine (45 kg)	30	16·8
Poultry	47·6	—
Turkey[a]	32·5	—
Rat[a]	15	—

[a] 50% mature weight.

Thus, in considering any quantification of a Bioplex system, many assumptions are needed. Before examining any potential Bioplex systems in detail, however, it is worthwhile considering the effect of the various conversion factors on the overall productivity.

The product yield $P = X/X + Y + Z$, where X = conversion to body weight (%), Y = conversion to energy (%) and Z = conversion to waste (%). If it is assumed that there is zero wastage it is possible to derive a graphical expression for productivity as related to energy and body conversion factors (Fig. 3). This shows, as might be expected, that product yield increases either as the body weight conversion is increased or as the percentage conversion to energy is decreased.

In addition to these conversion factors, the parameters which influence the choice of animals to be used in conversion stages are:

1. The marketability of the product (*i.e.* market size and price).
2. The acceptability of the intensive farming process to the population close to the complex.
3. The rate of feed conversion.

The rate of conversion is important as a large continuous stream of waste is coming forward. Also, to keep processing and farming plant to a reasonable size, high conversion rates are necessary.

Marketability, *i.e.* an outlet for all the products at a fair price, is an obvious necessity in choosing the animals for Bioplex. Most animals will be acceptable if they are to be sold as feedstuffs for other animals, but if they are to be sold directly for human food there will be obvious problems of sales resistance. This could be a serious obstacle to the concept. The acceptability will vary with the product;

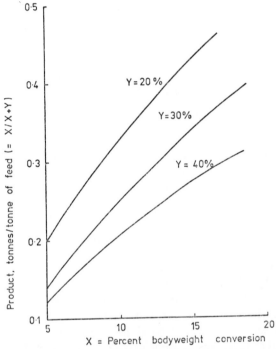

FIG. 3. The effect of varying the feed conversion parameters on the overall productivity.

for example, pigs bred on fractions of domestic refuse and incorporated into pork products would have less sales resistance than, say, ducks bred directly on sewage and sold for the table. Microbial protein produced from the cellulose fraction of refuse and used as protein enrichment in convenience foods would be more acceptable than rabbits, which had been fed on waste, sold as fresh meat. Market research will be necessary to aid the selection of animals, but it must also be stressed that to meet world food requirements, eating habits will have to undergo some changes. If we reflect on the changes we have accepted in foods over the past decade, we can see that our eating habits are not as conservative as some people would have us believe. However, if Bioplex research does proceed it must be supported at an early stage with a market research programme.

The acceptability of the Bioplex system to the community in the vicinity of the site will have a considerable influence on the choice of animals. Microbes grown in large tanks or fermenters, or fish farms in deep silos, will obviously be more acceptable to large urban communities than will intensive animal farms, whereas goats and geese will fit more readily into a rural Bioplex than will the relatively complex bioengineering equipment. The different locations will therefore produce different products and this is an advantage as far as not saturating a market by over-production is concerned.

Therefore the schemes suggested for large urban complexes will be mainly fermentation processes, and will be akin to the industrial processes already sited in these areas. They may, however, have an advantage over the industrial processes in that they produce no obnoxious fumes and little or no dangerous effluents. The rural Bioplex will be similar to intensive farms already operating in these areas.

PROPOSALS FOR BIOPLEX

Each year some 2×10^{11} t of carbon are fixed by photosynthesis, about half of this being in the form of cellulose. The amount of this which is wasted annually in the UK can be seen from the data in Table 3. However, although this would indicate that there is a plentiful supply of raw material for recycling units, it must be realised that these wastes are widely distributed and that there is a minimum viable size for a recycling unit to give a reasonable return on capital. It has been estimated that for a plant producing only microbial protein from waste, this minimum viable unit is one which produces 50 000 t of single-cell protein per year.[15] This means a feed rate of 160 000 t of cellulose per year. On this basis, a number of the wastes could not be used, as the quantities available, because of their geographical distribution, are insufficient. A Bioplex system, however, because of its greater productive power, would be able to utilise a greater proportion of the available wastes.

In the schemes described, it is assumed that mixed wastes such as domestic refuse can be fractionated automatically on site. There are essentially three types of process that could be used for this: a wet process similar to that developed by Black Clawson International;[16] a mixed wet/dry separation such as the one used by the city of Rome;[17] or a dry system (*e.g.* the Madison process or the TNO method).[18] Any of these techniques would produce an organic feedstock for Bioplex together with several inorganic fractions for which ready markets could be found. It could therefore be assumed that the separation stage would be self-financing and that the organics would reach Bioplex at nil cost.

TABLE 3
Major organic wastes in the UK
$(10^6$ t/year, dry weight)

Refuse organics	9·90
Sewage sludge	3·34
Forestry:	
Softwood	0·59
Hardwood	0·36
Sawmill	0·56
Paper processing	0·11
Farming:	
Vegetable	1·34
Cattle	16·70
Poultry	1·43
Pigs	2·80

Once processed in this way, the organic slurry would become the feedstock for a multiple production line (Fig. 4). The products could then be varied to suit the market requirements or the plant location and size. For example, the culture of oysters requires a saline environment, so that this scheme would be best operated in a Bioplex unit situated near the coast.

Bioplex schemes utilising sewage sludge would be similar to those using refuse as a feedstock but would generally start at a later stage as the pretreatment fractionation stage would not be required. Indeed some of the stages suggested in Fig. 4 are already being practised (*e.g.* direct feeding of fish). However, some fractionation may be advantageous. In its biochemical composition, sludge is more diverse than the refuse organics, containing proteins, fats and celluloses, so that a separation stage might facilitate some of the later production processes. There are some indications, for example,

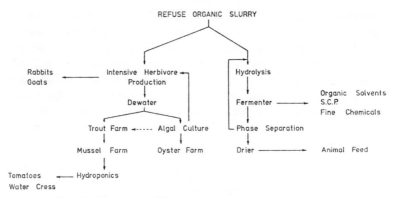

Fig. 4.   The potential for productivity from refuse organics.

that the presence of proteins may decrease the yield of the sugars obtained from celluloses by hydrolysis.[19] Probably one of the more common unit operations in a sludge-based Bioplex would be anaerobic digestion to produce methane. This is a well-established technique which is used at many sewage works. The fractionation processes (Fig. 5) have also been tested as separate stages and the combination of the various technologies is now being investigated further.[20]

The limits to growth of intensive farm units are frequently set by the capacity of the area near the unit which is available for waste disposal, since these wastes are usually spread as a form of organic

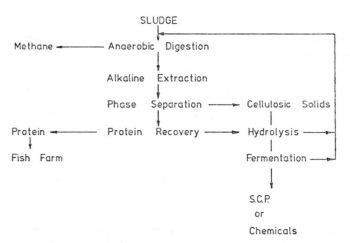

Fig. 5.   The potential for productivity from sewage sludge.

fertiliser or dumped in land fill sites. Thus, if these wastes could be utilised on site it is likely that intensive farm units could be increased in size. Therefore the design of a Bioplex system based on farm wastes has an advantage over those based on domestic wastes in that the animal population producing the waste can be increased to suit the economics of the waste-utilisation process. The animal species being farmed in the first case now becomes an integral part of the biological complex and the system is not a waste utilisation complex but a complex which makes use of food supplied through a system of internal recycling.

The simplest system of this kind is one where pig manure is fed direct to an oxidation ditch and the products of the ditch (*i.e.* microbial protein) returned as pig food. This system would probably be suited for both small and large pig farms by today's standards. If farms were established on a larger scale the wastes would be fed to an anaerobic digester for methane production and the digester residues dewatered and dried, using the methane as the energy source. The dried product could then be used as a feed supplement for the original animal.

One of the problems with this system, however, will be the large amounts of lignin and other materials arising from bedding and litter. These would either have to be removed from the system or the bedding and litter will have to be redesigned to suit the system. A synthetic bedding which could either be separated during processing or which could be washed free of manures in the first stage may be an answer. The liquid arising from the dewatering of digester residues could be used in aquaculture for some form of shellfish farming. The reason for the dewatering stage is to convert the residue to a form acceptable as an animal feed. This could be done by a biological method developed by the Dow Chemical Company.[21] In this, maggots are raised on the residue and fed to fish or chickens, leaving a dry material which can be dumped or recycled to the anaerobic digester. This system has the advantage that it could be used as a means of removing inert materials which would otherwise accumulate in the residues.

CONCLUSIONS

The modern world is facing four main problems: its population, its environmental pollution, its consumption of natural resources and its production of food. These are closely interrelated, the latter three being increasingly caused by the exponentially expanding population. Considering just one of these latter problems, food production, each additional person will require, on average, 0·4 ha of land for extra food production. However, 0·08 ha per head are required for additional housing, roads, waste disposal, etc., so that there is a steady erosion of the available arable land. Because of this exponential decrease in the availability of land, doubling or even quadrupling agricultural productivity, in its presently accepted form, will only gain perhaps 50 years before the available arable land runs out. In addition to this problem of production there is also the problem of food distribution, on a global scale, to be faced, and here we meet the problems, in the absence of any global policy, of over-production, stockpiling, production cutbacks and even wastage as attempts are made to balance supply and demand in localised areas.

The world is therefore faced with two alternatives, a self-imposed limitation to growth or a nature-imposed limitation to growth, and to avoid a natural catastrophe the former will eventually have to be accepted. This will involve the acceptance of many new philosophies and techniques and one of the most obvious is the return of as much as possible of our waste materials in the overall life-cycle. The productivity that can be achieved by utilising wastes in Bioplex units has already been outlined. However, the yields from these units could be improved further by using mixed waste streams and by extending the concept of intensivisation; for example, fish could be grown in cages, with a space of little more than the volume of the fish, and water moved through the cage. In applying these philosophies, we must not be bound by our past history of domestication of wild animals which limits us to those species handed down from Neolithic man, who could afford the agricultural inefficiencies of open-system farming. A search must therefore be made for species capable of high productivity on waste materials. Ways must then be found to introduce these animals into the human food cycle; tradition must not be allowed to define acceptability.

This work of domesticating new species, fully quantifying the various possibilities for incorporation in Bioplex systems and developing new technologies for waste reclamation, needs to be undertaken with considerable urgency. Probably the best way to ensure the proper integration of all the disciplines necessary for this would be the establishment of a National Research Centre for Recycling. The recent Green Paper, *War on Waste*,[22] stated: 'We all instinctively feel that there is something wrong in a society which wastes and discards resources on the scale which we do today.' Is it not time to follow our instincts and act?

REFERENCES

1. Porteus, A. (1971). *Public Cleansing*, **61**, p. 152.
2. Porteus, A. (1975). In: *Utilisation of Wastes*, British Paper and Board Industry Federation Symposium, Manchester.
3. Finnecy, E. E. (1974). *Waste Recovery and Recycle*, London Chemical Engineering Congress.
4. *Notes on Water Pollution*, No. 67 (1975). Department of the Environment, London.
5. Mueller, J. C. and Walden, C. C. (1970). *Process Biochemistry*, **5**(6), p. 35.
6. Romantschuk, H. (1973). 2nd International Conference on SCP, Massachusetts Institute of Technology, Cambridge, Mass.
7. Romano, A. H. (1958). *Tappi*, **41**, p. 687.
8. Forster, C. F. (1973). *Effluent and Water Treatment J.*, **13**, p. 697.
9. Long, T. A., Bratzler, J. W. and Frear, D. H. E. (1969). *Proc. Agricultural Waste Management Conference*, Cornell University, Ithaca, NY, p. 98.
10. Imrie, F. K. E. and Vlitos, A. J. (1973). 2nd International Conference on SCP, Massachusetts Institute of Technology, Cambridge, Mass.
11. Grant, R. A. (1974). *Process Biochemistry*, **9**(2), p. 11.
12. Lewin, D. C. and Forster, C. F. (1974). *Effluent and Water Treatment J.*, **14**, p. 142.
13. Jarl, K. (1971). *Socker Handlingar*, **25**(2), p. 4.
14. Edwards, T. H. and Finn, R. K. (1969). *Process Biochemistry* **4**(1), p. 29.
15. Peter Ward Associates Ltd and University College, Cardiff (1974). *Conversion of Organic Wastes into Marketable Protein.*
16. Kohlhepp, D. H. (1974). 78th National Meeting of the American Institute of Chemical Engineers, Salt Lake City, Utah.
17. Sabbatini, M. (1975). *Utilisation of Wastes*, British Paper and Board Industry Federation Symposium, Manchester.
18. Kenworthy, I. C. (1975). *Utilisation of Wastes*, British Paper and Board Industry Federation Symposium, Manchester.
19. Wimpenny, J. W. T. Personal communication.
20. Wimpenny, J. W. T., Kane-Maquire, L. A. P. and Forster, C. F. Unpublished data.
21. Ettinger, M. B. and Wade, L. L. (1971). *Proc. 26th Industrial Waste Conference*, Purdue University, Lafayette, Indiana, p. 266.
22. *War on Waste: A Policy for Reclamation* (1967). HMSO, London.

DISCUSSION

Tannenbaum: After listening to your talk I find myself somewhat perplexed, because frankly I don't see how what you are suggesting is any different from what people have been talking about all along, and to add to that I think we already have operating examples in the world that are exactly what you are talking about. For example, in Taiwan they are working with what you would call the Bioplex system.

Forster: I quite agree with you. The process is working in Taiwan. It is not working in the UK. We are still having to import grain at high prices. I would like to see Bioplex in a more advanced state than the Bioplex systems which again are operating in the UK. For example, we treat sewage, we produce sewage sludge, we put the sludge on land which produces grass, we feed animals on the grass and we eat the animals. This is a form of Bioplex. There are many of them working. What I am asking for is development of new species. Since the Bronze Age we have domesticated only one species—the turkey. There are still many more. Some of these could well have a high productivity, and need to be utilised. A greater intensification of fish farming, again, being based on waste, needs to be practised. But I agree with you, we are copying existing systems. We are merely intensifying them.

Tannenbaum: I somewhat dispute that in that I thought SCP processes were novel, in that essentially what you are doing is getting rapid production. In fact one of the advantages of SCP is that now, I think, people have in fact become educated. They are saying 'Let's steer away from animal systems because of their inefficiency'.

Forster: When you start to treat waste, if you take a processing system producing refuse you have got to hydrolyse it. That produces the waste stream. Then you have got to ferment it. That produces a waste stream. And to treat those waste streams you have to pay money which pushes up the price of your single-cell protein. You can utilise those waste streams to produce further protein or further useful products.

Tannenbaum: But the point is that people are doing this. For example, in the USA there are companies which take waste streams and produce products from them. So I think it is being done.

Forster: In part, yes, it is being done. I know there is recycling being done and I'm not saying Bioplex is the alternative.

Tannenbaum: I don't think it is anything different.

Forster: It is concentrating, if you like, all the technologies of recycling into one organised complex.

Chairman (Professor Aylward): In any new discovery it seems that first of all there is an argument, then people say it isn't necessary, and finally there is an even greater argument that it isn't new at all.

Wimpenny: I think one of the answers is possibly that this is more or less low technology as far as I understand it, and I don't think you could possibly operate in the same area as SCP production operates, which is high technology and requires, as you said, I think, Professor Tannenbaum, probably something like 10 000 tons per year of waste material. We have said up to 50 000 tons per year, as Dr Forster described, but I would say there is some element of tidy housekeeping about a process which rears animals and has essentially no waste. For example, one of the groups in Cardiff Zoology Department is in fact growing a thing called the zebra mussel. Now the zebra mussel was first discovered as a pest growing around outlets of sewage works and obviously is a very good candidate because it grows well on the sewage sludges. Therefore it is being grown at the moment in Cardiff Zoology Department on sewage sludges, and the idea hopefully is that the zebra mussel, which has a very high yield for an animal (poor for bacteria but very good for an animal), is then chopped up and used as a dog food or something like that. That is the idea of part of this Bioplex system as far as I understand it. One other scheme (I believe still a paper scheme) which is being mooted by somebody in Cardiff, and I believe he is actually building a plant in his own garden, is a fish pond over which is put a glasshouse and the fish are growing in this pond, and above this pond is a flock of poultry and these are defecating into the fish pond. Yes, I agree. It has been done before.

Tannenbaum: I don't dispute any part of the system. What I simply do not understand is why we need to call it a Bioplex system. This is the point I was trying to make. To me you have simply described what we are all trying to do. Professor Worgan, for example, grew fungi, and that is now a new domesticated species. It wasn't domesticated before and perhaps this mussel is. I don't see what we gain from making a new institute and putting all these things together.

Wimpenny: Professor Tannenbaum, you were the person who christened single-cell protein SCP, weren't you?

Tannenbaum: Yes.

Wimpenny: Well, why did you call it SCP? It is just as nice to call it single-cell protein. (*Laughter*)

Index